PAULINE WHITEHOUSE
QY50

Laborato nal Law

K

SThL (Jus

b

**Blackwell
Science**

© 2000 by
Blackwell Science Ltd
Editorial Offices:
Osney Mead, Oxford OX2 0EL
25 John Street, London WC1N 2BL
23 Ainslie Place, Edinburgh EH3 6AJ
350 Main Street, Malden
    MA 02148 5018, USA
54 University Street, Carlton
    Victoria 3053, Australia
10, rue Casimir Delavigne
    75006 Paris, France

Other Editorial Offices:

Blackwell Wissenschafts-Verlag GmbH
Kurfürstendamm 57
10707 Berlin, Germany

Blackwell Science KK
MG Kodenmacho Building
7–10 Kodenmacho Nihombashi
Chuo-ku, Tokyo 104, Japan

First published 2000

Set in 11/13pt Bembo
by DP Photosetting, Aylesbury, Bucks
Printed and bound in Great Britain
at the Alden Press, Oxford and Northampton

The Blackwell Science logo is a trade mark of
Blackwell Science Ltd, registered at the United
Kingdom Trade Marks Registry

DISTRIBUTORS

Marston Book Services Ltd
PO Box 269
Abingdon
Oxon OX14 4YN
(*Orders:* Tel: 01235 465500
         Fax: 01235 465555)

USA
Blackwell Science, Inc.
Commerce Place
350 Main Street
Malden, MA 02148 5018
(*Orders:* Tel: 800 759 6102
                781 388 8250
         Fax: 781 388 8255)

Canada
Login Brothers Book Company
324 Saulteaux Crescent
Winnipeg, Manitoba R3J 3T2
(*Orders:* Tel: 204 837-2987
         Fax: 204 837-3116)

Australia
Blackwell Science Pty Ltd
54 University Street
Carlton, Victoria 3053
(*Orders:* Tel: 03 9347 0300
         Fax: 03 9347 5001)

A catalogue record for this title
is available from the British Library

ISBN 0-632-05278-3

Library of Congress
Cataloging-in-Publication Data

Dolan, Kevin.
    Introduction to laboratory animal law/Kevin
Dolan.
        p.   cm.
    Includes bibliographical references and index.
    ISBN 0-632-05278-3
    1. Laboratory animals—Law and legislation—
Great Britain.   2. Animal experimentation—Law and
legislation—Great Britain.
    KD3426. D65   2000
    344.41′049—dc21   99-054972

For further information on
Blackwell Science, visit our website:
www.blackwell-science.com

Contents

Preface

The title of this book goes some way towards defining its scope. It is not intended to be a treatise on animal law in general. It was written for the use of those involved in animal studies especially those concerned with animals in research. It is hoped that it will give them an overall view of their legal obligations towards the animals in their care.

The main emphasis in the text will obviously be on the Animal (Scientific Procedures) Act 1986 (referred to throughout the text as the ASPA). Other legislation, e.g. the Protection of Animals Act 1911 (referred to throughout as the 1911 Act), the Veterinary Surgeons Act 1966, the Agriculture (Miscellaneous Provisions) Act 1968, the Animal Health Act 1981 and the European Belai Directive, will be commented upon in so far as they may be relevant to laboratory animals. The impact of European law on this area of legislation will be noted. Passing reference will be made to some animal laws e.g. the Wildlife and Countryside Act 1981, which are peripheral to the main theme of the book.

Numerous Statutory Instruments, both Orders and Regulations, along with Directives, Codes of Practice, Guidelines and the Stipulations of Good Laboratory Practice bearing on animal experimentation could be of interest to many scientists and technicians dealing with animals and often very relevant to their particular area of work. Unfortunately both space and time are limited. Where appropriate I will refer to such documents and attempt to indicate the best place to find them. In such specialised areas there is the obvious need to consult the actual documents themselves. Their details would be difficult to paraphrase in a work such as this. Furthermore, it must be stressed, that where there are actual legal problems or disputes of a litigious nature the appropriate legal experts must be consulted if an authoritative solution is being sought.

The order in which the material is presented corresponds with my own past lectures aligned to the Institute of Animal Technology's syllabus for the Fellowship Examination. Gratitude is due for the moulding of this text to the many students who listened patiently and sometimes spurred me on; Dale Holt, Jas Barley, Roger Francis, and Sué Jones among many others spring readily to mind. Thanks also to those who encouraged me along the way, Dr Marjorie Dinsley, Keith Millican Fraser Darling, Jim Wallace and Tim Betts certainly fall into this category.

Without fruitful consultation with ABCU and the Inspectorate, along with their generous supply of relevant material, this book would not have been possible. I would also like to acknowledge my indebtedness to the many pertinent publications of the The Stationery Office, so essential as source documents.

Acknowledgements

The Research Defence Society has generously made available to me a large amount of useful source material which I would like to acknowledge with gratitude. The Society stands out as a positive, outspoken force in the controversy surrounding biological research.

The material in Appendix 1 taken from the Guidance Notes is Crown copyright and reproduced with permission of the Controller of Her Majesty's Stationery Office.

Abbreviations

ABCU	Animals, Byelaws, Coroners Unit
APC	Animal Procedures Committee
ASPA	Animals (Scientific Procedures) Act 1986
BLAVA	British Laboratory Animal Veterinary Association
BMJ	*British Medical Journal*
CD	Certificate of designation
CH	Certificate holder
CITES	Convention on International Trade in Endangered Species
COP	Code of Practice
COPHCASP	Code of Practice for the Housing and Care of Animals used in Scientific Procedures.
COSHH	Control of Substances Hazardous to Health
DE	Designated establishment
DETR	Department of the Environment, Transport and the Regions
GLP	Good laboratory practice
HO	Home Office
HOI	Home Office Inspector
HOG	Home Office Guidance (on the operation of the ASPA)
IAT	Institute of Animal Technology
LASA	Laboratory Animal Science Association
MAFF	Ministry of Agriculture, Fisheries and Food
NACWO	Named Animal Care and Welfare Officer
NAVS	National Antivisection Society
NVS	Named Veterinary Surgeon
OJ	Official Journal of the European Union
PL	Personal Licence
PODE	Place other than a designated establishment
PPL	Project licence
RIDDOR	Reporting of Injuries, Diseases and Dangerous Occurrences Regulations 1995
SPCA	Society for the Prevention of Cruelty to Animals (Precursor of the R[oyal] SPCA)
SI	Statutory Instrument
SOP	Standard operating procedure
RDS	Research Defence Society
3 Rs	Replacement, Reduction and Refinement
UFAW	Universities Federation for Animal Welfare

I hope the above list will prove of some use. It can be annoying to be confronted in the middle of a text with a set of initials that look as if they belong to some esoteric code beyond human comprehension.

In connection with some of the above arcane terms I think an anticipatory apology may not be out of place. In any subject but particularly in law there is a tendency to become immersed in the associated jargon. Often we are so familiar with our own technical expressions, whose meanings seem so obvious, we tend to forget that to the outsider they may have an air of mystery about them.

This was brought home to me after lecturing for four hours on the ASPA. A Swiss scientist in Oxford expressed her appreciation of the instructive session. In answer to my concerned enquiry she assured me she understood all that was said. Only one oft recurring phrase puzzled her. She knew what 'Home' meant and what 'Office' meant. She could not comprehend what was the relevance of either term to laboratory animals. The fact that the term 'Secretary of State' applies equally to individuals as diverse as Mo Mowlam and Robin Cook indicates how baffling even this title can be to the uninitiated. In this book 'Secretary of State' refers to one of Her Majesty's Principal Secretaries of State – Secretary of State for the Home Department, popularly known as the Home Secretary. At the time of writing he is the Rt. Hon. Jack Straw MP.

Part I

Introduction

Chapter 1

The General Legal Protection of Animals

The growth of legislation

The main piece of legislation protecting animals in the UK is the Protection of Animals Act 1911 or in Scotland the Protection of Animals Act 1912. Most legal cases involving animals are prosecuted under either of these Acts. Unlike the Animals (Scientific Procedures) Act 1986, the 1911 Act allows for the process of private prosecution. This has rendered it a useful instrument for bodies actively involved in combating animal cruelty. However it was not until the twentieth century that such a comprehensive piece of animal protection legislation evolved. The first animal protection Act was of limited application – the Martin Act 1822. Richard Martin, a barrister and MP for Galway, was with William Wilberforce, one of the founding fathers of the movement in 1824 which blossomed into the RSPCA. Although entitled: 'an Act to prevent the cruel and improper Treatment of Cattle', it was somewhat wider in its scope than just the protection of cattle as the term is now generally understood, as the full text of the Act implies.

> 'Whereas it is expedient to prevent the cruel and improper Treatment of Horses, Mares, Geldings, Mules, Asses, Cows, Heifers, Steers, Oxen, Sheep and other Cattle: May it therefore please your majesty that it may be enacted; . . . and if the Party or Parties accused shall be convicted of any such offence . . . he, she or they so convicted shall forfeit and pay any Sum not exceeding Five Pounds nor less than Ten Shillings.'

By the time we come to 1911 such misdemeanours were viewed far more gravely and hard labour was included among the possible penalties which could be imposed on offenders. Modern sanctions under the 1911 Act are not so draconian. The numerous amendments, in which the 1911 Act abounds, moderated the penalties as well as introducing other features into the legal prevention of cruelty to animals. The penalties usually appear to be short terms of imprisonment, moderate fines or community service. A more recent amendment, the Protection of Animals (Amendment) Act 1988 did, however, increase the powers of the courts to deal with offenders in this area. It enabled the court to disqualify a person from having custody of an animal on a first conviction of cruelty and increased the penalties relating to animal fights. It made further provision with respect to attendance at such fights, in England and Wales and penalises attendance at such fights in Scotland.

The range of animals originally brought within the protection of Martin's Act was gradually extended. The Cruelty to Animals Acts 1835 and 1849 proved to be wider in their application. It appears that around the 1850s an enterprising lawyer was able to harness the breadth of this legislation to prosecute a person suspected of cruelty to some children. He used this approach as there was no specific legal protection of them at the time. Unfortunately I have been unable at present to trace a precise reference for this case. Any determined investigator could, I am sure, verify the details. Limited though Martin's Act was, a case under it brought by the RSPCA was instrumental in the success in the campaign to pass the Cruelty to Animals Act 1876 (the predecessor of the Animals (Scientific Procedures) Act). Dr. Magnan, a Frenchman, demonstrated at a public meeting of the BMA in 1874 that while injection of alcohol produced anaesthesia in a dog, absinthe caused convulsions. He wished to draw attention to the dangers of absinthe. Dr. Magnan had left the country before the prosecution was effective.

'Animal' in the 1911 Act

Within the 1911 Act the term 'animal' was not extended to all animals, just as in the Cruelty to Animals Act 1876 where the term 'animal' was intended to cover no more than vertebrates. Qualification for protection under the 1911 Act was restricted to domestic or captive animals.

Under s. 15 'domestic' includes animals commonly considered domesticated, such as horses, cattle, cats, dogs and birds as well as any other species which has been 'sufficiently tamed to serve some purpose for the use of man'.

The term 'captive' covers any other species, including any bird, fish or reptile, which is in captivity or under some form of control (such as caging or pinioning) to keep it confined. The captivity must be something more than temporary prevention from escape or inability (not caused by man) to escape. The precise meaning of the term 'captive' has been defined by case law. Unlike the 1876 and the 1986 Acts concerned with animals in research, the 1911 Act has produced abundant and fruitful precedents for the development of reliable case law.

In *Steele* v. *Rogers* (1912) 'captivity' had already been given a restricted meaning under the Wild Animals in Captivity Act 1900. In that case it was decided that 'captivity' had to mean more than a temporary inability to get away from a particular spot. Rogers had seriously mutilated with a knife a stranded whale on the sand at Penzance. An hour and half later the tide returned and the whale sank from sight. It was held that the whale was not 'captive'. It was in that position of its own accord; it could have escaped at high tide. Rogers was acquitted of the charge on the grounds that the whale was not 'captive'.

In a later case, this time under the 1911 Act, the connotation of 'captive' appeared to be further restricted. In *Rowley* v. *Murphy* (1964) a hunted stag became trapped under a stationary furniture van. The stag was dragged and carried six or seven yards into a compound where it was killed with a knife by Murphy. The whole operation took about five or ten minutes. The case was thrown out at the magistrates' court on the grounds that the stag was not 'legally captive' The prosecution appealed, but Lord

Parker held that a mere temporary inability to get away was not a state of captivity and accepted that 'in captivity' implied a state of affairs in which domination is exercised over an animal, beyond mere capture. Mr Justice Otton added that the 1911 Act does not cover the maiming of wild animals while they were still in that state, but only when such animals were in a state of captivity. Murphy was acquitted of any offence against the 1911 Act. A further case reinforced this interpretation of the 1911 Act. In *Hudnott* v. *Campbell* (1986), Campbell was charged under the 1911 Act. He had badly beaten a hedgehog which was quietly sitting on the side of the road. The hedgehog did not, and as the beating progressed, could not escape. A kindly person found the hedgehog the next day and took it to a veterinary surgeon but it died. Campbell admitted the facts of the case but the charge was dismissed since the hedgehog was not legally a captive animal. On appeal the Divisional Court upheld the decision of the lower court and rejected the prosecution's contention that the beating had reduced the hedgehog to such a state that Campbell 'had dominion over it'. Another aspect of this moot point in law had been established much earlier in *Water* v. *Meakin* (1916) where it was accepted that recapture would constitute a 'state of captivity'.

The above understanding of 'captivity' is still valid. The League against Cruel Sports brought a case against Jeffrey and Keith Colbert and John Fleming of causing unnecessary suffering to a fox cornered in a culvert by a terrier. The Court of Appeal held that the fact the fox went to ground did not give it the legal status of being in captivity. It was only temporarily restrained with a view to it being killed. The dog had been sent in to flush it out. It had locked its jaws into the fox and dragged it out. Then the fox was shot. The House of Lords upheld the ruling of the Court of Appeal. In refusing to allow the League against Cruel Sports to appeal, the Law Lords obviously considered established precedents in the matter acceptable in law (*Daily Telegraph* 14 May 98).

These cases have been quoted as an indication of the abundant and complex but useful casuistry involved in the interpretation of the 1911 Act. It illustrates how crucial terms in animal legislation may be understood by the courts. This diversion may appear rather irrelevant to our main theme but it must be remembered that laboratory animals are 'captive'. Universities, institutes, pharmaceutical companies etc. certainly have 'dominion over' the animals they use. These animals are therefore well within the protection of the 1911 Act.

The 1911 Act and the ASPA

Schedule 3 of ASPA

'In section 1(3) of the Protection of Animals Act 1911 for the words "the Cruelty to Animals Act 1876" there shall be substituted the words "the Animals (Scientific Procedures) Act 1986".'

The above statement transfers to the ASPA the exemption from the 1911 Act of possible cases associated with the Cruelty to Animals Act 1876. This exemption is further confirmed and clarified.

'3. In paragraph 1 of Schedule 1 to the Protection of Animals (Anaesthetics) Act 1954 for the words "Any experiment duly authorised under the Cruelty to Animals Act 1876" there shall be substituted the words "Any procedure duly authorised under the Animals (Scientific Procedures) Act 1986".'

A person cannot, therefore be charged with an offence under the 1911 Act for acts permitted under their project or personal licence or for actions allowed within the context of a certificate of designation. Even a dedicated laboratory animal is not always under a regulated procedure. Most of its life is spent undisturbed in its cage or pen. If in that situation it suffers unnecessarily, due perhaps to neglect, then those responsible could be charged with an offence under the 1911 Act.

Between 1986 and 1999 there have been four prosecutions involving animals used in research. Only two of these were under the ASPA and are noted in the appropriate place. Even so in the second case (*Lord Advocak* v. *Bairden*, July 1998) there had been offences charged under the (Scotland) Protection of Animals 1912 Act for which a plea of not guilty was accepted.

The first case between 1986 and 1999 involving laboratory animals was a prosecution, but not under the ASPA, of a company and one of its directors in 1989. They were found guilty of offences following an incident in which 79 beagles died en route by ferry to Sweden. The incident did not come directly within the scope of ASPA because it had occurred before s. 7 (apropos Schedule 2) had come into force. The second case, brought under the 1911 Act was against two animal technicians for causing dogs unnecessary suffering. It was first heard in Huntingdon on 7 June 1997 and resulted in their conviction. The evidence in the case came from a Channel 4 TV Programme on 26 March 1997 entitled 'It's a Dog's Life' in the *Countryside Undercover* series (APC Report, 1997). These cases will be referred to later in the chapter on prosecutions.

The need to take notice of the relevance of other legislation apart from the ASPA in the setting of animal units was highlighted by a case commenced in Bromley magistrates' court and completed in Croydon Crown Court. In *British Union for the Abolition of Vivisection* v. *The Royal College of Surgeons* (1985) the RCS was unsuccessfully prosecuted by the BUAV under the 1911 Act. The BUAV had accused the RCS of neglect of a female monkey in unsuitable environmental conditions as regards temperature and that due to this negligence the animal had consequently sustained an injury and had suffered unnecessarily.

Although the cases concerning wild animals may have seemed irrelevant they may be of some interest to researchers involved with PODEs. (A PODE is a place other than a designated establishment.) Here, a scientist may be involved with animals that are not captive. It could be a moot point whether in specific cases such animals would be protected by the 1911 Act.

Further comments on the 1911 Act

The Act gives various details of types of cruelty which are not appropriate here but s. 1 of the Act indicates the main theme of this law. It is illegal to cruelly treat, or being the owner, to permit ill treatment of an animal. This last phrase has relevance to the duty of employers within animal units. The general offence under s. 1 is to wantonly or unreasonably cause unnecessary suffering to an animal. This is an open-ended category which includes not only overt acts but also omissions such as the failure to provide necessary food, water or veterinary attention. In *Bernard* v. *Evans* (1925) 'cruelly' was equated with 'so as to cause unnecessary suffering'. Consequently to show an offence had occurred, it must be proved that the act caused suffering and that the suffering was unnecessary. The words 'wantonly or unreasonably' were described as being 'the callous disregard for or reckless indifference to the suffering of an animal' (*McEwan* v. *Roddick* (1952), a New Zealand case).

The use of anaesthetics on animals

The Protection of Animals (Anaesthetics) Act 1954 was amended in certain matters by the Protection of Animals (Anaesthetics) Act 1964. For easier understanding of the legal position I think it is preferable to present the final result of the fusing of the 1964 amendments with the original 1954 Act.

The principle on which the legislation is based is that any operation involving interference with sensitive tissues or the bone structure of an animal without a properly administered anaesthetic shall be deemed for the purposes of the 1911 Act to be performed without 'due care and humanity'. The provision does not apply to injections or extractions using a hollow needle nor to operations listed in Schedule 1 of the 1954 Act. The variations introduced in 1964 revoked or qualified aspects of this Schedule. The present exceptions, when anaesthetics need not be used on an animal, are:

(1) *Regulated procedures* in which the use of anaesthetics is not required under the authority of the ASPA. One must always be aware however of Schedule 2A of the ASPA.
(2) Emergency first-aid to save life or relieve pain.
(3) Docking of the tail of a dog before its eyes are open. Since July 1994 this operation can legally only be done by a veterinary surgeon but the Royal College of Veterinary Surgeons in 1974 had declared the practice unethical. Such an operation, therefore, would need to be justified in relation to the well-being of the puppy.
(4) Amputation of the dew-claws of a dog before its eyes are open.
(5) The provisions as regards castration of equidae were revoked by the 1964 amendment and are now redundant.
(6) Minor operations by a veterinary surgeon which because of their quickness or painlessness, are customarily so performed without an anaesthetic.
(7) Minor procedures which would not customarily be performed by a veterinary surgeon, These could include some procedures on agricultural animals.

The 1964 amendment stressed that castration, dehorning and debudding are not to be regarded *per se* as 'minor operations' or 'minor procedures' (as above in (6) and

(7)). The 1954 Act allowed for castration of a bull or ram under three months and a goat or pig under two months without the use of anaesthetics. The 1964 amendment specifically ruled out castration by the use of any device constricting the flow of blood to the scrotum unless applied within the first week of life. The amendment also ruled out the dehorning of cattle or the disbudding of calves without an anaesthetic, except by chemical cauterisation applied in the first week of life.

As regards other procedures on agricultural animals, lamb's tails can only be docked by a device constricting blood flow to the tail if applied within the first week of life. According to the Docking and Nicking of Horses Act 1949 such a practice with respect to a horse, pony, mule or hinny, was forbidden unless certified as necessary by a veterinary surgeon. (Hardly relevant here but it would be a pity to omit such a little statutory rustic gem.)

Deer antlers in velvet must be removed under anaesthesia sufficient to prevent pain unless done in an emergency or authorised under the ASPA (Removal of Antlers in Velvet (Anaesthetics) Order 1980).

Neither the 1954 Act nor the 1964 Amendment apply to 'fowl or other bird, fish or reptile'. Failure to use anaesthesia for an operation on a bird, a fish or a reptile would not automatically imply in law that an operation had been carried out without 'due care and humanity'. The operator could not be deemed to have breached the Protection of Animals (Anaesthetic) Acts, however a successful prosecution might be brought under the 1911 Act proving that in a specific case such an operation did *de facto* lack 'due care and humanity' or caused unnecessary suffering.

Part II

The Animals (Scientific Procedures) Act 1986 (ASPA)

Chapter 2

The Coming of the Law on Laboratory Animals

The Cruelty to Animals Act 1876

When in 1809 Lord Erskine introduced a Bill into the House of Lords concerned with the use of animals in research, he was regarded as eccentric and his suggested legislation was summarily dismissed as hardly worthy of serious consideration. Society at that time openly condoned cock fighting and bear baiting.

During the nineteenth century, however, there was a gradual build up of demands for legislation to protect animals used in research. The Society for the Prevention of Cruelty to Animals had been founded in 1824 and by the 1880s the Anti-Vivisection Society had been established. There were already strong feelings in high places on the matter as instanced by Disraeli's correspondence with Queen Victoria. Leading scientists were also concerned. A petition signed by Huxley, Jenner, Owen, the Presidents of the Royal Colleges of Physicians and Surgeons and other eminent scientists including Darwin, called for the control of animal experimentation.

A Royal Commission was set up in 1875 which ushered in the Cruelty to Animals Act 1876. This Act, the first of its kind in the world, controlled 'painful experiments' on animals for specific purposes and under certain conditions. This Act was a great leap forward in concern for animals. It was, however, far from perfect after all it was a 'first off'. Its use of the crucial phrase 'painful experiments' in an exclusive sense implied that some uses of animals in research which could be disturbing, were, as the lawyers would say 'outwith' the Act. Strictly speaking the term 'experiment', by definition could only include procedures by which new knowledge could be gained. Thus such practices as passaging tumours or the production of antibodies could be considered as outside the reach of the legislation. Furthermore the term 'painful' could not literally include experiments or other uses of animals in research which could give rise to great discomfort, short of pain as such. The confusion caused by these inadequacies in the legislative drafting of the 1876 Act were obviated by the skilful drafting (under the guidance of the then Home Office Minister, David Mellor) of the 1986 Act. The inapt phrase 'painful experiment' was replaced in section 2(1) of the 1986 Act by the crucial and more explicit term 'a regulated procedure':

> '...any experimental or other scientific procedure applied to a protected animal which may have the effect of causing that animal pain, suffering, distress or lasting harm.'

On account of the aforementioned deficiencies in the 1876 Act and continual and forceful agitation from pressure groups, an abortive attempt was made to produce consensus on the reform of the 1876 Act. A Departmental Committee on Experiments on Animals was set up which produced in 1965 the Littlewood Report. This was a lengthy and informative report, but unfortunately it was of little lasting consequence.

The use of animals under the 1876 Act rose steadily during the twentieth century reaching by 1973 the significant figure of 5.5 million per annum. This high number sparked off further controversy and caused some interested parties to call into question the ability of the 1876 Act to control animal experimentation.

At a deeper level than existing legislation, debate was provoked on the topic of ethical justification for the use of animals in research. Attitudes hardened, opinions crystallised and the various pressure groups intensified their activities. The lobbyists of various societies instigated numerous attempts to produce new, usually stricter, legislation on animal experimentation by means of Private Members' Bills throughout the 1970s.

In 1978 a Council of Europe Committee of experts started work on a draft convention for the protection of animals used for experimental and other scientific purposes. In 1980 the then Home Secretary invited his Advisory Committee on Animal Experiments to discuss framework legislation to replace the 1876 Act. In March 1986 the Council of Europe's Convention for the Protection of Vertebrate Animals used for Experimental and other Scientific Procedures was promulgated. In the UK a comprehensive supplementary White Paper to a previous 1983 White Paper on the subject, had already been issued with serious intent in May 1985. The 1985 White Paper was given legislative form in keeping with the European Convention as the Animals (Scientific Procedures) Act 1986 (ASPA).

The European Convention had been adopted by the Council of Europe (a supra-national body distinct from the EEC) in May 1985, opened for signatures on 18 March 1986 and had received sufficient signatures of Member States (including the UK), to bring the Convention into force on 1 October 1986 prior to ratification by individual nations. Ratification has not yet been forthcoming from all the signatories. The presence or absence of formal ratification is no reflection on the sincerity with which the provisions of the Convention have been applied in practice. The then EEC (now the EU) legislated for Member States. Directive 86/609/EEC demanded compliance with the Convention within three years from 1986. Up to the present (2000) application of the stipulations of the Convention have varied even within the EU.

The 1876 Act, a valediction

Before passing on to deal in detail with a consequence of that European Convention – our own ASPA, it may not be out of place to refer to the worth of the Cruelty to Animals Act 1876. Inadequate though it may have been it was a unique legal phenomenon, worldwide, certainly for nearly 50 years. Apart from Germany and

Italy it was not matched outside the British legal system for over a century (see *Ethics, Animals and Science*, K. Dolan, Blackwell Science, Oxford, 1999). In spite of its many critics the 1876 Act weathered the storms for over a century and did not lack effectiveness. In spite of rumours to the contrary there were in fact three prosecutions under this Act.

In 1876, Dr. Arbrath was prosecuted for advertising, obviously a case of public display, a lecture on poisons in which experiments would be shown. The advertisment appeared three days after the Act was passed. Although no experiment was actually performed there was a conviction with a nominal fine. Dr. Arbrath belonged to the local SPCA (a plebeian form no doubt of the RSPCA) who had refused to prosecute him (*BMJ* 1876 (ii) 545).

In 1881, Dr. David Ferrier was prosecuted by the Victoria Street Society (precursor of the NAVS) for performing experiments on the brain. The prosecution failed because the operations were actually performed by a Dr G.F. Yeo who held the required licence and certificates (*BMJ* 1881 (ii) 836–842).

In 1913 Dr. Warrington Yorke was prosecuted for cruelty to a donkey involving a drug possibly useful against sleeping sickness which produced a species of paralysis. The prosecution failed. Dr Yorke was properly licensed and the court decided that the suffering involved was not unnecessary (*Times Law Reports*, 29 May 1914).

A peculiar case prior to the 1876 Act ushered in the passing of the Act. In 1874, a Frenchman, Dr Magnan demonstrated at a public meeting of the BMA that while an injection of alcohol produced anaesthesia in a dog, an injection of absinthe caused convulsions. Although this procedure was done for the best of motives, to show the dangers of absinthe, an attempt was made to prosecute him under the Martin Act 1822. By the time the prosecution had got under way Dr. Magnan had left the country. It is difficult to understand why the prosecution was under the Martin Act which was primarily concerned with cattle (*cf. Valiant Crusade* pp. 77–78, Moss, Cassell, London, 1961).

Scope of the Animals (Scientific Procedures) Act 1986

The scope of this Act was clearly set out in the 1991 Report (p. 22) of the Animal Procedures Committee:)

> '8.2 The Act provides for the licensing of experimental and other scientific procedures carried out on protected animals, which may cause pain, suffering distress or lasting harm. Such work is referred to in the Act as a regulated procedure. This means that the Act controls the whole range of scientific procedures, from major surgery to the many thousands of scientific procedures which are so minor that they do not require anaesthesia, like the taking of a blood sample.
>
> 8.3 Protected animals are defined in the Act as all living vertebrate animals [and *Octopus vulgaris* since 1993] except man and the definition extends to foetal,

larval or embryonic forms which have reached specified stages in their development. Under the Act an animal is regarded as 'living' until the permanent cessation of circulation or complete destruction of its brain. It follows that procedures carried out on decerebrate animals are subject to the controls of the Act.

8.4 The Act extended controls to some scientific work not covered by earlier legislation. Such work includes, in particular, some breeding animals with genetic defects; production of antisera and other blood products; the maintenance and passage of tumours and parasites; and the administration for a scientific purpose of an anaesthetic, analgesic, tranquiliser or other drug to dull perception. The humane killing of an animal for scientific purposes requires licence authority in certain circumstances.

8.5 The controls do not extend to procedures applied to animals in the course of recognised veterinary, agricultural or animal husbandry practice, procedures for identification of animals for scientific purposes, if this causes no more than momentary pain or distress and no lasting harm; or clinical tests on animals for evaluating a veterinary product under authority of an Animal Test Certificate under the Medicines Act 1968.'

Further details of how the scope of this Act is expressed in practice are to be found in the 'Guidance on the Operation of the Animals (Scientific Procedures) Act 1986' These Guidance Notes are being revised in 2000. As this document is commonly referred to as the Home Office Guidance, it will be referred to in this text as HOG. Further details of changes as regards the administration of ASPA appear in Home Office communications.

Sections of ASPA

Each section of the Act is concerned with a specific area of the legislation on the use of animals in research. These are outlined in Table 2.1. '(A)' signifies that these sections have been amended in some way. Many of these amendments appeared in 1998 and will be dealt with later when appropriate.

An enabling Act

The adaptability of the 1986 Act arises from the fact that it is an enabling Act. By the power of enabling, indicated within the Act itself, the appropriate Minister, in this case the relevant Secretary of State, the Home Secretary, is authorised to issue Statutory Instruments clarifying or amending but not of course radically changing the law as made and approved by Parliament.

Table 2.1 Sections of the 1986 Act concerned with specific areas of the legislation on the use of animals in research

Section	Area of legislation covered
s. 1	defines 'Protected Animal'. (A)
s. 2	defines a 'Regulated Procedure'.
s. 3	outlines the nature of a personal licence in the setting of a project licence and specified place.
s. 4	gives details on the granting of a personal licence. (A)
s. 5	describes in detail the nature of a project licence. (A)
s. 6	deals with Designated Scientific Procedure Establishments, mentioning the NACWO (was 'named person') and the NVS.
s. 7	deals with Designated Breeding and Supplying Establishments. (A)
s. 8	calls for the paying of the fees by the CH.
s. 9	refers to those who may be consulted by the Secretary of State.
s. 10	refers to the conditions on licences and certificates. (A)
s. 11	is concerned with the variation or revocation of licences or certificates.
s. 12	outlines the process of making representation against an adverse verdict from the Secretary of State.
s. 13	allows for suspension of a licence or certificate and describes the process and possibility of appeal.
s. 14	forbids re-use of animals unless permission is given. (A)
s. 15	demands euthanasia at end of series of regulated procedures if suffering or likely adverse effects are present.
s. 16	prohibits use of protected animals in public displays.
s. 17	restricts the use of neuromuscular blocking agents.
s. 18	states the duties and powers of the Inspectors.
s. 19	describes the make up of the Animal Procedures Committee (APC).
s. 20	states the function of APC.
s. 21	presents miscellaneous and supplementary information on Guidance Notes, Codes of Practice, Information and Alterations by Parliamentary Resolutions, and the publishing of appropriate information.
s. 22	lists penalties under the Act.
s. 23	states penalties for making false statements.
s. 24	states penalties for disclosing confidential information.
s. 25	refers to entry of a constable with a warrant.
s. 26	refers to the process of prosecution under the Act.
s. 27	deals with repeal and consequential amendments in previous relevant Acts and transitional provisions in this Act, details of which appear in Sch. 3 and 4 of the Act.
s. 28	outlines the negative procedure associated with the enabling process of producing Statutory Instruments under this Act.
s. 29	deals with the application of the Act in N. Ireland.
s. 30	attends to routine legal matters e.g. the title, interpretation and coming into force of the Act.

Statutory Instruments

The definition of this term is complex and raises difficult points of interpretation. Broadly, the term covers delegated legislation made under:

(1) Powers conferred by statutes after 1947 on Her Majesty in Council, or on Ministers or Departments, to make, confirm or approve subordinate legislation where the enabling Act says that the power will be exercisable by Statutory Instrument;

(2) Powers conferred by statutes before 1948 on these authorities or other rule-making authorities (such as the Rule Committee of the Supreme Court) to make subordinate legislation, and on ministers to confirm or approve instruments of a legislative (but not of an executive) character which also have to be laid before Parliament;

(3) Regulations made by designated Ministers under the European Communities Act 1972.

Government statements of policy and intent, departmental circulars giving instructions and procedural rules issued by certain other public bodies may be legislative in effect and will usually be published; but they will not be published as Statutory Instruments even if made in pursuance of statutory powers.

Under a few statutes, the initiative in preparing draft rules and regulations is given to bodies representing persons engaged in the occupation, and occasionally to individuals so engaged; such schemes cannot normally be given legislative effect without the responsible Minister's approval.

Statutory Instruments may appear in the form of Orders, Regulations and Rules.

The method of producing Statutory Instruments

The parent Act may or may not require the instrument to be laid before Parliament. If there is no requirement as to laying before Parliament, a member who gets to know about it may put down a question about it to the responsible Minister. If the instrument is merely laid before Parliament, no opportunity is provided for it to be discussed, but at least it is brought to the notice of members. It is more common for the enabling Act to provide that an instrument shall be laid subject to the negative resolution procedure. It is then open to any member to move a prayer to annul the instrument within 40 days of it being laid.

A minority of instruments are required to be laid subject to an affirmative resolution of one or both Houses; unless a resolution approving the instrument is passed within the period (if any) prescribed by the enabling Act, the instrument ceases to have effect or, if only in draft, cannot be made.

Safeguards in respect to subordinate legislation

The most effective safeguard against the abuse of delegated legislation is caution with regard to the terms of delegation. The terms of delegation ought to be carefully worded. The established forms of prior consultation with advisory bodies and organised interest groups ought to be used to the full.

There is a Joint Select Committee whose remit since 1977 has been to consider instruments laid before Parliament by the the negative or affirmative procedure, with a view to deciding whether the special attention of the House should be drawn to the instrument.

Knowing about Statutory Instruments

'Does any human being read through this mass of departmental legislation?' asked Lord Hewart (*The New Despotism* (1929), pp. 96–97). Unfortunately, *ignorantia juris neminem excusat* (ignorance of the law is no exuse). Statutory Instruments must be printed, numbered, published and sold. They are also published in annual volumes. However, local or temporary instruments, instruments made available in a separate series to persons directly concerned, and very bulky schedules may be exampted from the requirement of publication.

An instrument may nevertheless have legal effect before it is published and available for sale at a government bookshop but Departments usually stipulate that an instrument shall not come into operation for 21 days after being laid before Parliament. It is, however, a defence to criminal proceedings for contravening an instrument to prove that the instrument had not been issued at the date of the contravention unless the prosecution proves that reasonable steps have previously been taken to bring its purport to the notice of the public or person likely to be affected (*Constitutional and Administrative Law*, S.A. de Smith, Penguin Books, 1978, pp. 328–335.)

Delegated legislation and the 1986 Act

Fortunately, there has not been an abundance of delegated legislation associated with this Act, although one Statutory Instrument, in the form of an Order concerning appeal procedures, was issued even before the end of 1986. It was the Animals (Scientific Procedures) (Procedure for Representations) Rules 1986 (SI 1986/1911).

The delegation of legislative power to the Secretary of State occurs frequently throughout the Act:

(1)   s. 1 (3) (a) and (b) – the protected animal;
(2)   s. 2 (9) – euthanasia;
(3)   s. 7 (9) – Sch. 2;
(4)   s. 12 (7) – representation.

The enabling process in practice and the changing pattern of practical aspects of ASPA are illustrated in Table 2.2.

Table 2.2   The enabling process and the changing pattern of practical aspects of ASPA

Year	Stage
1986	The first Statutory Instrument made under ASPA 'The Animals (Scientific Procedures) (Procedure for Representations) Rules 1986 (SI 1986/1911). It was made on 7 November 1986 and laid before Parliament on 18 November coming into operation on 10 December. This Statutory Instrument spelt out the details of the process for the relief of aggreived parties under the ASPA. Production of *Guidance on the operation of ASPA*, a Code of Practice for The Housing and Care of Animals used in Scientific Procedures.
1987	Guidelines on eye irritation/corrosion tests. Guidelines on the use of neuro-muscular blocking agents.
1989	Advice on research on psychological stress.
1990	Licensees past retirement age – restrictions.
1991	Antibody production – minimal severity. Advice guidelines on use of strychnine in research. Supplementary guidance notes on PPL for microsurgery training. Policy on laparoscopic surgery training.
1992	RCVS Code of Practice for NVSs.
1993	Quail (*Coturnix coturnix*) included in Sch.2. Scientific procedures listing endangered species. Guidance on brokerage. Act extended to *Octopus vulgaris*.
1994	Code of Practice on licensing and inspection. Policy on conflict of interests of named persons. Revised guidelines on eye irritation tests. Training requirements for PIL applicants. Guidance on transgenics and harmful mutants
1995	Training requirements for PPL applicants. Code of Practice for designated breeding and supply establishments. New policy on the use of non-human primates. APC recommendations on regulatory toxicology testing. Revised system for reporting of annual statistics. Training requirements for NVSs.
1996	Requirements for the importation of primates to be used under the Act. Revision of Schedule 1 of the Act and the introduction of a Code of Practice on humane killing.
1997	Named person renamed named animal care and welfare officer (NACWO) Ascites method ban. Cosmetic product testing ban. Alcohol and tobacco testing ban.

Cont.

Table 2.2   Contd

1998	Comprehensive amendment of ASPA, particularly of ss. 4,5,10,14 and the insertion of Sch.2a. These changes are given in detail in the Schedule to the Statutory Instrument, Animals (Scientific Procedures) Act 1986 (Amendment) Regulations 1998 which came into force in 1998. The main effects of this amendment appear to be a requirement for proven competency on the part of PL holders (s. 4), necessity always to consider seriously the 3 Rs (s. 5), provision for keeping animals after procedure, possibility of release, stipulations on the marking of animals and control of the use of animals from the wild (s. 10), greater restriction on the re-use of animals (s. 14) and emphasis on the need to use anaesthetics (Sch. 2a). These amendments have been introduced to bring our law into greater conformity with the Council Directive 86/609/EEC (OJ No L358 18 December 1986 p.1). This text will reflect the amendment as the occasion arises. In 1998 there were further moves regarding cosmetics. The testing of ingredients of cosmetics was banned. Upgrading of dog facilities were also introduced.
Early 1999	Call for listing in designated establishments of those competent in the operation of Sch. 1 methods. Compulsory local ethical review process as from 1 April.

The APC in its 1998 Report (p.2) has an apt note on the amendments

'15. In July, a further Order amending the 1986 Act was debated in both Houses of Parliament. The Order was laid under the provisions of the European Communities Act and amended the Act to bring it into full compliance with the European Directive on the approximation of laws, regulations and administrative provisions of the Member States regarding the protection of animals used for experimental and other scientific purposes (86/609/EEC). These amendments had no practical consequences as the requirements were already enacted through administrative measures such as licence conditions. The changes received cross-party support.'

Into the future

The evolution of the application of the ASPA is a continuous process, particularly under the stimulus of the APC. A salient feature of the reports of the APC has been recommendations on the development of the administration of the ASPA. The prospects for the more recent future were outlined in an address at the LASA winter meeting given by George Howarth MP, Parliamentary Under Secretary of State at the Home Office. The details of his speech can be found in the *LASA Newsletter*, Winter 1998–1999 pp. 4–7. Predicted features already translated into regulations will be referred to in this text. It would be inappropriate to list possible future legislation because in parliamentary procedure and political manoeuvres there can be 'a slip between the cup and the lip'.

Not just the Home Office

The administration of Statutory Instruments and other legislation regarding animals is not solely confined to the Home Office. Other organs of government are involved in controlling animal use and welfare, and in dealing with legal matters that are relevant to the proper running of animal units. In the future, no doubt some of these affairs will be dealt with by the devolved administrations of Scotland, Wales and Northern Ireland.

Some of the branches of government which should be considered as relevant, with examples of their area of concern, are shown in Table 2.3.

Table 2.3 Some of the branches of government and their areas of concern relating to animals

Department	Example
The Ministry of Agriculture, Fisheries and Food (MAFF)	The Animal Health Act 1981
The Department of the Environment, Transport and Regions (DETR)	The Environmental Protection Act 1990
The Nature Conservancy Council (NCC)	The Wildlife and Countryside Act 1981
The Department of Health (DoH) The Department of Health in Northern Ireland	The Medicines Act 1968 The Animals (Scientific Procedures Act 1986)
The Department of Trade and Industry (DTI)	The Export of Animals (Protection) Order 1981
Local government authorities	Collection and Disposal of Waste Regulations 1988
The local constabulary	The Firearms Act 1968
Commissioners of Customs and Excise	Endangered Species (Import and Export) Act 1976

If no specific arm of government is directly concerned with a piece of legislation then the usual legal processes come into operation in the prosecution of an offence e.g. prosecution by the Crown Prosecution Service or a private prosecution (for instance, under the Protection of Animals Act 1911) or in civil cases a suing of the defendant by a claimant (for instance, under the Animals Act 1971).

Chapter 3

The Protected Animal

'Protected animal' defined

The crucial definition of 'protected animal' in s. 1 of the ASPA was amended by a Statutory Instrument, in keeping with the enabling powers of the Secretary of State as stated:

> 's. 1 (1) Subject to the provisions of this section . . .'

and

> 's. 1 (3) The Secretary of State may by order:
>   (a) extend the definition of protected animal so as to include invertebrates of any description;'

The Animals (Scientific Procedures) Act (Amendment) Order 1993 extended the original definition of 'protected animal' (only vertebrates) to an invertebrate species. The new definition of 'protected animal' now reads:

> 'A "protected animal" for the purposes of this Act means any living vertebrate and Octopus vulgaris other than man.'

A comprehensive treatment of the arguments leading to the insertion of the *Octopus vulgaris* into this definition appeared in the 1992 APC Report pp. 7–8.

For the purposes of the Act, an animal is regarded as 'living' until the permanent cessation of circulation or the destruction of the brain. Brain destruction is not complete in decerebrated animals, these are considered to be living and protected under the Act.

For clarification of 'destruction of the brain' refer to the Code of Practice dealt with later in association with Sch. 1.

An animal becomes protected when it reaches the following stages of development:

- in the case of mammals, birds and reptiles halfway through gestation or incubation periods;
- in the case of fish, amphibians and *Octopus vulgaris* the time at which they become capable of independent feeding.

The Secretary of State is enabled by s. 1 (3)(b) to alter the stage of development at which an animal may become protected (HOG 1.6–9).

There are animals and animals

In the amended (1998) s. 5 (5)(b) of ASPA a sort of grading of animals was introduced:

> 'that the regulated procedures to be used are those which ... involve animals with the lowest degree of neurophysiological sensitivity,...'

In section 18 of the application form for a project licence, calling for a plan of work, it was previously required that one justified the choice of species. Special justification was looked for in the case of the use of cats, dogs, equidae and primates. In the amended s. 10 (6) of ASPA attention is drawn to the need for special identification of dogs, cats and primates.

Increasingly, and rightly so, emphasis has been laid on the need to avoid the use of primates in research whenever possible.

By 1996 the APC Primate Sub-committee reviewed its role so that new applications involving wild-caught primates or primates in substantial severity procedures were considered by the full Committee. On p. 10 (n. 78) of the same 1996 Report:

> 'No new applications to use wild-caught primates were considered.'

The *LASA Newsletter* (Winter 1997) refers to the limitations on the use of primates:)

> 'Great apes have never been used under the 1986 Act as laboratory animals. In future the Government will not allow their use. It is felt that the cognitive and behavioural characteristics of these animals means it is unethical to treat them as expendable for research.
>
> It was also confirmed that wild-caught primates of any species will only be allowed in scientific procedures if exceptionally justified. For wild-caught primates to be authorised, there must be no alternative tests appropriate, no suitable captive-bred animals available and the likely benefit must fully justify their use.'

The APC in its 1997 Report (p. 12 n. 80–81) continued to concentrate on concern for the proper treatment of primates.

> '80. Our advice was sought on the suitability of island breeding colonies (where the animals are effectively captive, but free to roam around the island). It was our view that, whilst it might appear preferable that the animals were not caged, the additional stresses of capture, caging and close human contact mean that island colonies are less preferable as a source of animals than captive-breeding centres.'
>
> 81. We are pleased to hear that the European Commission is turning its attention to the use, acquisition, transport and housing of primates and were

pleased to be able to offer advice on a draft European Union policy statement on the use of primates as laboratory animals. We are also delighted to hear that the UK was one of the first states to sign a Council of Europe Declaration of Intent on the use, transport, care and accommodation of laboratory animals (Appendix B). In relation to primates, this declaration requires precise information on the origin and provenance of the animals to be obtained with the objective of limiting the use of animals to those which are purpose-bred and encourages initiatives and measures to end the use of wild-caught primates.'

Chapter 4

The Regulated Procedure

Section 2 (1) of the ASPA states:

> 'Subject to the provisions of this section, "a regulated procedure" for the purposes of this Act means any experimental or other scientific procedure applied to a protected animal which may have the effect of causing that animal pain, suffering, distress or lasting harm.'

The Home Office Guidance on the Operation of the Animals (Scientific Procedures) Act 1986, slightly altering the wording of this definition goes on to expound on the connotation and extension of the term, 'regulated procedure' (HOG 1.10–15).

The terms 'pain, suffering, distress or lasting harm' include death, disease, injury, physiological and psychological stress, significant discomfort, or any disturbance to normal health, whether immediately or in the long term.

A procedure may be regulated if composed of a combination of non-regulated techniques which may cause pain, suffering, distress or lasting harm. The legal distinction between a procedure and a technique is not clarified.

A procedure is regulated if, following or during a procedure, an animal reaches the stage at which it becomes a protected animal and the procedure may have the effect of causing pain, suffering, distress or lasting harm.

A procedure which may result in pain, suffering, distress or lasting harm to a fetus or immature form at or beyond the stage at which it becomes protected is regarded as a regulated procedure, irrespective of any effect on the parent animal. Anything which may result in the birth or hatching of a protected animal with abnormalities which may cause it pain, suffering, distress or lasting harm (for instance, the breeding of animals with harmful genetic defects) is a regulated procedure. It follows that the term 'regulated procedure' can include genetic manipulation involving animals which will reach the stage at which they will become protected animals. The crucial term 'may' in the definition of regulated procedure is of importance in this context.

A procedure is still regulated even if any pain, suffering, distress or lasting harm which would have otherwise resulted is mitigated or prevented by anaesthetics or other substances to sedate, restrain, or dull perception, or by prior decerebation or other procedure for rendering the animal insentient.

The giving of an anaesthetic or analgesic or other substance to sedate or dull the perception of pain of a protected animal for scientific purposes is itself a regulated procedure. Likewise, decerebration, or any other procedure to render a protected animal insentient, if done for scientific purposes, is a regulated procedure.

The comments on the definition of a regulated procedure in HOG are useful and significant because a clear grasp of this term is crucial to the proper understanding of the ASPA. If one is involved in a regulated procedure one needs authorisation in the form of licences and the appropriate certificate. If what is being done to the animal is not a 'regulated procedure' no licence is required.

Variation in the acceptability of some procedures

A government policy announcement appeared in the 1997 Report (p.5, n.37) of the APC.

> '37. In November, the Government issued a supplementary note to its response on our interim report in which it published a policy statement on the use of animals in scientific procedures. It promised:
> - an end to the use of animals in the testing of finished cosmetic products had been secured through a voluntary agreement with the companies carrying out this type of work in the UK;
> - the possibility of ending the use of animals in testing finished household products and the testing of ingredients for the types of cosmetics which could be called 'vanity products' would be explored; [In 1998 a ban was imposed. on the testing of the ingredients of cosmetics on animals.]
> - tests which involved animals in the testing of offensive weapons, or of alcohol or tobacco products would not be allowed;
> - the use of ascitic animals in the production of monoclonal anti-bodies would be phased out.'

Procedures which are not regulated

'The words of the Act 'subject to the provisions of this section' (ASPA s. 2(1)). allow for exceptions in law as regards some scientific procedures on animals.

In keeping with subsections (5), (6), (7) and (8) of s. 1 there are procedures which appear to have the three essential elements of a regulated procedure – 'scientific', 'a protected animal' and 'pain'. They are not, however, regulated procedures because the law says they are not. Description of these exempt procedures are given in HOG 1.16–18 and 1.20.

(1) Ringing, tagging or marking of an animal or any other humane procedure for the sole purpose of enabling an animal to be identified, if it causes only momentary pain or distress or no lasting harm.

(2) Clinical testing on animals for evaluating a veterinary product in accordance with the Medicines Act 1968.

(3) Procedures carried out for the purposes of recognised veterinary, agricultural or animal husbandry practice are not regulated under the Act. For example, taking

blood or other tissue samples for diagnosis and giving established medicines by injection are recognised veterinary procedures, if done for the benefit of the animal. Similarly, husbandry practices which may cause pain, like castration, are not regulated procedures unless they form part of a scientific study. Where there is doubt, the Inspector should be consulted. This is wise advice. From experience it is apparent that official interpretation may vary in this matter.

(4)   Euthanasia by a Schedule 1 method is not a regulated procedure.

Chapter 5

Schedule 1 of the ASPA

Schedules are usually lists of relevant legislative detail appended to an Act. Although placed at the end of an Act they have equal legal force with any section of the Act. Indeed the sole prosecution under the Act for more than the first ten years of the ASPA was for a breach of Sch. 2. This case will be referred to later in association with Schedule 2. The current Schedules to the ASPA are shown in Table 5.1.

Table 5.1 The five schedules of the ASPA

Sch. 1	(Revised 1996) Appropriate methods of humane killing.
Sch. 2	(Revised 1993 and 1998) List of animals to be obtained only from designated breeding or supplying establishments. This Schedule will be commented upon in the chapter on certificates of designation.
Sch. 3	Consequential amendments. The aim of this Schedule was the replacement of references in earlier Acts to the Cruelty to Animals Act 1876 by references to the Animals (Scientific Procedures) Act 1986.
Sch. 4	Transitional provisions dealing with delays in bringing into operation certain parts of the Act. These adjustments are, of course, all now completed, Most of them, e.g. the implementation of Sch. 2 and replacements of 1876 licences were in place before 1990.
Sch. 2a	A requirement to use anaesthetics in all experiments on animals unless there are irrefutable reasons for acting otherwise. This new Sch. 2A, which is not associated with Sch. 2, was issued with the amended form of ASPA published towards the end of 1998. This Schedule will be expounded upon along with the amended and augmented conditions on the personal licence.

The force of Schedule 1

The implication of Sch. 1 is that if an animal in a designated establishment is killed by a method approved for that type of animal, that killing is not a regulated procedure and so no licence is needed to cause legally the death of that animal. The person, however, performing this procedure must be competent in that method of euthanasia. Any uncertainty consequent on the lack of a clear definition of 'competent' has now been obviated by the demand for the drawing up of a register in designated establishments of persons competent in the approved methods of killing in the particular establishment. There is a comment on this aspect of Sch. 1 in the 1997 Report (p. 109 n. 13–14) of the APC:)

'13 We also note that, for those who believe that their particular circumstances merit the use of a humane method not described in Schedule 1, the necessary authority can be granted in the relevant certificate.'

(If this is in the context of a dedicated breeding or supplying establishment it would seem there could be the possibility of a personal licensee operating outside the scope of a project licence, unless it was a case of killing animals of a mutant strain expressing a defective gene or genetically manipulated animals.)

'14. There were also concerns about the qualifications and competence of those undertaking Schedule 1 killing. The Home Office has already accepted the recommendations that we made in our interim report that those carrying out Schedule 1 killings should be appropriately trained and that establishments be required to maintain a register of those competent to humanely kill animals.'

Regarding the future

Again p. 109 of the APC 1997 Report says:

'15. It was also suggested that establishments using only Schedule 1 methods (those, for example, preparing carcasses for dissection or killing animals for tissue or to harvest organs) should be brought within the controls of the Act and should be designated. Some respondents went further: Schedule 1 killing should become a regulated procedure requiring licence authority. These have a bearing on our plans, as set out in Chapter 5, to look at animal use outside the terms of the 1986 Act and we will consider these issues further.'

Schedule 1 in detail

Appropriate methods of humane killing

(ASPA s. 2, 6, 7, 10, 15 (1) and 18(3))

'1. Subject to paragraph 2 below, the methods of humane killing listed in Tables A and B below are appropriate for the animals listed in the corresponding entries in those tables only if the process of killing is completed by one of the methods listed in sub-paragraphs (a) to (f) below:
(a)   confirmation of permanent cessation of the circulation
(b)   destruction of the brain
(c)   dislocation of the neck
(d)   exsanguination
(e)   confirming the onset of *rigor mortis*
(f)   instantaneous destruction of the body in a macerator.

small animals {(c) (d) (e) (f)}

2. Paragraph 1 above does not apply in those cases where Table A specifies one of the methods listed in that paragraph as an appropriate method of humane killing.

A. Methods for animals other than foetal, larval and embryonic forms	Animals for which appropriate
1. Overdose of an anaesthetic using a route and an anaesthetic agent appropriate for the size and species of animal	All animals
2. Exposure to carbon dioxide gas in a rising concentration	Rodents, rabbits and birds up to 1.5 kg
3. Dislocation of the neck	Rodents up to 500 g Rabbits up to 1 kg Birds up to 3 kg
4. Concussion of the brain by striking the cranium	Rodents and rabbits up to 1 kg Birds up to 250 g Amphibians and reptiles up to 1 kg (with destruction of the brain before the return of consciousness) Fishes (with destruction of the brain before the return of consciousness)

5. One of the recognised methods of slaughter set out below which is appropriate to the animal and is performed by a registered veterinary surgeon, or, in the case of the methods described in paragraph (ii) below, performed by the holder of a current licence granted under the Welfare of Animals (Slaughter or Killing) Regulations 1995 (a).
  (i)   Destruction of the brain by free bullet, or
  (ii) captive bolt, percussion or electrical stunning followed by destruction of the brain or exsanguination before return of consciousness.
	Ungulates

B. Methods for foetal, larval and embryonic forms	Animals for which appropriate
1. Overdose of an anaesthetic using a route and anaesthetic agent appropriate for the size, stage of development and species of animal.	All animals
2. Refrigeration, or disruption of membranes, or maceration in apparatus approved under appropriate slaughter legislation, or exposure to carbon dioxide in near 100% concentration until they are dead	Birds Reptiles
3. Cooling of foetuses followed by immersion in cold tissue fixative	Mice, rats and rabbits
4. Decapitation	Mammals and birds up to 50 g

[handwritten: Schedule 1 until day animal born Her need licence]

(a) S.I. 1995/731'

Code of practice for the humane killing of animals under Schedule 1 to the Animals (Scientific Procedures) Act 1986

One marked advantage of this new form of Schedule 1 has been the addition of a Code of Practice providing commentary on and explanation of the terms used in the Schedule.

For a full grasp of what is involved the actual text of both the Code and the Schedule should be studied. The material in Table 5.2 is merely intended to highlight more significant material from parts of the Code. Unfortunately the selection is bound to be subjective.

Table 5.2 Code of Practice under Schedule 1 to ASPA

Part 1 is a general introduction.

Part 2 refers to the various stipulations in the Act on euthanasia; most of this material occurs elsewhere in this work but some items call for special attention:

- 'Killing a protected animal for a scientific purpose at a designated establishment does not require a licence if a method listed in Schedule 1, appropriate to the animal, is used. However, if another method is used, the killing is a regulated procedure and requires personal and project licence authority.' (2.1) The statement (2.1) above is crucial to the proper understanding of the legal implications of Schedule 1.

Contd.

Table 5.2   Contd

- 'Under Section 10(2)(b) of the Act there is an inviolable termination condition applied as condition 14 to all personal licences. If an animal undergoing a regulated procedure shows signs of severe pain or distress which cannot be alleviated, the personal licensee must ensure that it is killed painlessly without delay . . .' (2.7)
- The executive power of the Inspector to require the killing of an animal if she/he considers it is undergoing excessive suffering carries a criminal sanction. (2.8)

Part 3 is concerned with safeguards for humane killing e.g.:

- Sympathetic handling is paramount. (3.1)
- Do not kill animals in the presence of others. (3.2)
- Adjust the method to cause the least amount of suffering, induce terminal unconsciousness. (3.3)
- Only those who are competent should use physical methods of killing animals. (3.4)
- The CH should ensure the competency of those members of staff who are required to kill animals. (3.5)
- Methods of killing must be appropriate to the species and stage of development of the animal. (3.6)
- 'It is accepted that killing a pregnant animal by a Schedule 1 method in the later stages of gestation normally leads to the death of the foetus. There is no evidence to suggest that the death of the unborn animal would be distressful and inhumane provided direct physical injury to the foetus is avoided. Killing the pregnant dam by a Schedule 1 method does not require licence authority. Project and personal licence authority is required to use the live foetus in a regulated procedure after the half-way stage of gestation.' (3.7)

Part 4 demands confirmation of death before disposal and describes ways of ensuring the animal is dead, e.g.:

- Check circulation has ceased from the absence of pulse or heart beat or make certain of death by section of the heart or great vessels. (4.2 & 4.5)
- The permanent loss of function rather than physical destruction of brain structure can be confirmed by no reflex to stimulus e.g. by touching the cornea, or by the cessation of breathing. (4.3)
- Death from dislocation of the neck can be confirmed by palpation. (4.4)
- Observation of rigor mortis can be used to ensure that death has occurred. (4.6)
- When macerators are used for the disposal of small carcasses, there must be confirmation that there is no longer any response to any painful stimulus. (4.7)

Part 5 refers to various obligations in respect of the disposal of carcases such as:

- To be sure the animal is dead. (5.1)
- To dispose on site if possible or discreetly. (5.2)
- To comply with all statutory legislation on the disposal of hazardous material. (5.3)
- To comply with special conditions in disposing of the carcasses of farm animals. (5.4)

Part 6 comments on the appropriate methods of humane killing in practice:

- Training or in some cases special qualifications (e.g. licensed slaughtermen or veterinary surgeons) are required (6.1)
- The guidance given in Part 6 is neither comprehensive nor mandatory. (6.2)
- When an anaesthetic is used the method, route and agent must be the most appropriate to the particular animal and there should be rapid loss of consciousness. (A.1)

Contd.

Table 5.2 Contd

- Direct injection into the heart can be painful and should not be used. (A.1)
- Anaesthesia induced by inhalation is not suitable for large animals nor diving animals. In the case of small animals care must be taken in administering anaesthetic inhalants and an effective scavenging system must be in place. (A.1)
- The recommended method of euthanasia for fish, amphibia and *Octopus vulgaris* is immersion in water containing an appropriate anaesthetic agent. (A.1)
- Details are given of the proper use of carbon dioxide gas for euthanasia e.g. the chamber should be emptied and flushed clear after each batch of animals has been killed. (A.2)
- Special training and skill is required for killing by dislocation of the neck. (A.3)
- Killing by concussion calls for special expertise and a great amount of care and attention is needed to ensure immediate death. (A.4)
- The use of a free bullet, captive bolt, percussion or electric stunning requires specialised equipment and approved expert operators. (A.5)
- Some small fetuses, embryos and larvae can be killed by immersion in anaesthetic agents. (B.1)
- Euthanasia by refrigeration of chick embryos can be by exposure to 4°C or below for more than 4 hours. (B.2)
- 'Chick embryos can be killed by passing the eggs through a macerator similar to those used for day old chicks and unhatched eggs' (EC Reg. COM(91)136.) Intact embryonated eggs and exposed embryos or larvae can be killed by keeping them in near 100% carbon dioxide gas for a long time until they are dead.' (B.2)
- In the case of reptilian embryos death should be ensured by an overdose of an anaesthetic agent, maceration or immersion in a tissue fixative. (B.2)
- Tissue fixative used in the euthanasia of foetuses should be 4°C. (B.3)
- Decapitation can be carried out with a strong pair of sharp scissors. (B.4)

Chapter 6

The Personal Licence

Definition of the personal licence

A personal licence is a certificate of competence permitting the holder to carry out the regulated procedure(s) authorised in the licence, subject to attached conditions and only in conjunction with a project licence permitting the performance of such regulated procedure(s).

Permitted procedures can only be performed in the stipulated designated establishment or establishments except in cases of the appointment of a specific PODE (place or places outside a designated establishment).

Except when issued to students and others for the purposes of study, personal licences generally remain in force indefinitely but are reviewed, at least every five years (ASPA s. 4(5)).

Qualifications

'Applicants for personal licences must be at least 18 years of age.' (HOG 5.4) The APC saw fit to recommend in its 1990 Report (nn. 28–33) restrictions limiting the licences of those approaching 70 years of age. 'It is normally expected that personal licensees should have at least the equivalent of five GCSEs at Grade C or above, or appropriate formal vocational training.' (HOG 5.5)

The crucial consideration taken into account in the issuing of the personal licence is competence. It is an appropriate skill or technique which is required. On the other hand in the case of a project licence the establishment of justification is demanded in the application and the ability to fulfil a managerial role is all-important.

Supposed competence is no longer taken for granted. By April 1994 a requirement came into effect for personal licence applicants to have satisfactorily undertaken mandatory training courses (of these more later). In the 1998 amendments to the ASPA:

> 'In Section 4 after subsection (4) there shall be inserted – "(4A) The Secretary of State shall not grant a personal licence to a person unless he is satisfied that the person –
> (a) has the appropriate education and training (including instruction in a relevant scientific discipline) for the purpose of applying the regulated procedures to be specified in the licence; and

(b) is competent to apply those procedures in accordance with the conditions which are to be included in the licence and to handle and take care of laboratory animals." '

Sponsorship

Sponsorship is a crucial feature of the application for and in the granting of a personal licence. The sponsor must be someone in authority at the place where the licence will be used. She/he must know and certify the qualifications, training, experience, competence and character of the applicant.

The personal licence is issued on the basis of the assessment of the sponsor and the Inspector. In special cases the Secretary of State before granting a licence, may if considered appropriate, consult an independent assessor or refer the application to the APC.

HOG contains various comments on sponsorship.

'5.6   Applicants who have not previously held a licence must provide a certificate [in which the requirements referred to above are vouched for] signed by a sponsor . . . The sponsor will . . . often be a project licence holder and hold or have held, a personal licence.'

5.7   The sponsor must . . . be able to give an opinion on their suitablility to hold a licence and take responsibility for the care of the animals. Sponsors must list their own qualifications.

5.8   In the case of applicants who do not have English as a native language, the sponsor must confirm the apppplicant's ability to understand English, the Act's provisions, the conditions of the project and personal licences, and the responsibilities of the personal licensee.'

Supervision

'. . . Most new licensees will be expected to work under supervision initially and, if so, conditions to this effect will be attached to the personal licence.'

(HOG 5.5)

The nature, extent and intensity of this supervision will vary e.g. according to whether the applicant is an undergraduate or has not lived in the UK for the previous five years or is seeking authority for extra techniques etc. The terms of supervision in the individual case will be clarified in conditions on that licence. The level of supervision is a matter for the supervisor, in consultation with the Inspector if necessary. As time goes on the supervision may become more a matter of monitoring or even eventually a discussion of methods of work. In the case of undergraduates, however, supervision remains until the completion of their degree course. In other cases a period of one year has been normal.

The imposition of a supervision condition will not lessen an individual's responsibility to comply with the provisions of the ASPA.

> 'Since a personal licence is a certificate of competence to perform regulated procedures on animals, personal licensees are not generally restricted to working on particular projects. However, new licensees will sometimes be confined to particular projects initially.'
>
> (HOG 5.9)

Responsibilities of the personal licence holder

> 'It is particularly important for personal licensees to appreciate that, as set out in para. 3.4. of the COPHCASP, they bear primary responsibility for the care of animals on which they have carried out scientific procedures.'
>
> (HOG 5.11)

This demands the licence holder's presence at any time when an animal is most likely to be in pain or distress, especially when recovering from a procedure or is under an anaesthetic.

> 'It is the responsibility of the personal licensee to familiarise themselves with the severity limit of procedures listed in the project licence (section 19a) and the constraints upon adverse effects described in the protocol sheets (section 19b).'
>
> (HOG 5.12)

> 'Personal licensees should ensure that the cages, pens or places in which the animals are held carry labels indicating the project licence number, the personal licensee, the procedures which the animals are undergoing and any additional information which may be required by the Inspector.'
>
> (HOG 5.13)

Larger animals as well as cats, dogs and all non-human primates, must be individually identified.

An understanding of the subordinate position of some personal licensees within some structures is shown in the ASPA (s. 22 (4)).

> 'A person shall not be guilty of an offence under section 3 or 17(a) above [these sections stipulate the need for the authority of a project licence to perform a regulated procedure and for the authority of a project licence to use a neuro-muscular blocking agent] by reason, only that he acted without the authority of a project licence if he shows that he reasonably believed, after making due enquiry, that he had such authority.'

This is not a complete reneging on the solid legal principle. *Ignorantia juris neminem excusat* (ignorance of the law excuses no man), but is rather a very sensible provision for cases of ignorance of fact where juniors might be unduly influenced and misled by forcefully expressed opinions of their seniors.

Conditions on a personal licence

All personal licences are governed by conditions. Those reproduced here are the standard conditions as increased from 19 to 22 (7/10/98) and later revised (22/4/99). They replace those found in the 1990 edition of HOG under Appendix VI. Similar revised conditions (22/4/99) on the project licence and on Certificates of Designation replace the previous ones under Appendices II, III and IV in the 1990 edition of HOG. These Conditions are reproduced below in their appropriate place under their appendix heading. The number of standard conditions on both the project licence and on the certificates of designation was increased on 7 October 1998. These standard conditions are applicable on every licence or certificate to which they are attached. The Inspectorate is, however, free to impose additional appropriate conditions on any licence or certificate of designation if circumstances demand it.

Breaches of conditions 1–9 and condition 10 on the personal licence may be criminal offences under the ASPA. There is a nice legal distinction between 1–9 and 10. In the case of 10, a one to one authoritative order is envisaged which would be personal to the individual addressed and only applicable in those circumstances.

Guidelines on neuromuscular blocking agents

The HO issued guidelines on the use of neuromuscular blocking agents in April 1988. The following quotations are from the APC Report 1988 pp. 26–28. (The actual text should be consulted for further details.)

'3. In section 17 of the Animals (Scientific Procedures) Act 1986 it states that "no person shall in the course of a regulated procedure:

(a)   use any neuromuscular blocking agent unless expressly authorised to do so by the personal and project licences under which the procedure is carried out; or

(b)   use any such agent as an anaesthetic."

To do so would constitute an offence under the Act. But should a person be able to show that he reasonably believed after making due enquiry that he had appropriate authority, he would not be guilty of the offence in (a) above.

4. Neuromuscular blocking agents may be classified according to their action at the motor endplate:

(a)   depolarising – including suxamethonium.

(b)   non-polarising – including tubocurarine, gallamine, alcuronium, pancuronium, atracurium, and vecuronium.'

5. There are other naturally occurring biological compounds, such as venoms (e.g. Black Widow Spider) and toxins (e.g. *Clostridium botulinum* toxin) which when used systemically block neuromuscular transmission. There are also other agents (e.g. neomycin, high concentrations of magnesium ions) which have

non-specific effects at the motor endplate. Such agents are not used clinically as neuromuscular blockers, and neither is it intended that they should be used instead of an anaesthetic. They will not be regarded specifically as neuromuscular blocking agents for the purpose of the Animals (Scientific Procedures) Act 1986; however, they must not be administered to living animals for an experimental or other scientific purpose unless authorised by a project licence.'

Applicants intending to use muscular blocking agents will need to understand their use as set out in the relevant guidelines. They will normally be required to have witnessed their use and be familiar with the procedures for achieving and maintaining anaesthesia under such regimes. Where a licensee has been given permission to use neuromuscular blocking agents for the first time, she/he will, unless specifically exempted by the Home Secretary, be required to give the Inspector 48 hours' notice of the procedure. This restriction may be extended to further occasions if the Inspector considers it appropriate.

'8 These personal and project licence requirements do not apply to the use of such blocking agents during licensed work performed on decerebrate animals'

Conditions 19A, 19B and 19C resulted from the introduction of Schedule 2A and the October 1998 amendment of ASPA (s. 10 (2a)). This amendment was an implementation of Article 8 of Council Directive No. 86/609/EEC.

The text of Schedule 2A

'1. All experiments shall be carried out under general or local anaesthesia.
2. Paragraph 1 above does not apply when:
    (a) anaesthesia is judged to be more traumatic to the animal than the experiment itself;
    (b) anaesthesia is incompatible with the object of the experiment. In such cases appropriate legislative and/or administrative measures shall be taken to ensure that no such experiment is carried out unnecessarily.
    Anaesthesia should be used in the case of serious injuries which may cause severe pain.
3. If anaesthesia is not possible, analgesics or other appropriate methods should be used in order to ensure as far as possible that pain, suffering, distress or harm are limited and that in any event the animal is not subject to severe pain, distress or suffering.
4. Provided such action is compatible with the object of the experiment, an anaesthetised animal, which suffers considerable pain once anaesthesia has worn off, shall be be treated in good time with pain-relieving means or, if this is not possible, shall be immediately killed by a humane method.'

Condition 19A enforces paras 1 and 2 of Sch. 2A but 'authorised procedure' (with a wider connotation) replaces 'experiment'. Condition 19B enforces para. 4 of Sch. 2A. Condition 19C enforces para. 3 of Sch. 2A.

Non-technical procedures

'If the conditions of a personal licence permit the holder to use assistants to perform, under his direction, tasks not requiring technical knowledge nothing done by an assistant in accordance with such condition shall constitute a contravention of section 3 above.'

(ASPA s. 10(4))

Permission to use assistants is sought by ticking the 'yes' box in section 16 of the application form for a personal licence. The specific authority to delegate, granted in response to this request will be contained in the personal licence. The terms of such a condition on the personal licence must be strictly observed.

Appendix VII of HOG provides a list, but not an exhaustive list, of 'some examples' of the kind of tasks which may be delegated. There is no attempt to define these 'non-technical procedures'; rather it is a matter of giving 'for instances'. Perhaps rightly so, because rigid definitions fossilise law and obviate desirable flexibility in its application. The Inspector will readily advise on these matters. Some examples of permitted assistance in transgenic work might not be regarded by some as non-technical in ordinary parlance.

Where the list below of the non-technical procedures in Appendix VII refers to tasks 'previously' carried out, those tasks will have been specified by a suitably qualified personal licensee, who must be within reach for assistance or advice if required.

'1) The filling of food hoppers and water bottles with previously mixed diets or liquids of altered constitution or to which test substances have been previously added.

2) The placing of animals in some previously set-up altered environments e.g. inhalation chambers, pressure chambers, aquatic environments.

3) Pressing the exposure button to deliver previously determined doses of irradiation to an animal.

4) Pairing/grouping associated with the breeding of animals with harmful genetic defects.

5) Withdrawal of contents from an established ruminal fistula.

6) Operating automated machinery which carries out inoculation of eggs.

7) Placement of animals in restraining devices, as defined by the project licence.

8) Withdrawal of food and/or water, as defined by the project licence.

9) Placement of avian eggs into previously-set chillers at the termination of a procedure.'

A special proviso is applied, over and above the initial caveat demanding permission to delegate these non-technical procedures, in the case of the two final categories of non-technical procedures which a personal licensee can delegate.

The following tasks can only be undertaken by assistants in the presence of a suitably authorised personal licensee.

‘10) In animals rendered insentient by decerebration or general anaesthesia which is to persist until death, and through an established catheter, administration of a substance(s) as defined by the project licence or removal of body fluids.

11) In animals rendered insentient by decerebration or general anaesthesia which is to persist until death, the administration of electric stimuli through electrodes implanted by a personal licensee.’

Figure 6.1 displays the various relationships of the personal licence holder to other members of staff involved with experimental animals.

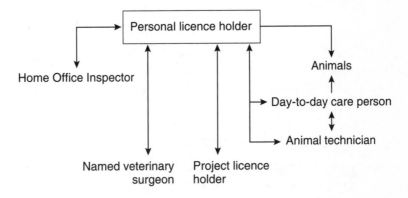

Fig. 6.1 Relationships of personal licence holder to other members of staff.

Chapter 7

The Project Licence

Definition of 'project licence'

The official definition of a project licence is to be found in the Animals (Scientific Procedures) Act 1986 itself.

> 's. 5 (1) A project licence is a licence granted by the Secretary of State specifying a programme of work and authorising the application, as part of that programme, of specified regulated procedures to animals of specified description at a specified place or places.'

Salient features of the project licence are:

- authorisation of a programme including regulated procedures
- description of background, objectives and potential benefits of a project
- description of techniques entailed in each procedure
- statement of species and estimation of numbers of animals used
- the fixing of severity bands
- the naming of the establishment where the work is done
- statement of the name of the licensee and named deputies.

The licence itself and the application for it are issued to parties concerned when required so copies of them hardly belong within this text.

The application for a licence is by no means a simple matter. The process involved is more in the nature of making a case – justifying the performance of suggested procedures – rather than merely filling in an official questionnaire, or establishing appropriate qualifications, as may be required for the acquisition of other types of licence. The complicated nature of the application is well illustrated by the fact that time must be set aside in the training of applicants, for specific instruction in dealing with the application form. Special useful and illuminating seminars were provided by the HO Inspectorate on this topic in 1999. Literature distributed by the ABCU containing indications on the type and form of information required by the inspectors who consider applications has proved extremely helpful. In some institutes involved in animal experimentation dedicated staff are employed in the important area of liaison with the HO regarding project licences. Some short notes on application for a project licence may not, however, be out of place in this text.

Application for a project licence

Required details include:

'(i)   the purpose and scientific justification for the work; (s. 17)

(ii)   a full description of the procedures which would be involved; (s. 19b)

(iii) an estimate of the number of animals of each species which may be required; (s. 19a)

(iv)   a statement of the status, qualifications and experience of the project licence holder, so that an assessment can be made of the suitability of the applicant to supervise, manage and take responsibility for the project; (s. 2, 5, 10, 17)

(v)   an assessment of potential severity'. (s. 19a, 19b)

(HOG 4.3)

and further:

'(i)   the suitability of the design of the project in relation to its stated objects; (s. 17, 18.)

(ii)   the considerations which have been given by the applicant to reducing the number of animals used, refining procedures to minimize suffering and replacing animals with alternatives; (s. 18, 21)

(iii) the justification for using the animals which are proposed, including the special justification required by section 5(6) for the use of primates, cats, dogs and equidae; and the sources from which schedule 2 animals are to be obtained; (s. 18)

(iv)   whether the proposed anaesthetic techniques or other methods for mitigating or preventing pain and distress are appropriate to the animals and procedures; (s. 19b)

(v)   whether the facilities at the establishment are adequate for the scientific procedures; (s. 21, 22)

(vi)   whether the place where the work is to be done has adequate facilities in accordance with the Code of 'Practice, for the species involved.' (s. 22)

(HOG 4.32)

An 's' in brackets refers to the relevant section on the application form.

Guidance on the Administration of the ASPA points out that regulated procedures performed under contract are usually under a project licence of the organisation doing the work. A project licence holder must be a person working in the UK. (HOG 4.33)

The licence application and the 3 Rs

The 3 Rs – replacement, reduction and refinement – are a crucial feature in both the application for and the granting of a project licence. The whole subject of the 3 Rs has dominated, and perhaps rightly so, the ethical discussion on animal experimentation (*Ethics, Animals and Science*, K. Dolan, Blackwell Science, Oxford, 1999, pp. 188–210).

The constant obligation to seek for more acceptable expressions of the 3 Rs in practice is not only ethical, it is solidly grounded in the Animals (Scientific Procedures) Act 1986:

> 'The Secretary of State shall not grant a project licence unless he is satisfied that the applicant has given adequate consideration to the feasibility of achieving the purpose of the programme to be specified in the licence by means not involving the use of protected animals,'
>
> (s. 5(5))

and

> 'The conditions of a personal licence shall include . . . a condition to the effect that the holder shall take precautions to prevent or reduce to the minimum consistent with the purposes of the authorised procedures any pain, distress or discomfort to the animals to which those procedures may be applied;'
>
> (s. 10(2)(a))

The Home Office Guidance (HOG) is equally insistent on the importance of the 3 Rs.

> 'Besides weighing the benefits of a project licence against the likely adverse effects on the animal concerned, a number of other considerations are taken into account before a project licence is granted. These include: . . .
> (ii)   The consideration which has been given by the applicant to reducing the number of animals used, refining procedures to minimise suffering and replacing animals with alternatives;
>
> (4.32)

and

> In applying for a licence (education and training) applicants must show that they have carefully considered alternatives, such as video material and computer simulations, and that none is suitable.'
>
> (4.40(5))

Among the official instructions on the project licence application is the following instruction:

> 'Consider alternatives, particularly with reference to reduction and refinement.'
>
> (s. 18)

Section 21 demands a signature to this effect. The legal importance of the 3 Rs might be further stressed by moving this demand to consider them, to an earlier section of the application.

A Home Office communication (HO/PCD-H Nov 1997) reiterates the significance of alternatives:

> 'This government will insist that applicants for licences demonstrate their efforts at finding alternatives before the use of animals is proposed.'
>
> (Response to the APC Report on the matter)

Furthermore since April 1999 this demonstration of a comprehensive consideration of the 3 Rs and non-animal alternatives is an essential element in every application for a project licence.

This stress on the importance of finding alternatives to animals in research expresses fully the spirit of the 1998 amendment of the ASPA:

> '3. In section 5 (project licences), for subsection (5) there shall be substituted –
>   "(5) The Secretary of State shall not grant a project unless he is satisfied –
>   (a) that the purpose of the programme to be specified cannot be achieved satisfactorily by any other reasonably practicable method not entailing the use of protected animals; and
>   (b) that the regulated procedures to be used are those which use the minimum number of animals, involve animals with the lowest degree of neurophysiological sensitivity, cause the least pain, suffering, distress or lasting harm, and are most likely to produce satisfactory results".'

Our domestic legal requirements in respect to the 3 Rs fully implement European legislation on the matter.

> 'An experiment shall not be performed if another scientifically satisfactory method of obtaining the result sought, not entailing the use of an animal, is reasonably and practically available.'
>
> (Directive 86/609/EEC, Art. 23)

Statements on the scientific validity of the Rat Skin Transcutaneous Electric Resistance (TER) Test and the EPISKIN test signed by Michael Balls, Head of ECVAM and Guy Corcelle, Head of DGXI/E/2, European Commission, Brussels were quickly approved, accepted and applied in the UK in an official letter by Steve Wilkes, head of the Animal Procedures Section (29/6/1998):)

> 'The European centre for the Validation of Alternative methods has validated two replacement skin–corrosivity tests; rat skin TER and EPISKIN. Authority to use animals to test skin corrosivity will only be given if a regulatory requirement can be established. All those with existing authorities to use animals in such tests should only do so where the in vitro alternative can be demonstrated to be inadequate.'

An ever increasing number of such directives may be anticipated in the future.

Researchers need to be aware of these advances. There is an indication here of possible conflict between the requirements of different authoritative bodies.

The APC in its 1997 Report particularly highlights the demand for the use of alternatives:)

> '31. In drafting applications, potential project licence holders are responsible for ensuring that reduction, refinement and replacement alternatives are fully considered in research programmes and that the project is designed to ensure that the chances of achieving the desired objectives are not compromised.'
>
> (p. 92)

> '61. Each year, the Home Office makes available to the Committee a budget to sponsor work aimed at developing or promoting the use of alternatives which replace animal use, reduce the number of animals used or refine the procedures involved to minimise suffering. Work aimed at improving the environmental conditions in which laboratory animals are kept and transported outside procedures has also been sponsored.'
>
> (p. 7)

During 1997 six projects funded by the Home Office were completed:

(1)   Development of *in vitro* assay for *Clostridium botulinum* neurotoxins.
(2)   Evaluating the potential of a human lymphoid explant in screening immuno-modulatory reagents of clinical interest.
(3)   Biochemical characterisation of plasma neurotoxins involved in equine grass sickness monitored by using neural cell lines.
(4)   Development of organ cultures from salmonids.
(5)   *In vitro* methods of identifying toxin producing *Corynibacterium dyptheriae*.
(6)   Development of rapid immunosensor assays for routine surveillance of paralytic and diarrhetic shellfish poisons (PSP and DSP).

The concept of the 3 Rs presented by Russell and Burch in *The Principles of Humane Experimental Technique* (1992) has been presented in various forms over the last few decades. The most recent authoritative interpretation of and outline of the application of the 3 Rs in practice is to be found in *Selection and Use of Replacement Methods in Animal Experimentation* (1998). This publication was issued under the auspices of FRAME (Fund for the Replacement of Animals in Medical Experiments) and UFAW (Universities Federation for Animal Welfare).

Duration of a project licence

A project licence is valid for five years. Application for renewal should be made well in advance of the expiry date. The licence is not transferable and terminates on the death of the holder. It may continue in force temporarily if the Home Office is notified within seven days by an appropriate representative who has learned of the death of the licence holder.

If it is necessary to transfer the licence to another holder a fresh application must be made and will be considered accordingly. (HOG 6.3–5.)

> 'Where a project licence is granted to a person aged 70 or more, this will be for 12 months only and will be reviewed at the end of that period. Particular attention will also be paid during inspections to the work of any licence holder aged 70 or more.'
>
> (APC Report 1991 p. 7, n. 2.11)

> 'In future, project licences, including new project licences for the continuation of previously authorised work, which are applied for by those aged 65 or more will only be granted for that period which takes the applicant up to his or her 70th. birthday.'
>
> (APC Report 1991 p. 7, n. 2.13)

Justification – cost/benefit

The establishment of justification of the programme suggested and for the regulated procedures involved, must be the main theme of any application for a project licence.

That requisite justification is arrived at by a careful weighing up of the relationship between the possible suffering of the animal and the desirable consequences which are the hoped for results of the research – the cost/benefit assessment.

Crucial to the granting of a project licence is the assessment stating the proposed severity limits and the potential benefits of the work. This assessment of cost against benefit is dealt with in paragraphs 4.4–6 of HOG:

> 'Section 5 (4) of the Act requires that a project licence cannot be granted unless the likely adverse effects (pain, suffering, distress or lasting harm) of the procedures have been weighed against the benefit likely to accrue as a result of the proposed programme of work.'

> The benefit of work may sometimes be difficult to assess in advance and fundamental research where no immediate benefit is sought other than the increase in knowledge is valid and permissible. There is no intention of seeking to control or direct research by ascribing greater intrinsic merit to one area of research than to another so, in all cases, applicants should set out the potential benefit of their specific project, rather than for instance, the importance of the project in general.

> Although it inevitably involves an element of subjectivity, applicants for project licences must assess the likely severity resulting from the procedures in order that this may be balanced against the potential benefit. It is, therefore, necessary to distinguish between assessment of the potential severity of individual procedures (or series of procedures) and the overall severity of the project. No work, however mild will be permitted unless it can be justified. It is recognised

that research into life threatening disease may necessitate a degree of severity which might be difficult to justify in other research.'

The future of cost/benefit assessment

It would seem appropriate at this point to indicate the continuing evolution in the interpretation in practice of the ASPA. This useful feature of the legislation is well illustrated by the consideration given to this theme in the 1996 Annual Report of the Animal Procedures Committee (pp. 27–28).

'18 The submissions we received revealed that there is considerable degree of interest in how the cost/benefit assessment is deployed under the 1986 Act. Some of the submissions from animal protection groups were explicitly critical that very few applications for licences apparently "failed" the cost/benefit assessment. This suggested to them that the analysis is not strictly applied, or that the Inspectorate colludes with licence applicants. We do not accept this conclusion or the premises on which it is based.

19 Some submissions to the review, both from animal protection groups and the user community suggested that there was uncertainty about how the cost/ benefit assessment operated in practice: what factors were examined in the assessment, how was cost evaluated, what kind of benefits were considered and how were costs and benefits weighed against each other? In other words, there are questions about the standard that is applied and about the method of its application.

20 These are issues that the statement on cost/benefit will explore. Our proposal is to discuss these matters with the Inspectorate so that this statement can be built upon and be a critique of existing Home Office practice. In the end, the statement will represent the view of the Animal Procedures Committee and not necessarily that of the Home Office. Among other things, it will situate the Home Office cost/benefit at the end of the chain of events that lead up to an application for a licence; and will examine whether the cost/benefit assessment functions more as a controlling standard than providing a pass/fail examination of applications. One of the effects of a controlling standard is to improve scientific design and ensure that alternatives are employed whenever possible.

21 As for the method of application, there was the recognition that the cost/ benefit assessment would always involve, in the end, a value judgement (but not an arbitary, personal judgement with which it is commonly confused). Judgements are based on interpretation of agreed rules and on previous judgements and are informed by the management processes whereby the Home Office achieves consistency – all features introducing a high degree of objectivity into the decision making process.

22 It is also proposed to examine examples of cases which involve high costs to

animals and others which involve low benefits for humans, other animals or the environment. We will also need to consider work aimed at advancing knowledge where the benefits may only accrue some way into the future and are less easy to identify. These "case studies" will show the cost/benefit assessment operating at the margins of what is acceptable under the Act – the assumption being that, if it operates effectively in these cases, it will do so in less marginal cases.'

This attempt at incipient casuistry by the APC is most timely and could prove to be of great advantage to those involved both in the application and observance of the ASPA. Throughout the history of English law, case law has played a crucial role in legal interpretation.

The delicacy of the casuistry called for in the assessment of cost/benefit is well illustrated in the APC 1997 Report (pp. 13–14) comment on the (1997) report produced by the Advisory Group on the Ethics of Xenotransplantation (the Kennedy Committee).

'96 ... The Kennedy Committee ruled out the use of primates as source animals, but concluded that it would be justifiable, under a cost/benefit analysis, to use such animals in research, where the benefit for a large number of humans would flow from the use of a much smaller number of primates. The Kennedy Committee also concluded that the use of pigs as sources of organs may be acceptable, but that the acceptability lay in balancing the benefit to humans against the costs to the pig.

97. These were views of some significance when it came to our own consideration of applications to use animals in xenotransplantation research, most obviously in the sense that the Kennedy Committee's conclusions were based on a method of cost/benefit assessment which is comparable to our own. As the passages in this report on xenotransplantation reveal, we are particularly sensitive to the issues arising from the use of wild–caught baboons in such research.'

More notes on the cost/benefit assessment

(APC report 1997 pp. 43–59)

'2. The question of whether the benefits derived outweigh the costs is a starting point for many people when contemplating the issues surrounding the use of animals for experimental purposes.

3. It is not surprising, therefore, that a cost/benefit assessment is central to the provisions of the Animals (Scientific Procedures) Act 1986 and to the framework which it establishes for the protection of animals. In some cases, it serves to prohibit certain experiments and, in all cases, it encourages an awareness of the welfare costs which experimentation may involve. It is a key element, then, in ensuring a responsible and critical use of animals in scientific procedures, and provides the backbone of the current regulatory regime.

4. Although the application of a cost/benefit assessment has been a statutory requirement in the consideration of project licences only since 1986, the understanding and practice of this assessment has evolved since then, and we expect that it will continue to evolve.'

The following 1993 quasi-algebraic portrayal of cost/benefit was, however, a worthwhile beginning:

(i) $\text{Justification} = \dfrac{\text{Benefit}}{\text{Cost}}$

(ii) $= \dfrac{\text{Importance of objectives} \times \text{Probability of achievement}}{\text{Cost to animals in suffering}}$

(iii) $= \dfrac{\text{Background/Objectives potential benefits} \times \text{Scientific quality}}{\text{Adverse effects} - \text{Coping strategies}}$

(iv) $= \dfrac{\text{Section 17} \times \text{Section 18}}{\text{Section 19}} \text{ of PPL}$

'5. In giving attention to the issue of the cost/benefit assessment, we have not meant to suggest that it is always difficult to find a consensus about costs and benefits. If we think of cases as lying on a spectrum, at one end we shall find a band where the costs are plainly great and the benefits small and, at the other end, a band in which the benefits are great and the costs small. There are other cases, however, where things are more finely balanced, and where the necessary exercise of judgement will be more open to question.'

In the 1997 APC Report, the Chief Inspector expanded and advanced the notion of the cost/benefit assessment:

'1.2 The cost/benefit assessment is applied at the project licence level, and is a process rather than an event. It generally begins before a formal application is made and continues throughout the duration of the programme of work, rather than being applied only at the time authorities are granted or refused. An outline is given of how the Inspectorate both assesses new proposals and ensures the 3 Rs are properly implemented.

2.3. The 1993 paper [produced by the Inspectorate and published in the APC 1993 Report] stated that the cost/benefit assessment is applied at the project licence level, and argued that factors regulated by other parts of the system did not form part of this consideration. This is one area where thinking has changed. Although no cost benefit assessment is conducted when advising on personal licence or certificate of designation applications, technical competence and standards of care and accomodation are now considered during the project licence cost/benefit assessment.

3.8. Although a considerable body of precedent and case law has been established which is applied to new applications, the framework for the cost/benefit assessment is not, and should not be, a static system. Assessments reflect precedent, but also accomodate developments in welfare, science, ethics, political thinking and informed public opinion.

4.4. Applications set the animal-based research in the context of other activities and collaborative work being performed to meet the stated objectives. Experimental design must be sound and clearly suited to meeting the stated objectives. Justification is required for the animal models to be used and the specific endpoints requested (reflecting both welfare and scientific outcomes). It must be clear that the cost has been minimised and the benefits maximised.

4.5. A considerable proportion of Inspectorate resources is devoted to ensuring that project licence applications cannot be further refined, and that authorities are drafted in such a way that projects are reviewed if progress is not made or if unexpected welfare problems occur.'

Benefits

Following on the consideration of the cost/benefit assessment it would seem more appropriate to consider 'cost' before 'benefit'. Benefits with objectives, however, are considered in section 17 of the application for the project licence before the consideration of the cost in section 19 and the starting point of the assessment is whether benefits outweigh costs. The following legislative material lists the acceptable categories of benefits.

Purposes for which a project licence may be granted

There are legal restrictions on the granting of a project licence. Both the European Convention (Art. II) and the ASPA (s. 5 (3)) stipulate that a project licence can only be granted for one or more of the following reasons:

(i)   the prevention, diagnosis or treatment of disease; ('targeted research')
(ii)   the study of physiology; ('blue sky research')
(iii)   environmental protection benefiting health and welfare;
(iv)   advancement of biological or behavioural sciences;
(v)   education and training (factors such as the level of education, an in depth consideration of alternatives and the level of severity (usually unclassified), enter into the consideration of the granting of a licence under this heading);
(vi)   forensic enquiries;
(vii)   breeding animals for scientific purposes (an application for a licence under this

heading will not be concerned with the ordinary breeding of animals for research, but will be associated with the production of mutant strains of animals expressing a genetic defect or breeding involving genetic manipulation).

Comments on benefits

The seven reasons listed above categorise the possible benefits for which a project licence may be granted. In an actual application for a licence the hope for benefit of the project must obviously be spelt out in more detail. It will not always be easy to indicate precisely the actual as opposed to the potential benefit of any particular piece of research but there ought to be a realistic presentation of the beneficial results anticipated, commensurate with the use of the animals involved.

> '2.4. The essential determinants of "benefit" remain the likelihood of success, and how the data (or other product) generated by the programme of work will be used, rather than the importance of the field to which the research relates: for example, the long term goal may be to find a cure for cancer, but the "benefits" relate only to those which might reasonably be expected to arise directly from the programme of work for which licence authorities are sought. Expressed in these terms, the gulf between "fundamental" and "applied" research is narrower than many people perceive.'
>
> (APC Report 1997 p. 50)

Further comments by the Chief Inspector on benefits appear on p. 56 of the APC 1997 Report:

> '5.20 While the socio-economic advantage of cheaper healthcare (including "me too" products) is not ruled out as a legitimate benefit, the profitability of the company applying for authorities and the researchers' career prospects are not considered by the Inspectorate to be legitimate potential benefits for the purposes of the cost/benefit assessment required by the 1986 Act.
>
> 5.21. Every effort must be made to maximise the expected benefits. No useful data should be ignored or discarded, and resources and findings should be shared with others. The Inspectorate seeks improvements in study design which increase the potential benefits of the study without increasing the cost; encourage communication between research groups in an attempt to identify and spread best practice; and can make use of knowledge of practical problems which have not been reported in the literature.
>
> 5.24 However, different benefits apply in the context of regulatory toxicity and safety testing. For example, the testing of chemicals under the Dangerous Substances Directive allows for proper precautions to be taken during the manufacture, storage and transport of materials. Here, the issue is protection of

the work-force, the public and the environment – not consumer safety. The justification for such testing relates not to the finished products in which the chemicals are used, but to the public and ecological safety – regardless of the end use.'

In section 17 of the application for a project licence the term 'objective' occurs in tandem with 'potential benefits'. The 'objectives' of the project must be clearly defined. They are the definitely achievable and measurable outcome of the experiments. The 'potential benefits' are exactly that, the potential desired advantages which it is hoped will follow from the research.

Disbenefits

'5.25 Potential disbenefits (that is, the potential misuse of the resulting information or technologies) may be recognised. The Inspectorate considers that potential disbenefit does not, strictly speaking, form part of the cost/benefit assessment; but that, when foreseen, it must nevertheless be clearly signalled in the advice offered to the Secretary of State to facilitate any necessary wider consultation and consideration.'

APC 1997 Report

Perhaps the controversial areas of genetic manipulation or warfare research may fall within the shadow of this notion of disbenefit.

Cost

This term 'cost' in the sense in which it is used in this context, that is, 'the cost in animal suffering', is the pivotal concept in the whole assessment process. Only if there may be some pain, suffering, distress or lasting harm is there a need to embark on a cost/benefit assessment. No explicit definition of a specific level of hurt (a code term for pain, suffering, distress or lasting harm) permitted in law is to be found in the legislative material associated with the ASPA. Indications, however, are given of limits to permissible hurt – a hurt too far, as it were.

With regard to the minimal qualifying hurt to rank among regulated procedures, we may perhaps think in terms of a single injection.

ASPA s. 10(2)(b) requires all personal licences to be issued with an 'inviolable termination condition'. This effectively sets a level of suffering for which licence authorities are not granted.

The 1997 APC Report (p. 52) refers to the introduction of administrative controls that further outline limits on the scope of work which can be permitted on animals:

'3.5.1 Unjustifiable "costs": for example, the prohibition on the use of Great Apes.

3.5.2 Alternative methods available; examples include the safety testing of finished cosmetic product; the exceptional and specific justification required for the production of monoclonal antibodies in ascitic fluid; and the restriction of authorities for training of surgeons in manual skills for microvascular work.

3.5.3 Morally or ethically objectionable; for example, the prohibitions on the use of animals for the development or testing of offensive weapons, alcoholic products or tobacco products.

3.6 These limits are superimposed on the system of case-by-case assessment which requires that submissions for authorities maximise benefit and minimise cost, and that the potential benefits are desirable, attainable and clearly exceed the expected welfare cost.'

The APC 1997 Report (p. 58) sheds further light on the factors considered in regards to 'cost'.

'7.3 The resources and track record of the research group are important considerations which can be relevant either to the cost (in terms of the standards to which the work can be done) or the benefit, when the likelihood of success may be affected. Thus, the outcome of the cost/benefit assessment may be determined by the technical expertise of the available personal licence holders or the standards of the available facilities. Although these are regulated by the controls applying to personal licences and Certificates of Designation, they are nevertheless legitimate considerations when performing the cost/benefit assessment for application.

7.4 In some instances the "costs" which are taken into account begin before any regulated procedure has been performed and extend in time beyond the completion of the study for which authorities are sought. For example, when non-human primates are to be taken from the wild or transported from overseas, the stresses of capture and transport are deemed to be relevant, and from some "field studies" the incidental effects on the local ecology are legitimate concerns.

7.5 The assessment of ("costs") is performed and advice is formulated using:
- information on the form of application;
- knowledge of the research group, its track record, facilities, resources and published work;
- specialist knowledge of the area of science and other work being conducted in the same field;
- the likely adverse effects; and
- knowledge of policy, precedent, practice and refinements.

Number and species of animals as a feature of 'cost'

The 1998 amendment of ASPA states:

'3. In section 5 (project licences), for subsection (5) there shall be substituted –
"(5) The Secretary of State shall not grant a project licence unless he is satisfied ...

(b)   that the regulated procedures to be used are those which use the minimum number of animals, involve animals with the lowest degree of neurophysiological sensitivity, cause the least pain, suffering, distress or lasting harm, and are most likely to produce satisfactory results".'

This is the first introduction into UK legislation on animal experimentation of an attempt to grade animals in general in respect to the 'hurt' of which they may be aware. In the 1980s this need to consider the sentient grade of the experimental animal had been enshrined in Danish law. The demand for special justification for the use of primates, cats, dogs and equidae has always been a feature of section 18 on the UK application.

Recently, and rightly so, the use of non-human primates has attracted special attention. In 1999 a supplement was added to section 18 of the application requiring special justification in greater detail for the use of non-human primates and in the case of the use of non-human primates taken from the wild it will only be acceptable in exceptional cases.

The APC has been exceptionally vigilant regarding non-human primate use.

'84. In addition to xenotransplantation research ... the Committee saw three applications during 1997 for authorities to use non-human primates.

85. The first was for an amendment to an existing project licence concerned with the study of Parkinson's disease. The licence had been referred to the Committee because the amendments related to protocols with substantial severity limits. Whilst some members had strong feelings against the use of primates in scientific experiments or felt that not enough was being done to address the causes of this condition, it was agreed this was a well structured study and that there were good grounds for the amendment. The Committee endorsed it.

86. The second involved the use of wild-caught primates in a study to provide regulatory safety information for a drug therapy to be used in the treatment of osteoporosis. Initial studies had been carried out using a rodent species, but there was a regulatory requirement to carry out tests using a non-rodent species too. The study required the use of ageing animals and suitable captive-bred animals were not available in sufficient quantity.'

APC 1997 Report (p. 12)

'12. The Committee advises on applications to the Home Secretary for particularly significant licences for animal experimentation, especially ones which involve the use of primates caught in the wild or in procedures of substantial severity. In 1998 it saw one application for the use of wild-caught primates and two for their use in substantial procedures.

13. All raised complex scientific and ethical issues. The Committee referred one back for further information. The other two involved xenotransplantation – the transplanting of an organ into the primate subject from another species (in both cases, pigs) – and the Committee asked the Home Office to seek advice about the work from the United Kingdom Xenotransplantation Interim Regulatory Authority (UKXIRA).'

APC Report 1998 (p. iii)

In 1998, s. 10 of the ASPA was extensively amended with a view to alleviate possible 'hurt' and so minimise the 'cost' to the animals involved in research. Innovations include:

- the demand for anaesthesia in Schedule 2A
- special protection for endangered species and animals from the wild
- the release of animals
- provision for the preservation of animals after procedures
- need for trained animal care staff
- stricter control of the killing of animals
- special requirements on identification and
- stipulations on the essentials of good husbandry.

The main text of the amendment is set out below. Readers should note that the drafting of the amendment leaves something to be desired in the use of 'above' and 'below' in cross-references.

'10.(1) Subject to the provisions of this section, a licence or certificate under this Act may contain such conditions as the Secretary of State thinks fit.

(2)   The conditions of a personal licence shall include –

(a)   a condition to the effect that the holder shall take precautions to prevent or reduce to the minimum consistent with the purposes of the authorised procedures any pain, distress or discomfort to the animals to which those procedures may be applied; and

(b)   an inviolable termination condition, that is to say, a condition specifying circumstances in which a protected animal which is being or has been subjected to a regulated procedure must in every case be immediately killed by a method appropriate to the animal under Schedule 1 to this Act or by such other method as may be authorised by the licence.

(2A) Without prejudice to subsection (2)(a) above, the conditions of a personal licence shall include such conditions as the Secretary of State considers appropriate to ensure that the authorised procedures are carried out in accordance with Article 8 of Council Directive No. 86/609/EEC[b], the text of which is set out in Schedule 2A to this Act.

[b] OJ No. L358. 18.12.86, p.1.

(3) The conditions of a project licence shall, unless the Secretary of State considers that an exception is justified, include a condition to the effect –

(a) that no cat or dog shall be used under the licence unless it has been bred at and obtained from a designated breeding establishment; and

(b) that no other protected animal of a description specified in Schedule 2 to this Act shall be used under the licence unless it has been bred at a designated breeding establishment or obtained from a designated supplying establishment; but no exception shall be made from the condition required by paragraph (a) or (d) above [sic] unless the Secretary of State is satisfied that no animal suitable for the purpose of the programme specified in the licence can be obtained in accordance with that condition; and

(c) that no vertebrate of an endangered species shall be used under the licence; and

(d) that no protected animal taken from the wild shall be used under the licence;

and no exception shall be made from the condition required by paragraph (c) above unless the Secretary of State is satisfied that the use of animals of the species in question will be in conformity with the Council Regulation and that the purposes of the programme of work specified in the licence are either research aimed at preservation of the species in question or essential biomedical purposes where the species in question exceptionally proves to be the only one suitable for those purposes.

(3A) In subsection (3) above –

"endangered species" means a species listed in Appendix 1 of the Convention on International Trade in Endangered Species of Fauna and Flora (which is set out in Annex A to the Council Regulation) or in Annex C.1 to the Council Regulation: and "essential biomedical purposes" has the same meaning as in Council Directive No. 86/609/EEC, and in subsection (3) above and this subsection "the Council Regulation" means Council Regulation (EEC) No. 3626/82 as amended by Commission Regulation (EEC) No. 869/88 and Commission Regulation (EEC) No. 1970/92.

(3B) Where a project licence authorises the setting free of a protected animal in the course of a series of regulated procedures, that licence shall include a condition requiring the prior consent of the Secretary of State to the setting free of the animal.

(3C) The Secretary of State shall not give his consent to the setting free of an animal in pursuance of a condition included in a project licence under subsection (3B) above unless he is satisfied –

(a) that the maximum possible care has been taken to safeguard the animal's well-being;

(b) that the animal's state of health allows it to be set free; and

(c) that the setting free of the animal poses no danger to public health or the environment.

(3D) The conditions of a project licence shall include such conditions as the Secretary of State considers appropriate to ensure –

    (a)   that where a protected animal has been subjected to a series of regulated procedures for a particular purpose, at the conclusion of the series a veterinary surgeon or, if none is available, another suitably qualified person determines whether the animal should be killed or kept alive;

    (b)   that, if that person considers that it is likely to remain in lasting pain or distress, the animal is killed by a method appropriate to the animal under Schedule 1 to this Act, or by such other method as may be authorised by the personal licence of the person by whom the animal is killed; and

    (c)   that where the animal is to be kept alive, it is kept at a designated establishment (subject to subsection (6D) below).

(4)   If the conditions of a personal licence permit the holder to use assistants to perform, under his direction, tasks not requiring technical knowledge nothing done by an assistant in accordance with such a condition shall constitute a contravention of section 3 above.

(5)   The conditions of a certificate issued under section 6 above shall include a condition prohibiting the killing otherwise than by a method which is appropriate under Schedule 1 to this Act or approved by the Secretary, of State of any protected animal kept at the establishment for experimental or other scientific purposes but not subjected to a regulated procedure or required to be killed by virtue of section 15 below; and the conditions of a certificate issued under section 7 above [sic] shall include a condition prohibiting the killing otherwise than by such a method of an animal of a description specified in Schedule 2 to this Act which is bred or kept for breeding or as the case may be kept at the establishment for the purposes of being supplied for use in regulated procedures but not used or supplied for use, for that purpose.

(5A) The conditions of a certificate issued under section 6 above shall include such conditions as the Secretary of State considers appropriate to ensure –

    (a) . that sufficient trained staff are provided at the establishment; and

    (b)   that the persons who take care of protected animals at the establishment and those who supervise such persons have appropriate education and training.

(6)   The conditions of a certificate issued under section 6 or 7 above [sic] shall include conditions requiring the holder of the certificate –

    (a)   to secure that a person competent to kill animals in the manner specified by conditions imposed in accordance with subsection (5) above will be available to do so; and

    (b)   to keep records as respects the source and disposal of and otherwise relating to the animals kept at the establishment for experimental or other scientific purposes or, as the case may be, bred or kept for breeding there or kept there for the purposes of being supplied for use in regulated procedures.

(6A) The conditions of a certificate issued under section 6 or 7 above shall, if the certificate permits dogs, cats or primates to be kept or bred at the establishment in question, include conditions requiring the holder of the certificate to ensure –

    (a) that particulars of the identity and origin of each dog, cat or primate kept or bred at the establishment are entered in the records referred to in subsection (6)(b) above;

    (b) that before it is weaned, every dog, cat or primate in the establishment not falling within paragraph (c) above [sic] is provided with an individual identification mark in the least painful manner possible;

    (c) that where a dog, cat or primate is transferred from one establishment to another before it is weaned and it is not practicable to mark it beforehand, the records kept by the establishment receiving the animal identify that animal's mother until the animal is provided with an individual identification mark: and

    (d) that any unmarked dog, cat or primate which is taken into the establishment after being weaned is provided as soon as possible thereafter with an individual identification mark.

(6B) The conditions of a certificate issued under section 6 or 7 above shall include such conditions relating to the general care and accommodation of protected animals bred, kept or used at the establishment as the Secretary of State considers appropriate in order to ensure –

    (a) that the environment, housing, freedom of movement, food, water and care provided for each such animal are appropriate for the animal's health and well-being;

    (b) that any restrictions on the extent to which each such animal can satisfy its physiological and ethological needs are kept to the absolute minimum;

    (c) that the environmental conditions in which such animals are bred, kept or used are checked daily;

    (d) that the well-being and state of health of such animals are monitored by a suitably qualified person in order to prevent pain or avoidable suffering, distress or lasting harm; and

    (e) that arrangements are made to ensure that any defect or suffering discovered is eliminated as quickly as possible.

(6C) When considering what conditions are appropriate to ensure the matters specified in subsection (6B)(a) and (b) above, the Secretary of State shall have regard to the guidance in Annex II to Council Directive No. 86/609/EEC.

(6D) The conditions of a certificate issued under section 6 or 7 above shall include such conditions as the Secretary of State considers appropriate to ensure that any animal kept alive after being subjected to a series of regulated procedures will continue to be kept at the establishment under the supervision of a veterinary surgeon or other suitably qualified person unless it is moved to another designated establishment or a veterinary surgeon certifies that it will not suffer if it ceases to be kept at a designated establishment.

(7)   Breach of a condition in a licence or certificate shall not invalidate the licence or certificate but shall be a ground for its variation or revocation.'

The severity of procedures

The evaluation of the 'cost' of the cost/benefit assessment is expressed in practice in terms of degrees of severity or severity bands:

Unclassified
Mild
Moderate
Substantial.

The Home Office Guidance is comprehensive and clear in its notes on this topic.

'4.7. In assessing the severity of a series of regulated procedures, account should be taken of the effect of all the procedures (whether regulated or not) applied to each animal or group of animals; the nature of any likely adverse effects; the action taken to mitigate these effects; and the endpoints applying to the procedures.

4.8. Such an assessment should reflect the maximum severity expected to be experienced by any animal. It should not take into account the numbers of animals which might experience the maximum severity or the proportion of the animal's lifetime for which it might experience severe effects. Procedures throughout which the animal is either decerebrate or under general anaesthesia and is killed without recovering consciousness are regarded as unclassified.'

Only the level of severity referred to as unclassified can be so simply defined. The concepts of mild, moderate and substantial severity are far more difficult to define.

Some examples of the severity of different procedures (HOG, 4.9–11) are shown in Table 7.1.

Some limiting clinical signs (rodents and rabbits)

As already indicated there are few clear criteria for deciding levels of animal pain but there are some publications which may prove useful:

The assessment and control of the severity of scientific procedures on laboratory animals, LASA Report. *Laboratory Animals* (1990) **24**, 97–130.
Guidelines for the Recognition and Assessment of Pain in Animals, Association of Veterinary Teachers and Research Workers, UFAW 1989.

Table 7.1 Examples of the severity of different procedures (HOG 4.9–11)

MILD	It is not possible to lay down hard and fast rules about how potential severity should be assessed but the following procedures may be considered mild:
	The taking of small or infrequent blood samples Skin irritation tests with substances expected to be only mildly irritant; Minor surgical procedures under anaesthesia such as laparoscopy, small superficial tissue biopsies or cannulation of peripheral blood vessels, are likely to be regarded as mild unless there is significant combination or repetition of procedures using the same animal. So will other procedures terminated before the animal shows more than minor changes from normal behaviour.
MODERATE	This could include: much of the screening and development of potential pharmaceutical agents, toxicity tests avoiding lethal endpoints; most surgical procedures, povided that suffering can be controlled by reliable post-operative analgesia and care.
SUBSTANTIAL	Procedures that result in a major departure from the animal's usual state of health or well-being.
	These are likely to include: acute toxicity procedures where significant morbidity or death is an endpoint; some efficacy tests of antimicrobial agents and vaccines; some models of disease; major surgery where significant post-operative suffering may result.
	If it were expected that a single animal would suffer substantial effects, the procedure would warrant a severity limit of SUBSTANTIAL.

Note: Condition 6 of the project licence states: 'In any procedure, the degree of severity imposed shall be the minimum consistent with the attainment of the objects of the procedure.'

John Finch and Tony Buckwell have produced a useful relevant appendix of examples of appropriate clinical signs in respect to rodents and rabbits. The lists in Table 7.2 are summaries of the work published in the *LASA Newsletter.*

Further notes on severity from the Home Office Guidance

The overall severity of a project

Besides the assessment of individual procedures the project licence holder must give an assessment of the overall severity of the whole project in section 20 of the application form:

'4.14. The assessment of the overall severity of a project will reflect the cumulative effect of each procedure; the number of animals used in each

Table 7.2   Clinical signs in rodents and rabbits

Level	Limiting clinical signs
MILD	Reduced weight gain. Food/water intake 40–75% of normal for 72 hours. Partial piloerection. Subdued but responsive – normal provoked behaviour. Hunched – transient, especially after dosing. Vocalisation – transient. Oculo-nasal discharge (mild/transient). Tremors – transient.
MODERATE	Weight loss up to 20% of bodyweight. Food/water intake less than 40% of normal for 72 hours. Marked piloerection – staring coat. Subdued behaviour even when provoked, little peer interaction. Hunched – intermittent and pallor. Vocalisation – intermittent. Oculo-nasal discharge – persistent. Altered respiration. Tremors – intermittent. Convulsions – intermittent. Prostration – transient (say less than one hour).
SUBSTANTIAL	Weight loss greater than 25%. Reduced food/water intake less than 40% for 7 days or anorexia. Marked piloerection – dehydration. Unresponsive to provocation. Hunched – 'frozen' with pallor and cold. Vocalisation – distressed and unprovoked. Oculo-nasal discharge – copious. Laboured respiration. Tremors – persistent. Convulsions – persistent. Prostration for more than an hour. Self-mutilation.

procedure; the frequency of use of each procedure; the proportion of animals that are expected to be exposed to each procedure; and the length of time that the animals might be exposed to the upper limits of severity.

4.15. This assessment of overall severity will be used to weigh the likely adverse effects on all the animals against the benefits likely to accrue, as required by s. 5(4) of the Act.

4.16. The assessments of severity are not immutable and may be varied in the light of experience, for instance, when it transpires that an earlier endpoint would be equally acceptable scientifically, but would involve a lower level of suffering by the animal.'

Notes on the severity condition

'4.17. Licence holders are required by conditions in both project, and personal licences to minimise pain, suffering or distress and they should approach the limit of severity which has been authorised only when absolutely necessary.

4.18. All project licences contain a condition controlling the severity of procedures, This will reflect the severity limits which have been given to the procedures and the upper limit of severity which will be allowed on any one animal. The severity condition on the licence will be regarded as breached if the Inspector has not been notified when any protected animal has suffered significantly more as the result of a regulated procedure than has been authorised.

4.19. It is not regarded as a breach of the condition if an animal has suffered more than authorised either, unexpectedly or for extraneous reasons, for instance as the result of an intercurrent infection unrelated to the procedures. In all such cases, steps must be taken to alleviate the suffering at once.

4.20. If it seems likely that the severity limit for a procedure may be exceeded, the project or personal licence holder will either terminate the procedure or advise the Inspector, who may, in certain circumstances, temporarily authorise a higher severity limit for a period of up to fourteen days. If necessary, an application should be made to amend the project licence.'

APC views on severity

The 1997 APC Report states:

'5.1 The administrative system distinguishes between the "severity limit" of procedures and the "severity band" of projects. When discussing "cost", it is important to understand how these differ, and to distinguish between them.

5.2 The severity limit for a procedure is based on the potential single worst case. This may have a very low incidence; indeed, it may never be seen in practice. Thus a procedure banded as substantial because 100% of experimental animals may suffer severe adverse effects would not be re-banded if the design was improved to reduce this to less than 1%.

5.3 Severity limits for procedures must reflect fully the potential for suffering, rather than lay judgement. Specifically, outcomes which would be significant handicaps in, or cause great distress to, man may have different effects in animals: for example, in poorly sighted species, some additional degree of visual impairment may have little welfare cost and, similarly, sterility is not considered likely to be distressing to animals. Conversely, apparently minor effects in man can have serious welfare implications: for example, partial facial weakness has serious consequences for cud-chewing animals.

5.4 The best insight into the true severity of a procedure (that is, the true welfare costs likely to be encountered) is to be found not in the procedure "severity limit" stated at 19a of the project licence form of application, but in the section 19b(vi) for each procedure which outlines the likely adverse effects; their expected incidence; details of how they will be avoided, recognised and managed; and the endpoints to be applied.

5.6 The overall severity of the project, the severity band, is determined by the degree of suffering expected to be experienced by the average animal used during the study. It reflects the numbers, species and stage of development used in each procedure, the frequency of each procedure, the endpoints to be applied, the proportion of animals that are expected to be exposed to the upper limits of severity in each procedure, and the length of time that the animals might be exposed to the upper limits of severity.

5.8 It is possible to have a project licence with a "mild severity band" composed of "substantial severity limit" procedures when there is only a small risk of significant adverse effects in practice.

5.9 No matter how great the justification for the use of animals for experimental or other scientific purposes, the resulting animal suffering must be kept to the minimum. For this to be achieved, judgements must be informed by the precise scientific objectives and the range of animal and other model systems which can be used to generate the required data.

5.10 Consideration extends beyond the numbers of animals used and must take into account the species, stage of development, nature of the interventions performed, means of preventing or controlling adverse effects and the endpoints to be applied. Many different factors (all of which can be described but some of which cannot easily be quantified) must be balanced to determine the protocols which actually minimise the "cost". This remains an area for judgements, using criteria with both objective and subjective components.'

'5.14.1 In principle, the numbers of animals used should not be reduced if further reduction can only be attained at a disproportionally high welfare cost. A good example is the use of animals to grow (passage) tumours or parasites where this cannot as yet be done using in vitro methods. Models which allow the resulting material to be harvested from asymptomatic animals are preferred to those which, in order to harvest the same amount of material, require that a smaller number of animals are allowed to become symptomatic. Similarly there will be occasions when preference is shown to designs allowing the post mortem harvesting of material from animals humanely killed at fixed time points, to other study designs which require repeated, invasive biopsy procedures during life.'

Additional conditions on licences may be used to limit severity. The scale and nature of the permitted work may have to be precisely defined or reports on work in progress may be required which would detail welfare costs.

Table 7.3 indicates percentages of the different severity bands in practice.

Table 7.3 Severity bands in practice (APC Report 1997)

| | Project licences in Great Britain | | | | | |
| Severity band | In force on 31/12/1997 | | Granted during 1997 | | Revoked during 1997 | |
	Number	%	Number	%	Number	%
Mild	1546	41.1	358	39.0	432	42.2
Moderate	1990	52.9	490	53.3	515	50.3
Substantial	66	1.7	20	2.2	20	2.0
Unclassified	163	4.3	51	5.5	56	5.5
Total	3765		919		1023	

Humane end points

The proper fixing of human end points is an essential aspect of the refinement of any procedure in a realisic application of the principles of the 3 Rs. In spite of a certain amount of opposition, humane end points became a salient feature of the European Convention on Animal Experimentation and was given special emphasis in UK legislation on animal research.

'4.13. It is often possible to reduce the severity of procedures by the use of appropriate endpoints and project licence applications involving procedures which may have specific adverse effects should, wherever possible, specify the particular action which the applicant intends to take in order to mitigate these effects. This will include, where appropriate, withdrawing the animal from the procedure or humane killing.'

(HOG).

In practice, humane end points may vary greatly from, for example, geriatric status regards some primates in defined cases to much more specific conditions as illustrated in a relevant publication on this matter – *UKCCCR Guidelines for the Welfare of Animals in Experimental Neoplasia* (UKCCCR, 20 Park Crescent, London W1N 4AL) (1988).

'3.1. Considerable care should be given to the judicious choice of end point for tumour growth. This should take into account predictable indications of pain, distress or significant deviation from normal behaviour. Unless specified otherwise on the project licence, animals should be killed before:
(i)   predictable death occurs;
(ii)   they get into poor condition;
(iii) the tumour mass becomes over-large, likely to ulcerate or unacceptably limits normal behaviour.'

'3.10 Humane end points and other procedures should be refined in the light of experience.'

(UKCCCR, 1988)

The managerial role of the project licence holder

Supervision is among the most onerous duties of the project licence holder (Fig. 7.1). The project licence holder, unfairly perhaps, and even unrealistically in some circumstances, may be deemed to be aware of all occurrences within her/his programme of research. She/he may, consequently, be liable to sanctions for misdemeanours committed by others within her/his project. Particularly important in this context is condition 14 requiring supervision of personal licensees.

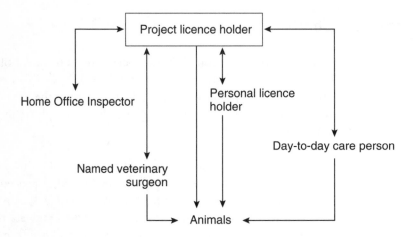

Fig. 7.1   Relationships of project licence holder with other interested parties.

Besides the attention to the overall control of the project the project licence holder should take cognisance of:

(a)   the provision of requisite facilities (HOG 4.32 v & vi)
(b)   proper animal care (Code of Practice 3.4)
(c)   observance in full of all the conditions on the licence (HOG Appendix IV)
(d)   the need for permission to move, transfer (between projects) or release animals included in the project (HOG Appendix IV, Conditions 5 & 15)
(e)   the obligation legally to conduct the project under the terms of the Act (HOG 4.35 (i))
(f)   the duty to keep the programme within the permitted purposes stated in the application (HOG 4.35. (ii))
(g)   the limit set on the species and number of animals to be used (HOG 4.35 (iii))
(h)   the need for personal licensees to have authority for the regulated procedures they perform (HOG 4.35. (iv))

(i)   the awareness of and compliance with the severity conditions on the part of all licensees working within the project licence (HOG 4.35 (v))

(j)   the appropriate training and guidance of personal licensees involved in the project (HOG 4.35 (vi))

(k)   the requirement for full and accurate records (HOG App. V)

(l)   the obligation on personal licensees to ensure all animals are identified. (HOG 4.35 (vii)).

The deputy project licence holder

It is indicative of the importance of the managerial role of the project licence holder that special significance is given in HOG to the need for deputy licence holders. This is particularly the case if there could be a lacuna or gap in the impact of management on any area of the research programme.

The scope of the authority assigned to the deputy will vary. In some cases it may be appropriate, for example, for the project licence holder to delegate to the deputy the power to sign on his/her behalf documents pertinent to the project.

It is apparent from the wide responsibilities associated with a project licence that it is usually advisable that the project licence holder have a deputy or deputies since joint project licences are unacceptable. In some circumstances a deputy project licence holder will be required:

'(i)   where the nature or scope of the project is such that control is best exercised through one or more deputy project licence holders;

(ii)   where work is to be done at more than one place so that a deputy is available locally to supervise the work on the project licence holder's behalf;

(iii)   where the project licence holder is likely to be absent for more than a month at a time;

(iv)   where the project licence holder does not hold a personal licence, in which case at least one deputy who holds a personal licence is required.'

(HOG 4.38)

'The deputy licence holder must be in position to exercise day-to-day control over the work and to cover for the project licence holder's absence. His or her identity must be made known to those working on the project. A deputy licence holder will normally hold, or have held, a personal licence.'

(HOG 4.39)

Amendments to licences

The availability of amendments to both licences and certificates is a beneficial effect of flexibility in the administration of the ASPA. What is written here about amendments applies equally, allowing for variations according to circumstances, to other amendments of obligations under ASPA in keeping with s. 11 thereof. An application form for amendments is provided whenever a certificate or licence is issued.

Requests for amendments should include two copies of the amended replacement or additional pages, Each should be signed and dated by the project licence holder at the top of the page, near the place where the surname has been inserted.

The complete unaltered licence and schedule should accompany any request for an amendment.

In 1999, a new form of application for an amendment was issued. This new form requires a signature by the certificate holder confirming that the amendment has completed the local ethical review process.

The submission of requests for amendments to existing licences allows enquiries to be made on progress to date – effectively reviewing the cost/benefit assessment. It is essential to ensure that amendments which increase the cost are not made without the cost/benefit assessment being reconsidered. Liaison with the inspector which can arise in this situation is most valuable. The significance of such liaison with the Inspector cannot be over stressed especially in the initial stages of an application for a licence. False starts or unacceptable proposals can be obviated by this early liaison. The Inspector, however, will step aside while the application as such is within the local ethical review process. The Inspector can however attend a local ethical review process or consult documents associated with it. Details concerning the local ethical review process which is concerned with other matters besides projects, for example, welfare, appear in the section in this book on the responsibilities of the certificate holder.

Chapter 8

Training of Those with Responsibilities Under The ASPA

The five modules

The introduction of mandatory education and training of project and personal licence holders appeared in the 1992 APC Report.

> 'n. 6.3. From 1 April 1994 applicants for personal licences will be required to have completed successfully an accredited training programme. In addition to this, from 1 April 1995, those project licence applicants seeking a project licence for the first time will require further pre-licensing training to be acquired from accredited training programmes ... All training programmes for applicants for personal and project licences are to be accredited under a scheme recognised by the Home Office.'

In practice this training takes the form of five modules:

Module 1 Elements
(1) Historical background
(2) An introduction to ethical aspects of the use of animals in scientific pro-
     cedures
(3) The Animals (Scientific Procedures) Act 1986
(4) Other relevant legislation

Module 2 Elements
(1) Recognition of well-being, pain, suffering or distress
(2) Handling and restraint
(3) Humane methods of killing
(4) Local procedures
(5) Personal health and safety

Module 3 Elements
(1) Biology and husbandry
(2) Common diseases and recognition
(3) Health monitoring and disease prevention or control
(4) Introduction to anaesthesia and analgesia
(5) Conduct of minor procedures

Module 4 Elements
(1) Surgical anaesthesia and analgesia
(2) Conduct of surgical procedures

Module 5 Elements
(1) Ethical aspects of the use of live animals
(2) Analysis of the literature
(3) Alternatives
(4) Project design
(5) Project licence management
(6) Legal aspects – the European and wider international context.

An applicant for a personal licence is required to complete an accredited training programme including Modules 1, 2 and 3 and also Module 4 where appropriate (see Table 8.1 for more detail).

Table 8.1 Training of personnel under the ASPA

Target audience	Module				
	1	2	3	4	5
Those not applying for a licence					
Personnel with administrative responsibilities only	★				
Non-licensed animal users; Those killing by a Schedule 1 method	★	★			
Licence applicants					
Undergraduates applying for limited personal licences to work under close supervision	★	★			
Personal licence applicants who will be performing minor non-surgical procedures; brief terminal procedures under anaesthesia	★	★	★		
Personal licence applicants who will be performing major surgical procedures under terminal or recovery anaesthesia	★	★	★	★	
Project licence applicants	★	★	if apt		★

The training requirements of former personal licensees who are applying for reinstatement of their licences will be determined by many factors including previous formal training and the length of time away from the use of animals in procedures. In such circumstances the person involved should discuss the matter with the Inspector.

Personal licensees seeking significant amendments to the species authorised on the licence which involve additional skills (e.g. extension from rodents to dogs or to farm animals) will be expected to undergo additional practical training as provided by the relevant parts of Modules 2, 3 and/or 4 before application for such amendment.

New applicants for project licences are required to have successfully completed at least modules 1, 2, and 5 and also modules 3 and 4 when appropriate to the procedures in the project.

Exemptions from mandatory training requirements

Appendix B of the 1992 APC Report states:

> 'All exemptions are discretionary on a case-by-case basis and should be discussed with the Inspector before application for a licence is made. The following examples indicate the types of circumstances in which exemptions will be considered.'

Personal licence applicants

> 'Exemption from all training requirements will be considered only for those persons with formal training in laboratory animal science, for example holders of the Certificate or Diploma in Laboratory Animal Science of the Royal College of Veterinary Surgeons, the MSc in Laboratory Animal Science of the University of London or the Associateship [now the Membership] or Fellowship of the Institute of Animal Technology.

> Completion of module 1 only will be considered:
> - for applicants for personal licences valid only for practical work on a micro-surgery training course, the licence to be surrendered immediately upon completion of the course. The contents of this module may be incorporated into the micro-surgery course itself;
> - for veterinary surgeons with practical experience of the relevant species;
> - for animal technicians highly experienced with the relevant species;
> - for holders of qualifications in laboratory science from outside the UK. They will be expected to complete module 1 to ensure familiarity with UK law.

> Completion of modules 1 and 2 only will be considered:
> - for applicants for very limited species and techniques (e.g. one species, oral dosing only);
> - for undergraduates who will be under close supervision and with limited authorities; the contents of these modules may be integrated into the undergraduate course;
> - for experienced overseas researchers.'

> Completion of modules 1 and 3 only will be considered:
> - for applicants with extensive experience of the relevant species.'

Project licence applicants

Project licence applicants who already hold a project licence will not normally be expected to undertake further training. On a more voluntary basis (at present – 2000) training courses and seminars are recommended for the NACWO, the NVS and the CH.

An obvious flaw in the efficient implementation of these very worthy schemes for the enlightment of those involved, arises from the fact that frequently inter-mingled with extremely fluent and highly educated scientists are equally highly educated and intellectual research workers who find real difficulty in understanding English, not only in dealing with legal matters but even in ordinary conversational parlance.

This *contretemps* calls for serious and realistic consideration from the APC. This, unusual in a dry law book, is a cry from the heart. It comes from one who talks from experience, having presented module 1 more or less weekly for the last six years.

Development of relevant training

The 1968 amendment of the ASPA has strengthened the legal demand as regards training. In s. 10 of the amended Act:

'(5A) The conditions of a certificate issued under section 6 above shall include such conditions as the Secretary of State considers appropriate to ensure –
   (a)   that sufficient trained staff are provided at the establishment; and
   (b)   that the persons who take care of protected animals at the establishment and those who supervise such persons have appropriate education and training.

The APC view

The APC has been deeply concerned with the need for appropriate training of all involved with animals in research. A sub-committee was formed to monitor and develop the concept of training in this area.

'The Education and Training Sub-Committee advises on the requirements for training and education of those who hold responsibilities under the Act. In doing so, it liaises with the two bodies which accredit licensee training courses – the Institute of Biology and the Universities Group for the Accreditation of Training.'

(1997 Report p. 11 n. 74)

The APC in its 1997 report commented forcefully on the education and training of licensees:

'The formal training requirements cannot guarantee prior competence. Nor can they overcome the disadvantages of experienced licensees ceasing to work with animals for periods of time or focusing their practice within a narrow band of particular techniques. Training remains the explicit responsibility of the designated establishment and supervision the responsibility of the project licence holder.'

(p. 97 n. 10)

The APC anticipates that in future there will be training for certificate of designation holders, named animal care and welfare officers and those killing animals using the methods listed in Schedule 1 of the Act. It is also indicated that sponsors will be required to make more focused declarations about applicants' training and, possibly eligibility. This assessment of competency would be noted in the personal licensee's records. (1997 Report p. 97 nn. 8 and 14)

A full and informative 'Working party report of the Federation of Laboratory Animal Science Associations working group on education of specialists (Category D)' accepted by the FELASA Board of Management appeared in *Laboratory Animals* (1999) **33**, 1–15. This report is a basis for FELASA guidelines for education of specialists in laboratory animal science (Category D). FELASA is the Federation of European Laboratory Animal Science Associations and recognises four competence categories:

Category A – Animal technicians
Category B – Research technicians
Category C – Scientists
Category D – Specialists

Chapter 9

Certificates of Designation

Designated establishments

Every regulated procedure must be performed within the provisions of a project licence, a personal licence and a certificate of designation. The requisite authorisation for the use of experimental animals may be indicated thus:

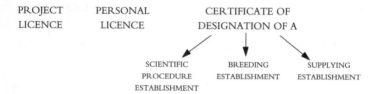

PROJECT LICENCE   PERSONAL LICENCE   CERTIFICATE OF DESIGNATION OF A

SCIENTIFIC PROCEDURE ESTABLISHMENT   BREEDING ESTABLISHMENT   SUPPLYING ESTABLISHMENT

The interdependence and interlocking of the two forms of licences have already been discussed. The three forms of certificates are, however, discrete, one in no way depends upon the other, they exist separately and various establishments may have only one or all three.

The Home Office Guidance on the ASPA expounds on the law as regards establishments:

> '2.1. All places where regulated scientific procedures are performed must be designated under section 6 of the Act ...' It is possible for certain regulated procedures to be performed in a place which is not a designated establishment, referred to as a 'PODE' (place other than a designated establishment). The 'PODE' comes into the frame (project licence application form section 13), when authority may be required for a temporary period or when it would be unrealistic or inappropriate to designate such places as rivers or woods. Authority to carry out procedures at a 'PODE' will be included in the project and personal licences. Special conditions may be imposed, for example, as regards a 'rendezvous' or a need to obtain permission of the land owner.

> 2.2. The certificate of designation will be issued to the person who represents the governing authority of the establishment and who is ultimately responsible to the Home Office for ensuring that the conditions of the certificate are observed.

> 2.3. Under section 6(5), all applicants for certificates must nominate:
>   (i)   one or more persons responsible for the day-to-day care of the animals; [known since March 1997 as the named animal care and welfare officer (NACWO)]

(ii)   one or more veterinary surgeons to provide advice on animal health and welfare.'

Therefore on every certificate of designation at least three persons must be nominated – the certificate holder, the named animal care and welfare officer(s) and the named veterinary surgeon(s).'

I have encountered various individuals who have been concerned with the fact that they have various roles as regards the animals and worry about possible conflicts of interest. The APC comments on this situation as follows.

'The 1986 Act makes provision for up to five different individuals being responsible for different aspects of the well being of protected animals at designated establishments; certificate holders; project licence holders; personal licence holders; named animal care and welfare officers; and named veterinary surgeons. There may be occasions when more than one individual fulfils more than one of these roles. We continue to take the view that at least three individuals should fulfil these five roles, and that a named veterinary surgeon who has a substantial interest in the outcome of a programme of work should make alternative provision for oversight of the animals in question. This is existing Home Office policy.

2.5. If the facilities provided are appropriate and those persons nominated for the care of the animals are suitably qualified, a certificate will be issued with certain standard, and where necessary, additional conditions.'

Section 7 of the Act legislates in a similar manner to s. 6 for breeding and supplying establishments, for example, requiring the naming of the three responsible persons.

The early edition of HOG (Question 3. p. 3) defines each type of establishment in reference to its function:

'User establishments will include premises where animals are held, before during and after procedures, but not bred. These will need certificates of designation as scientific procedure establishments.

If animals are bred for use in the same establishment or somewhere else, the premises will need certificates of designation as breeding establishments.

If animals are kept at an establishment where they have not been bred, for supply elsewhere, the premises will need certificates of designation as supplying establishments.'

Establishments which qualify for more than one of the certificates must apply for each designation which is appropriate. An establishment which breeds animals with harmful genetic mutations or genetically manipulated animals or supplies surgically prepared animals must also be designated as a scientific procedure establishment.

Section 7 and Schedule 2 of the ASPA

Section 7 of ASPA regulates breeding and supplying establishments.

> 's. 7. (1) A person shall not at any place breed for use in regulated procedures (whether there or elsewhere) protected animals of a description specified in Schedule 2 of this Act unless that place is designated by a certificate issued by the Secretary of State under this section as a breeding establishment.'

and

> '(2) A person shall not at any place keep any such protected animals which have not been bred there but are to be supplied for use elsewhere in regulated procedures unless that place is designated by a certificate issued by the Secretary of State under this section as a supplying establishment.'

Under Schedule 2 animals may be obtained only from a designated supplying establishment. If a scientific procedure establishment does not breed its own animals (if it does, it would presumably already be designated as a breeding establishment), the animals listed below must be obtained only from a designated breeding establishment:

Dog
Cat

The animals listed below must be obtained from a designated breeding or supplying establishment:

Mouse
Rat
Guinea-pig
Hamster
Rabbit
Quail★

Non–human primates.

Added to this second list from 1/1/1999 were:

Ferret
Gerbil
Genetically modified pig
Genetically modified sheep

★ This restriction only applies to *Coturnix coturnix*; the European Quail, not, for example, to *Coturnix japonica*.

Consequences of Schedule 2

An overseas breeding or supplying establishment cannot be certified under the Act. Consequently, consent is required for the use of all imported cats and dogs and, also for the use of imported Schedule 2 species unless they have been acquired from a supplying establishment. The Secretary of State can grant an exemption from the demands of Schedule 2. (Code of Practice for the Housing and Care of Animals used in Scientific Procedures (later referred to as CODHCASP) 3.5.)

While there is no restriction in the Act on importation as such, it would be prudent to seek Home Office approval to ensure that animals may be used once they have been imported.

> 'The importation of animals from overseas is controlled by the Animals and Animal Products (Import and Export) Regulations 1995 which is in keeping with the Belai Directive 92/65/EEC and the Animals (Post-Import Control) Order 1995. In some cases there may be involvement with the Endangered Species (Import and Export) Act 1976. Details about licences, health certificates, rabies and other quarantine requirements should be obtained from the Animal Health Division, MAFF.'

Since 1996 primates can be acquired from overseas breeding centres only if these centres have been approved by the Home Office. (APC Report 1997, p. 78 n. 4)

Termination and variation of certificates

There is clear and ample information on these topics in HOG:

> '6.1. Certificates of designation remain in force until suspended or revoked. The holder of a certificate of designation may apply at any time for a variation of the certificate, for instance when permission is required to keep different animals or to alter the rooms where they are kept. A change of certificate holder, for instance on retirement will require the issue of a new certificate.
> 6.2. Applications for permanent changes to the certificate of designation must always be in writing with, where necessary, plans showing any proposed alterations to the premises. The Inspector has authority to grant temporary changes such as permission to hold animals in particular rooms overnight.'

> '6.7. Because of the detail in certificates and licences, it will often be necessary to amend them. An application form for this purpose will be provided whenever a certificate or licence is granted. Significant amendments, like the initial application, should be discussed in the first instance with the Inspector.
> 6.8. Certificates of designation, project licences or personal licences may be varied on the authority of the Secretary of State at any time under section 11 of the Act and the procedure for making any representations against this under section 12 is set out in Appendix VIII and Appendix IX.'
>
> (HOG)

This readiness of official variation of stipulations under the ASPA gives a welcome flexibility in its practical application. The availability of the staff of the Inspectorate ensures the efficient achievement of this flexibility in practice.

1998 amendments and designated establishments

The amendments to s. 10 of the ASPA had important implications for welfare obligations associated with designated establishments.

In subsection 3:

'(3B) Where a project licence authorises the setting free of a protected animal in the course of a series of regulated procedures, that licence shall include a condition requiring the prior consent of the Secretary of State to the setting free of the animal.

(3C) The Secretary of State shall not give his consent to the setting free of an animal in pursuance of a condition included in a project licence under subsection (3B) above unless he is satisfied –

 (a) that the maximum possible care has been taken to safeguard the animal's well-being;

 (b) that the animal's state of health allows it to be set free; and

 (c) that the setting free of the animal poses no danger to public health or the environment.

(3D) The conditions of a project licence shall include such conditions as the Secretary of State considers appropriate to ensure –

 (a) that where a protected animal has been subjected to a series of regulated procedures for a particular purpose, at the conclusion of the series a veterinary surgeon or, if none is available, another suitably qualified person determines whether the animal should be killed or kept alive;

 (b) that, if that person considers that it is likely to remain in lasting pain or distress, the animal is killed by a method appropriate to the animal under Schedule 1 to this Act, or by such other method as may be authorised by the personal licence of the person by whom the animal is killed; and

 (c) that where the animal is to be kept alive, it is kept at a designated establishment (subject to subsection (6D) below).'

(6D) refers to the need for supervision by and the approval of the NVS if an animal is kept alive after regulated procedure.

In subsection 5:

'(5A) The conditions of a certificate issued under section 6 above [sic] shall include such conditions as the Secretary of State considers appropriate to ensure –

 (a) that sufficient trained staff are provided at the establishment; and

(b)   that the persons who take care of protected animals at the establishment and those who supervise such persons have appropriate education and training.'

In subsection 6:

'(6A) The conditions of a certificate issued under section 6 or 7 above [sic] shall, if the certificate permits dogs, cats or primates to be kept or bred at the establishment in question, include conditions requiring the holder of the certificate to ensure –

(a)   that particulars of the identity and origin of each dog, cat or primate kept or bred at the establishment are entered in the records referred to in subsection (6) (b) above; [that paragraph deals with general animal records]

(b)   that before it is weaned every dog, cat or primate in the establishment not falling within paragraph (c) above' [sic] 'is provided with an individual identification mark in the least painful manner possible;

(c)   that where a dog, cat or primate is transferred from one establishment to another before it is weaned and it is not practicable to mark it beforehand. The records kept by the establishment receiving the animal identify that animal's mother until the animal is provided with an individual identification mark; and

(d)   that any unmarked dog, cat or primate which is taken into the establishment after being weaned is provided as soon as possible thereafter with an individual identification mark.'

'(6B) The conditions of a certificate issued under section 6 or 7 above shall include such conditions relating to the general care and accommodation of protected animals bred, kept or used at the establishment as the Secretary of State considers appropriate in order to ensure –

(a)   that the environment, housing, freedom of movement, food, water, and care provided for each such animal are appropriate for the animal's health and well-being;

(b)   that any restrictions on the extent to which each such animal can satisfy its physiological and ethological needs are kept to the absolute minimum;

(c)   that the environmental conditions in which such animals are bred, kept or used are checked daily;

(d)   that the well-being and state of health of such animals are monitored by a suitably qualified person in order to prevent pain or avoidable suffering, distress or lasting harm; and

(e)   that arrangements are made to ensure that any defect or suffering discovered is eliminated as quickly as possible.

Some extracts (Fig. 9.1 and Table 9.1) from the 1997 APC Report are useful illustrations of arrangements within designated establishments and the number and types of establishments in 1997.

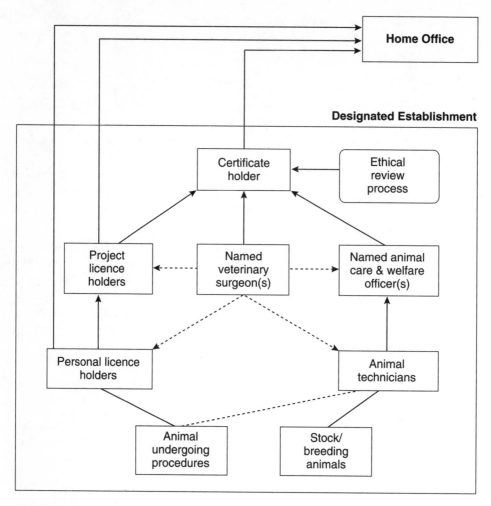

Fig. 9.1   Relationships within designated establishment. *Note:* for simplicity, the advisory roles of persons other than the named veterinary surgeon (NVS) and the named animal care and welfare officer (NACWO) are not shown. *Source:* APC Report (1997), p.26

The certificate holder

The function of this nominated person has evolved from, in some cases being a distant cypher, far removed from the animal house, for example, the vice-chancellor of a university or the bursar of an institution, to being a pivotal figure in the overall management of the animal facilities. In some establishments the role of certificate holder has become a crucial office in its own right.

Section 6(4) of the ASPA implies that the certificate holder be a person of authority. Responsibilities of the certificate holder feature in the amendments to s. 10 of the ASPA dealt with above.

Table 9.1   Certificates of designation in Great Britain

Establishment type	In force on 31/12/1997	Granted during 1997	Revoked during 1997
Commercial concern	108	6	9
Higher education	102	—	1
QUANGO	35	—	2
Government	18	1	2
Non-profit making organisation	15	1	2
NHS hospital	11	—	—
Public health laboratory	3	—	—
Total	292	8	16

Responsibilities of the certificate holder

ASPA s. 8 imposes the obligation of paying the relevant fees on the certificate holder (CH). HOG 2.7 stresses that both the amount of and basis on which these fees are charged may be varied from time to time in line with any changes in the cost of regulatory arrangements. At present they are charged annually and consist of a flat rate annual fee on the designation/s of the establishment and a fee for each personal licensee.

Other responsibilities of the CH are given in detail in HOG 2.6. They include ensuring the following matters:

- The Inspector is provided with reasonable access to all parts of the establishment.
- The NACWOs discharge their duties.
- The NVSs discharge their duties.
- The fabric of the establishment is maintained in accordance with the COPH-CASP and other relevant codes e.g. on euthanasia.
- All scientific procedures are authorised by project and personal licences and records are maintained.
- The establishment is appropriately staffed and licensees trained.
- Competent persons are available to kill animals humanely.
- Animals are obtained from appropriate sources.
- All primates, dogs and cats are marked by a method agreed with the Inspector.
- A protected animal is issued only to a suitably authorised person.
- Source, use and disposal records of the animals are kept.
- The Inspector is notified of any changes to personnel or the use of rooms within the designated establishment.

A new and onerous responsibility was imposed on certificate holders from 1 April 1999. The Home Office Circular PCD/2/98 which outlined the establishing of ethical review processes indicated that:

'The CH will be responsible for the operation of the local ERP [ethical review process] and will appoint the members of a committee or group (or where appropriate, more than one such body) to implement the procedure.'

(Annex n. 4)

and

'The CH should ensure as wide an involvement of establishment staff as possible in a local framework acting to ensure that all animal use in an establishment is carefully considered and justified; that proper account is taken of all possibilities for the reduction, refinement and replacement (the 3 Rs); and that standards of accomodation and care are maximised.'

(Annex 2)

The involvement of outside people in the ERP must be considered by the CH. (PCD Circular n. 3.5)

It may be significant that the term 'committee' is only one word among others such as 'body' used regarding the ERP. The acronym LERP is now used more frequently than ERP. Is this stressing the local arrangements of the present situation? Will there be regional ethical review processes?

A further responsibility of the CH has appeared in the form of an obligation to draw up a list or register of members of staff competent in the various methods of Schedule 1 killing. This is a welcome innovation which guarantees appropriate care in the administration of euthanasia.

APC and the role of the certificate holder

The APC 1997 report states at p. 90:

'11. Certificate holders must be visible to, and approachable by, those who work with animals in the establishment. They must actively set the tone of, establish, nurture and reflect the "culture of care" which should pervade each and every designated establishment, and provide the time and other resources required to discharge properly their responsibilities under the Act.

12. Certificates of designation are issued to persons occupying positions of authority at designated establishments who are then personally accountable to the Home Office for compliance with the conditions of issue on the certificate. These include the provision of appropriate standards of care and accomodation; effective internal management to prevent the performance of unauthorised procedures; and the training, performance and conduct of staff with responsibilities under the Act or who interact with the protected animals in other ways (for example, animal care staff and those performing humane killing).'

The report goes on to deal with the diagram of internal arrangements within the establishments already presented.

'14. The certificate holder should be the person who can take effective action to discharge properly these responsibilities – i.e. someone with sufficient seniority and authority, and who can also take an active interest in the work in animal units. The "right person" must be combined with the right management systems. Certificate holders should be selected on the basis, not of their job title, but by their ability and determination properly to discharge the responsibilities.

15. It is not a role which can be passively discharged – active, visible and effective leadership and management are essential. The Committee has been disappointed, when considering infringements and other departures from best practice, that "laissez faire" attitudes and practices on the part of some of the certificate holders involved have too often been aggravating factors.

16. Tighter internal controls often have to be introduced following infringements, or at least existing controls have to be applied more rigorously. Tighter controls might include, for example, requiring that certificate holders endorse personal licence applications; providing additional means for ensuring that animals are only issued and used in accordance with specific licence authorities; and requiring that users not in the certificate holders' employ be subjected to all the normal institutional controls. We recommend that certificate holders ensure that internal controls are regularly reviewed to identify any deficiencies which might lead to infringements. This is a possible role for the ethical review process.

17. All certificate holders should reflect on whether their current systems represent "all reasonable attempts" to prevent unauthorised work at their establishment. The prevention of infringements should not, however, be the only objective. It is just as important that certificate holders promote the right culture, one in which animal use and suffering is minimised and welfare maximised.

(APC 1997 Report, n. 13)

The above is not, of course, law, but the history of the ASPA as an enabling Act portrays a tendency for recommendations and even suggestions to eventually become closely associated, sometimes imperceptibly, with legislation.

Local ethical review process (LERP)

The Secretary of State requires an ethical review process to be established in each designated establishment under s. 6 or 7 of the ASPA. The requirement for a LERP is a standard condition on a certificate of designation of user, breeding and supplying establishments.

Although much of the discussion concerning LERPs tends to be concerned with project licence applications and the 3 Rs, the fact that both breeding and supplying establishments, where there may be no project licence holders, must have LERPs, is a clear indication that the review process must be seriously concerned with animal welfare as such.

The Annex to the Home Office Circular PCD 4/98 outlines clearly the nature of and requisites for a viable LERP:

'Ethical review process
2. The certificate holder should ensure as wide an involvement of establishment staff as possible in a local framework acting to ensure that *all use of animals in the establishment, as regulated by the Animals (Scientific Procedures) Act 1986*, is carefully considered and justified; that proper account is taken of all possibilities for reduction, refinement and replacement (the 3 Rs); and that *high* standards of accommodation and care are *achieved*.

Aims
3.1 To provide independent ethical advice to the Certificate holder, particularly with respect to project licence applications and standards of animal care and welfare.
3.2 To provide *support* to named: people and *advice to* licensees *regarding* animal welfare and ethical issues arising from their work.
3.3 To promote the use of ethical analysis to increase awareness of animal welfare issues and develop initiatives leading to *the widest possible* application of the 3 Rs.

Responsibility of the certificate holder
4. The certificate holder will be responsible *to the Home Office* for the operation of the local ethical review process and *for the appointment of people* to implement its procedures.

Personnel
5. A named veterinary surgeon and representatives from among the named animal care and welfare officers should be involved. In user establishments, project licensees and personal licensees should also be represented. As many people as possible should be involved in the ethical review process. Where possible, the views of those who do not have responsibilities under the Act should be taken into account. One or more lay persons, independent of the establishment, should also be considered. Home Office inspectors should have the right to attend any meetings and have access to the records of the ethical review process.

Operation
6. These people should deliberate regularly and keep records of discussions and advice. All licensees and named animal care and welfare officers must be informed of the ethical review process and should be encouraged to bring matters to its attention. An operating description should allow for input by colleagues and other people from outside the establishment. It should be clear how submissions can be made. The people involved should be regarded as approachable, dealing in confidence with complaints and processing all suggestions for improvement.

7. Specifically, the process should allow (where appropriate) the following:

    7.1   promoting the development and uptake of *reduction, replacement and refinement* alternatives in animal use, where they exist, and ensuring the availability of relevant sources of information;

    7.2   examining proposed applications for new project licences and amendments to existing licences, with reference to the likely costs to the animals, the expected benefits of the work and how these considerations balance;

    7.3   providing a forum for discussion of issues relating to the use of animals and considering how staff can be kept up to date with relevant ethical advice, best practice, and relevant legislation;

    7.4   undertaking retrospective project reviews and continuing to apply the 3 Rs to all projects, throughout their duration;

    7.5   considering the care and accommodation standards applied to all animals in the establishment, including breeding stock, and the humane killing of protected animals;

    7.6   regularly reviewing the establishment's managerial systems, procedures and protocols where these bear on the proper use of animals;

    7.7   advising on how all staff involved with the animals can be appropriately trained and how competence can be ensured.

8. Commonly, there should be a promotional role, seeking to educate users (in applying the 3 Rs) and non-users (by explaining why and how animals are used), as appropriate. There should be some formal output from the ethical review process for staff and colleagues in the establishment, made as widely available as security and commercial/intellectual confidentiality allow.

9. Receipt of a project licence application signed by the certificate holder will be taken by the Home Office to mean that the application has been through the ethical review process for that establishment.

10. Once the system is established, Inspectors will still be happy to discuss early ideas with prospective project licence holders *and will be available for advice and clarification at any point. But an application will not be considered for formal authorisation by the Home Office until the prospective project has been considered appropriately within the ethical review process.* The Inspector will not negotiate with any advisory group. Local arrangements and the individual case will dictate whether amended applications must re-enter the ethical review process. *It will be a matter of judgement in the particular case how best to balance the inputs of the ethical review process and the Inspectorate without duplicating effort or creating undue delay.'*

(HO 01/04/1998)

It is hardly the place in a legal text to expound on the evolution in practice of LERPs. The topic is referred to more fully in *Ethics, Animals and Science* (K. Dolan, Blackwell Science, Oxford, 1999). Suffice here to quote an apt comment of the APC (1997 Report p. 5).

'41. It is axiomatic that the ethical review process should serve the certificate of designation holder and become a means for helping ensure responsibilities under the 1986 Act are properly discharged. Ethical considerations should pervade and reinforce managerial processes. The aim is not to increase bureaucracy or cause delay but to promote the ethical consideration of animal use and to exploit the potential for applying the 3 Rs and the highest standards of animal care.'

Named animal care and welfare officer (NACWO)

There is an abundance of literature on this topic concerning the named person in day to day care – known since March 1997 as the named animal care and welfare officer (NACWO). Particularly useful for study is the IAT booklet *Guidance notes on the role of the named animal care and welfare officer in establishments designated under the Animals (Scientific Procedures) Act 1986* (Spring 1998). In a similar fashion the Royal College of Veterinary Surgeons has published ample material on the role of the named veterinary surgeon in a Code of Practice and a Guide. Relevant material eminating from both these informed bodies will be referred to but it is important initially to consider the basis in law for the required functions as expressions in practice of the legal responsibilities of the NACWO and the NVS.

The NACWO, the NVS and the law

The ASPA deals with the roles of the NACWO and the NVS in s. 6 and 7. The subsections involving the NACWO and the the NVS in both these sections are subsections (5), (6) and (7). Section 6 is concerned with scientific procedure establishments and Section 7 is concerned with breeding and supplying establishment.

Section 6 (5) and s. 7 (5) read the same except the obvious variation called for, in s. 7 (5) (a), on account of the differing purposes of the establishments involved. Merely a case of *mutatis mutandis* as the lawyers say.

> 'A certificate under this section shall specify –
> (a) a person to be responsible for the day-to-day care of the protected animals kept for experimental or other scientific purposes at the establishment; and
> (b) a veterinary surgeon or other suitably qualified person to provide advice on their health and welfare;'

In special circumstances, a non-veterinarian is not excluded from being specified for this post.

> 'and the same person may, if the Secretary of State thinks fit, be specified under both paragraphs of this subsection.'

This implies the possibility, but hardly the likelihood in practice, of the NACWO and the NVS being one and the same person.

There is an important variation between subsection 6 (6) and subsection 7 (6) because of the involvement in scientific procedure establishments of personal licensees:

'6 (6) If it appears to any person specified in a certificate pursuant to subsection (5) above that the health or welfare of any such animal as is mentioned in that subsection gives rise to concern he shall –
  (a) notify the person holding a personal licence who is in charge of the animal; or
  (b) if there is no such person or it is not practicable to notify him, take steps to ensure that the animal is cared for and, if it is necessary for it to be killed, that it is killed by a method which is appropriate under Schedule 1 to this Act or approved by the Secretary of State.'

'7 (6) If it appears to any person specified in a certificate pursuant to subsection (5) above that the health or welfare of any such animal as is mentioned in that subsection gives rise to concern he shall take steps to ensure that it is cared for and, if it is necessary for it to be killed, that it is killed by a method appropriate under Schedule 1 to this Act or approved by the Secretary of State.'

Subsection (7) is identical in both ss 6 and 7:

'In any case to which subsection (6) above applies the person specified in the certificate pursuant to paragraph (a) of subsection (5) above may also notify the person (if different) specified pursuant to paragraph (b) of that subsection; and the person specified pursuant to either paragraph of that subsection may also notify one of the inspectors under this Act.'

In short, if there is concern about an animal the NACWO may notify the NVS or in such a situation either the NACWO or the NVS may notify the Inspector.

In greater detail and more clearly HOG outlines the role of both the NACWO and the NVS.

HOG on NACWO

HOG refers to the named person in day to day care but to better reflect changes in, and the development of, this important role since its inception under the ASPA the title was changed in 1997 to named animal care and welfare officer. This named person will often be a senior animal technician. Usually several such persons will be named for each establishment. Each individual will be responsible for a discrete area of the establishment. These areas should be clearly defined and communication routes put in place to ensure a standard approach across the establishment. The daily responsibilities assigned by HOG to the NACWO implies a need to appoint deputies.

Responsibilities of the NACWO

'(i)   being aware of the standards of husbandry and welfare set out in the Code of Practice and taking steps to ensure that these are met;

(ii)   ensuring that suitable records are maintained of the health of the animals, in a form determined by the named veterinary surgeon with the agreement of the Inspector;

(iii)   ensuring that suitable records are maintained of the environmental conditions in the rooms in which animals are held, and of all the animals bought, bred, supplied, issued, used, killed or otherwise disposed of;

(iv)   knowing which areas of the establishment are listed in the certificate of designation and the purposes for which they are designated;

(v)   ensuring that every protected animal in all designated areas is seen and checked at least once daily by a competent person;

(vi)   being familiar with the project licences in use, including severity limits and severity conditions, adverse effects and humane endpoints;

(vii)   knowing how to contact all project or personal licence holders, the named or deputy veterinary surgeon(s) and the certificate holder;

(viii) being aware of appropriate methods of killing listed in Schedule 1, together with any other approved methods listed in the certificate of designation and either being competent in their use or knowing how to contact someone who is.'

(HOG, 2.10)

The NACWO adequately performs her/his requisite functions by conscientiously fulfilling the above responsibilities.

The APC Report 1996 appears to envisage an extension of the role assigned by HOG to the Named Persons:

'The guidance notes for the completion of project licence applications (and where necessary, the form itself) be revised to ensure that;

● Named Persons are consulted by project licence applicants;'

(p. 23, n. 2)

'(d) Named Animal Care and Welfare Officers
38. Part of the framework for the effective management of animal work within an establishment relies on the Named Animal Care and Welfare Officer (formerly known as the Named Day-to-Day Care Person). It is vital that this person is appropriately trained and qualified and promotes throughout the animal unit a sympathetic, compassionate and professional attitude to animal care, welfare and use. The Named Animal Care and Welfare Officer must be given the necessary authority and management support to ensure best practice is maintained, and that the terms and conditions of licences are strictly adhered to.'

(p. 30)

'Recommendation 7:
It is recommended that the Home Office give consideration to ensuring that

Named Animal Care and Welfare Officers are appropriately trained and qualified, and that the importance of this role be promulgated to all who work under the Act.'

(p. 30)

IAT NACWO guidelines

These guidelines supplement with more practical details the demands made upon the NACWO in respect of the requisite functions, responsibilities and qualities associated with the office:

'... statutory duties, performed by the NACWO on behalf of the certificate holder, are directed towards minimising suffering and optimising the welfare of animals being bred or used for scientific procedures at the establishment.

The contribution of the NACWO, and the named veterinary surgeon (NVS), towards the Three Rs – refinement, reduction and replacement – can and should be made during the planning stage of project licences and as part of an ethical review process. Further opportunities to contribute will occur during the five year life of the project. These include improvements to care regimes, enhancement of housing standards and notifying the personal licence holder when the condition of an animal gives cause for concern or, if this is not possible, caring for or, if necessary, humanely killing the animal.

The provision of the highest standards of animal welfare and husbandry is explicit in this often challenging and demanding role. The NACWO will be called upon to advise and assist others working under the legislation, including the certificate holder, personal and project licensees and the NVS. Expertise in all areas of animal care and husbandry is a pre-requisite and will include areas such as health, nutrition, caging and housing, biology, breeding and legislation. A certain maturity, coupled with tact and diplomacy, may be needed in some dealings.

Selection of the right person with the right qualifications and the right attitude to animals and others within the establishment, coupled with management support and an opportunity to maintain and further develop the necessary skills and attitudes, is seen as key to the successful functioning of an individual in the NACWO role. Whilst it is vital to establish good lines of communication with all people working within the legislation, the provision of a means of direct access between the NACWO and certificate holder is particularly important.'

(p. 1.)

'The skills and knowledge required to fulfil this vitally important animal welfare position are both numerous and varied. Normally the person to whom responsibility is given for the day to day care of protected animals will have the following qualities.

- An extensive knowledge of the welfare and husbandry requirements of the species housed at the establishment. Such knowledge will include the caging or housing needs for different group sizes, optimum environmental conditions including enrichment opportunities, nutritional requirements and expert knowledge of the physiological and ethological needs of the species maintained. This person will normally be a qualified and senior animal technician but in some establishments may be an experienced stockman or a veterinary or biological graduate with the appropriate experience and training.

- A detailed understanding of the various legislation under which the use of animals at the establishment is regulated together with the knowledge and ability to act as advisor to other individuals working within it. The NACWO may also be called upon to give advise on local procedures within the establishment including such areas as health and safety and the acquisition, transportation and disposal of animals.
- Familiarity with the content of project licences operating in their area of responsibility and, in particular, the types of procedures, severity limits, conditions and humane endpoints contained therein.
- Good verbal and written communication skills and sufficient standing and authority at the establishment to enable them to access the appropriate persons, offer advice and obtain timely action whenever necessary.
- The ability to recognise any variance from normal health and behaviour in the animals under his/her care, determine the action that must be taken along with its degree of urgency and be conversant with all methods of euthanasia listed under Schedule 1 of the Act, together with any other methods approved by the Home Secretary for use at that establishment.'

(pp. 2–3)

'... It is a pivotal position and it is incumbent upon the person appointed to establish, and nuture, a culture of care within the establishment. The NACWO, irrespective of his/her position in the establishment, must promote the right caring attitude, amongst all those coming into contact with animals, regarding welfare and use of animals.

It is vital that the NACWO be not only appropriately trained and qualified but that he/she constantly updates this knowledge and skills base to remain at the forefront of new and emerging technologies. The NACWO must have the necessary status, authority and management support within the establishment to ensure high standards of welfare are maintained and that the terms and conditions of all licences are strictly adhered to. In short the NACWO must be acknowledged and accepted as a valued expert on animal husbandry, care, welfare and legislation.'

(p. 4)

'The NACWO may also be given delegated authority for the organisation of training for all animal care personnel, thus guaranteeing best standards of animal welfare. He/she should also be prepared to make, and progress, improvements to the care and welfare of animals whenever the opportunity arises. The NACWO must, therefore, keep abreast of developments and advances in the field of laboratory animal science and welfare. This continued professional development is crucial to the role and can be achieved by regular attendance at scientific meetings or discussion groups, reading scientific literature and communicating with his/her peers. Membership of professional laboratory science organisations, such as the Institute of Animal Technology (IAT) and/or the Laboratory Animal Science Association (LASA) is strongly recommended.'

(p. 5)

Enrolment on the Register of Animal Technicians could also be appropriate.

'The NACWO must be able to advise a licensee what rooms in his/her area of responsibility are authorised for animal use and the types of procedures and species that may be used within them. It is imperative the NACWO has access to all designated rooms within his/her responsibility at all times.'

(p. 6)

'In summary the NACWO will make an important contribution to the control of severity of procedures by;
- advising the certificate holder and project licensee on matters of animal welfare and husbandry during the construction of the project licence;
- alerting the appropriate individual to an animal that is experiencing, or is likely to experience, pain and suffering.'

(p. 7)

Named veterinary surgeon (NVS)

The 1998 amendment of the ASPA stresses a facet of the role of the NVS as regards animals to be kept alive at the conclusion of a series of procedures.
Section 10 states:

'3(D) The conditions of a project licence shall include such conditions as the Secretary of State considers appropriate to ensure –
(a) that where a protected animal has been subjected to a series of regulated procedures for a particular purpose, at the conclusion of the series a veterinary surgeon or, if none is available, another suitably qualified person determines whether the animal should be killed or kept alive;
(b) that, if that person considers that it is likely to remain in lasting pain or distress, the animal is killed by a method appropriate to the animal under Schedule 1 to this Act, or by such other method as may be authorised by the personal licence of the person by whom the animal is killed; and
(c) that where the animal is to be kept alive, it is kept at a designated establishment (subject to subsection (6D) below).'

'(6D) The conditions of a certificate issued under section 6 or 7 above [sic] shall include such conditions as the Secretary of State considers appropriate to ensure that any animal kept alive after being subjected to a series of regulated proce- dures will continue to be kept at the establishment under the supervision of a veterinary surgeon or other suitably qualified person unless it is moved to another designated establishment or a veterinary surgeon certifies that it will not suffer if it ceases to be kept at a designated establishment.'

It is to be presumed that the 'veterinary surgeon' in the above text is the NVS of the designated establishment. It could be supposed that 'another qualified person' is the approved non-veterinarian replacement of a NVS, as allowed for in section 5(b) of the ASPA.

Responsibilities of the NVS

Home Office Guidelines on ASPA (n. 2 11–15) stipulate the NVS's responsibilities as follows:

'(i)   visiting all parts of the establishment designated in the certificate at a frequency which will allow the effective monitoring of the health status of the animals;

(ii)   having regular contact with the certificate holder and the named day-to-day care person(s);

(iii)   having a thorough knowledge of the prevention, diagnosis and treat- ment of disease which may affect the species kept, and of their hus- bandry and welfare requirements;

(iv)   providing a comprehensive veterinary service at all times of the day or night throughout the year;

(v)   supplying and directing the use of controlled drugs and other pre- scription only medicines for use on protected animals in the establish- ment;

(vi)   supervising the maintenance of health records relating to all protected animals in a form agreed with the Inspector: this should include a written record of advice or treatment given: these records should be kept at the establishment and be readily available to the named day-to- day care person, the certificate holder and the Inspector;

(vii)   being familiar with the project licences in use, including severity limits and severity conditions, adverse effects and humane endpoints;

(viii) being able to advise licensees and others on appropriate methods of anaesthesia, analgesia and euthanasia, surgical technique, choice of species, and on the recognition of pain, suffering, distress or lasting harm;

(ix)   being familiar with all methods of killing listed in Schedule 1 to the Act, together with any additional approved methods set out in the certificate of designation;

(x)   certifying where appropriate, that an animal is fit to travel to a specified place; to be used in further regulated procedures; to be released to the wild; or to be released for non-scientific purposes.'

(HOG n. 2. 11–15)

The NVS should nominate deputies and make sure they are known to other relevant members of the establishment. (2.12)

NVS involved in research

'2.13. Where the named veterinary surgeon also holds a project licence, a different veterinary surgeon should be nominated to perform the duties of the named veterinary surgeon for the project.

2.14. Where the named veterinary surgeon holds only a personal licence, there is no need for a different person to be named as the veterinary surgeon for this work, unless there is a risk of a conflict of interest between the scientific outcome of the research and the welfare of the animals. If such a conflict of interest is thought likely to arise, it will be necessary to obtain the opinion of another veterinary surgeon (who should be identified on the certificate of designation) on matters relating to the health and welfare of the animals involved.

2.15. Only in exceptional cases will these requirements be relaxed and this will require prior agreement of the Inspector.'

HOG elucidates the apparent anomaly of a non-veterinarian NVS posited in subsection (5) of section 6 and 7 of the Act.

'2.4 A person other than a veterinary surgeon may be accepted in respect of certain species when, after consultation with the Royal College of Veterinary Surgeons, it appears that no appropriate veterinary surgeon is available. In practice, this is unusual and has arisen mostly in relation to establishments in which work is confined to fish or avian embryos.'

Further material on the role of the NVS

As already mentioned there is an amount of relevant literature on the duties of the NVS. The Royal College of Veterinary Surgeons in its *Guide to Professional Conduct* (Third Draft) gives useful information on the responsibilities of the NVS:

'3.7.1 NVS's must be full members of the RCVS. Those on the temporary register may not be NVS's.

3.7.2 A full Code of Practice for NVS's, available from the RCVS, has been drawn up after consultation with the British Laboratory Animals Veterinary Association (BLAVA), the BVA and the Home Office. Although the species of animals cared for and the level of involvement may vary, all veterinarians taking on NVS duties should read the full Code of Practice, understand the Home Office Guidance on the Operation of the Act and consult with other NVS's.

3.7.3 An introductory course for NVS's, approved by the RCVS, is run by BLAVA each year. All veterinarians expecting to undertake NVS duties should undertake further training appropriate to the subject and keep up to date through a formal course of continuing professional development. With effect from 1 April 1996, all those taking on full-time or part-time appointments as NVS's, for the first time, and who have no higher professional qualification in the subject, will have to show evidence of satisfactory completion of the BLAVA introductory course or any equivalent course approved by the RCVS.

3.7.4 An NVS is employed in a professional capacity by the Certificate Holder ... NVS's are responsible to the Certificate Holder ...

3.7.6 ... other veterinarians must be available to provide an NVS service during periods of absence. Prior arrangements must be made. The names and telephone numbers of the other "on-call" veterinarians must be available in the establishment; ... NVS's must be clear at the outset which protected animals in the establishment are to be considered "animals under their care" under the terms of the Medicines Act 1968.' (This caution in respect to the Medicines Act is seemingly relevant to the NVS's direct involvement with the controlled drugs and prescription only medicines in the establishment, and to accepted veterinary practice.)

3.7.6 ... It is essential ... for the NVS to understand the scientific objectives and be familiar with the terms agreed in project licences ...'

As regards euthanasia the direct involvement of the NVS with the killing of animals was increased in March 1997 by the new version of Schedule 1. A registered veterinary surgeon may, without a personal licence, kill ungulates by:

(i)   destruction of the brain by free bullet; or
(ii) captive bolt, percussion or electrical stunning followed by destruction of the brain or exsanguination before return of consciousness.

An extra note

The Banner Committee was established to consider the ethical implications of emerging technologies in the breeding of farm animals and reported in 1995. It was concerned with the welfare of animals involved in such techniques and its comments could be of interest to veterinarians involved in research. Prof. Banner was concerned about the adverse effects in genetically modified animals and posited unacceptable 'intrinsically objectionable' modifications which might fall outside the category of 'adverse effects'. The APC Reports 1995 and 1996 (pp. 12–13) commented on the Banner Report which as yet has no direct specific impact on the responsibilities of named persons under the ASPA.

Overlapping responsibilities of the NACWO and NVS

The NACWO and NVS are closely associated in both s. 6 and s. 7 of the Act. On both of them is laid the responsibility of dealing with an animal the health or welfare of which gives rise to concern by subsection (6) of ss 6 and 7. Both the NACWO and the NVS are obliged to notify the relevant personal licence holder, if appropriate, or care for the animal or see that it is killed. Subsection (7) of ss 6 and 7 of the Act suggests the NACWO might notify the NVS when there is concern about an animal's health and welfare.

It also suggests either the NACWO or the NVS might notify the Inspector in such circumstances.

The very nature of the roles ascribed in law to the NACWO and NVS imply involvement one with the other as well as an amount of overlapping of the duties assigned to either of them. The most onerous duty of the NACWO, the daily checking of every animal, is a prerequisite for the NVS to adequately fulfil her/his main responsibility of monitoring the health and welfare of the animals. The awareness of the NACWO alerts the NVS to attend immediately to the care of specific animals.

HOG refers to the required interrelationship between NACWO and NVS: (2.10, 2.11 and 2.12).

- The NACWO must ensure health records are maintained in a form determined by the NVS.
- The NACWO must know how to contact the NVS or her/his deputy.
- The duties of the NACWO and NVS as regards euthanasia overlap.
- The NVS must have have regular contact with the NACWO.
- The NVS should make the health records available to the NACWO.
- The NVS should make known the identity of nominated deputies to the NACWO.

Background literature on both the NACWO and NVS reinforce the need for these two named persons to be closely associated. The duties of both overlap particularly in the area of training:

> 'The NACWO may also be given delegated authority for the organisation of training for all animal care personnel . . .'
>
> (NACWO Guidelines, p. 5)

> 'The NVS is in the best position to advise on improvements in anaesthesia, surgical techniques and the control of pain and will be expected to do so. An NVS will also be expected to advise on methods of humane killing and train technicians and scientists in these and other skills.'
>
> (*Guide to Professional Conduct*, 3.7.6)

The NACWO guidelines also state:

> 'The NACWO will be called upon to advise and assist others working under the legislation including . . . the NVS.'
>
> (p. 1)

The *Guide to Professional Conduct* comments:

> 'An NVS must establish a professional working relationship with the Named Persons Responsible for Day-to-Day Care, who will normally be senior animal technologists with considerable experience in the husbandry of laboratory animals and their use in research, ...'
>
> (3.7.5)

Figures 9.2 and 9.3 perhaps more clearly illustrate the overlapping and inter-dependence of the NACWO and NVS.

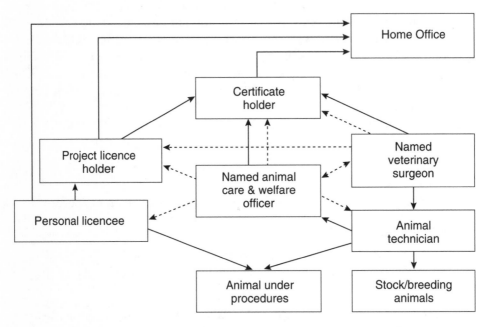

Fig. 9.2 Relationships of named animal care and welfare officer (NACWO) to other members of staff.

Home Office correspondence on the role of the NVS

The use of animals for education and training in agriculture

There follow extracts from Home Office correspondence on various matters germane to the application of the ASPA in agriculture and veterinary practice.

> 'Section 5(3)(e) of the Animals (Scientific Procedures) Act 1986 permits the application of regulated procedures which may cause pain, suffering, distress or lasting harm to animals for the purpose of education or training otherwise than in primary or secondary schools.
> It is Home Office policy to grant project licences authorising regulated

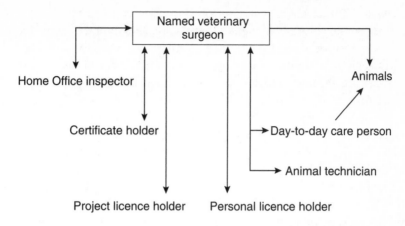

Fig. 9.3 Relationships of named veterinary surgeon (NVS) with other interested parties.

procedures only for educational purposes in a scientific context and to restrict the use of animals for training (i.e. the acquisition of manual skills) only to the practice of microsurgery in defined training courses.

This policy precludes the use of animals for demonstrations or practice of techniques in veterinary medicine and agriculture where the aim is to become proficient in performing such techniques. Thus project licences under the Animals (Scientific Procedures) Act cannot be granted for this purpose.

Section 2(8) of the Act has the effect of excluding from control procedures carried out for the purposes of recognised veterinary, agricultural or animal husbandry practice. The use of animals to demonstrate and practise routine techniques such as blood sampling and simple injections for veterinary or agricultural students must comply with legislative controls such as the Veterinary Surgeons Act and the Veterinary Surgeons (Practice by Students) Regulations, 1981.

In general, this use will need to be restricted to animals which have a perceived need to undergo the sampling or treatment for a specific veterinary or animal husbandry reason. For example, blood samples may be taken for biochemical analysis for diagnosis (or 'profiling' with a view to diagnosis) of trace element status and injections may be given if these form part of the routine husbandry of the herd or flock as in vaccination programmes in sheep or iron administration in piglets. The guiding principle in the use of animals in training courses must be that the use must benefit the individual animal or the herd directly.'

(HO, March 1990)

The Animals (Scientific Procedures) Act, 1986 and recognised veterinary practice

'The Act provides for the licensing of experimental and other scientific procedures applied to living vertebrate animals which may cause pain, suffering, distress or lasting harm. The controls do not extend to procedures applied to animals in the course of recognised veterinary, agricultural or animal husbandry practice; to procedures for the identification of animals for scientific purposes and which cause no more than momentary pain or distress and no lasting harm; or to clinical tests on animals for evaluating a veterinary product under authority of an Animal Test Certificate (Medicines Act, 1968).

In the years since the Act was introduced, the interpretation of "recognised veterinary practice" has caused some difficulties. However, in most cases, the difficulties have been resolved by considering two questions about the proposed action (Fig. 9.4). Is what you wish to do being performed essentially for a scientific or experimental purpose? If the answer to this is yes, then it is likely that licences under the Animals (Scientific Procedures) Act are required before the work is carried out. The second question should resolve any remaining

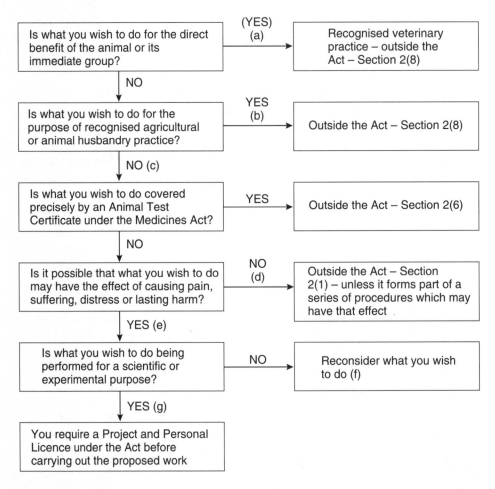

Fig. 9.4 The Animals (Scientific Procedures) Act 1986 and the performance of procedures by veterinary surgeons. Letters in brackets refer to examples of procedures falling within the particular decision and explained in Table 9.2. *Source:* Home Office.

difficulty; is what you wish to do for the direct benefit of the animal or its immediate group? If the answer to this is yes, then the work could reasonably be considered to be "recognised veterinary practice".

For example, if you wish to take a series of biopsies from an animal for the prime purpose of diagnosis and subsequent monitoring of the effectiveness of treatment, then this would be "recognised practice". If, however, the biopsies are taken primarily to study the pathogenesis of the condition, then licences would be required as the purpose is now one of scientific enquiry. It is accepted that there will be cases where the difference between these circumstances is less clear but the consideration of the question of benefit to the animal will usually resolve the difficulty.

The status of blood sampling may often be in doubt, particularly in educational and training establishments. Here again, the questions of purpose and benefit will usually provide a clear answer. If the samples are being taken from an animal, or animals within a herd or flock, for the purpose of diagnosis, or for metabolic profile test etc. and, as a result of the analysis of the samples, action will be taken for the benefit of the animal or animals, then the sampling is clearly "recognised practice". If the samples are intended essentially for laboratory use or for teaching purposes and there is no real prospect of direct benefit to the animal from which the sample was taken, then this would not be considered to be "recognised practice" and would require licences under the Act. The particular case of blood donor animals in clinical practice has been considered by the Preliminary Investigation and Advisory Committee of the Royal College. Their advice is set out in the Guide to Professional Conduct, 1990 Edition, Appendix 12.2.

Special problems in interpretation may arise for veterinary surgeons when dealing with animals undergoing a scientific procedure under the Act. The administration of an anaesthetic agent as part of the procedure described in the project licence or the performance of any other part of the procedure can only be legally carried out if the veterinary surgeon holds a personal licence. However, if the animal undergoing the scientific procedure requires clinical attention from the veterinary surgeon, usually from a cause extraneous to the scientific procedure itself, then no licence is necessary for carrying out the clinical procedure on the animal.

In any case of difficulty where you are unable to reach a decision in this matter, you should seek advice from the Home Office Inspectorate. The addresses of the Regional Offices are shown in Appendix 10 of the RCVS Register and Directory.'

(Jeremy Roberts, HO Inspector, 10 October 1990)

Further guidance

The list of examples in Table 9.2 is illustrative and not exhaustive. The advice of the Home Office Inspector should always be sought in cases of doubt.

Table 9.2   Some terms and examples of their use in practice

Term	Example(s)
(a) direct benefit	taking blood samples from an animal, or animals within a herd, for diagnosis, metabolic profile test, etc. taking a series of biopsies from an animal for diagnosis and monitoring the efficacy of treatment giving veterinary treatment to an experimental animal when treatment is for animal's benefit and not part of the scientific procedure use of drugs in ways other than described in product licence but for direct benefit of animal concerned NB; anaesthesia for a scientific purpose is regulated
(b) recognised practice	embryo transfer testing for halothane susceptibility in pigs restraint in commercial systems laparoscopy for A.I. laparoscopy for observation of the gonads for sexing birds removal of gonads or hormone administration for control of reproduction in non-experimental situations
(c) not recognised practice	laparoscopy for observation of the ovaries for a scientific purpose feeding of diets at variance with normal practice restraint in non-commercial or experimental systems
(d) no adverse effect	feeding of diets at variance with normal practice but which are not intended to result in deficiencies or excess of any dietary component and will maintain body weight within 85% of normal growth or starting weight reasonable restraint for short periods, for example a metabolism crate for up to 14 days
(e) adverse effect	any penetration of the integument, i.e. use of needle any procedure requiring sedation or anaesthesia maintenance in close restraint for any period and in restraint for long periods feeding of haematophagous insects
(f) think again	taking into account the provisions of the Veterinary Surgeons Act, the Veterinary Surgeons (Practice by Students) Regulations, 1981, the Animal Health Act, 1981, the Medicines Act, 1968 and the Wildlife and Countryside Act, 1981
(g) scientific purposes	taking blood for blood products or laboratory use. taking blood for teaching purposes taking biopsies for studying pathogenesis of a condition inoculation of material into an animal for diagnosis of disease in another animal use of substances, drugs, etc. other than as described in product licence, for research/development and not covered by an ATC

An informative warning letter on 'The Veterinary Surgeons Act 1966 and the Animals (Scientific Procedures) Act 1986 – acts of veterinary surgery performed by non-veterinarians' was sent by the Royal College of Veterinary Surgeons on 7 September 1998. It was accompanied by a BLAVA Position Paper on *The Veterinary Surgeons Act 1966 and the Animals (Scientific Procedures) Act 1986 – a conflict of legislative requirements*. Both these documents, available from the Royal College or BLAVA, could be of interest to the NVS. Another worthwhile publication of the Royal College of Veterinary Surgeons is *Legislation Affecting the Veterinary Profession in the UK*, (6th. Edition).

Chapter 10

Codes of Practice

At present (1998) there are four codes of practice which have been issued under s. 21 of the ASPA.

- for the Housing and Care of Animals used in Scientific Procedures (1989)
- Licensing and Inspection under the Animals (Scientific Procedures) Act 1986 (1994)
- for the Housing and Care of Animals in Designated Breeding and Supplying Establishments (1995)
- for the Humane Killing of Animals under Schedule 1 to the Animals (Scientific Procedures) Act 1986 (1997)

The codes of practice concerned with the operation of the Inspectorate and with euthanasia are referred to in Chapters 14 and 20. The two welfare codes: (a) for the Housing and Care of Animals in Scientific Procedures; and (b) for the Housing and Care of Animals in Designated and Supplying Establishments, have as their scope the outlining of the requisites of good husbandry, the basis of any effective animal welfare. These codes are the legal expression in practice of Article 5 of the European Convention for the Protection of Vertebrate Animals used for Experimental and other Scientific Procedures.

> 'Any animal used or intended for use in a procedure shall be provided with accommodation, an environment, at least a minimum degree of freedom of movement, food, water, care appropriate to its health and well being. Any restriction on the extent to which an animal can satisfy its physiological and ethological needs shall be limited as far as practicable.'

It would be of little practical avail in this text (August 1999) to expound in detail upon these welfare codes since the position is fluid. In, perhaps, the not too distant future at least some details will have been altered and additions may be made. Indications are given of these future developments in the APC 1997 Report (p. 41):

> 'Recommendation 10:
> The Committee recommended that the Home Office "Code of Practice for the Housing and Care of Animals Used in Scientific Procedures" be revised and consolidated at the appropriate time; and that the user community is consulted and informed about this process. Accepted by the Home Secretary – awaiting revised European standards, due in 2000.'

At this juncture, therefore, it suffices merely to outline the present codes and indicate their main drift while strongly urging that interested parties carefully peruse revised versions whenever they will be published.

Present welfare codes

These codes are of the utmost practical importance to all involved with the care of animals in designated establishments. It would be neither appropriate nor convenient to reproduce them in full in this text nor is it necessary since they should be readily available in any animal unit. Selective extracts could prove misleading and any attempt at an overall paraphrase of these source documents on welfare would no doubt fall short of providing comprehensive information on the good husbandry which both of the codes provide.

All students of law in this area should be fully conversant with the material in these codes. It would be difficult to retain in one's memory the complex details e.g. cage sizes, produced in the codes but the parts relevant to ones own responsibilities need to be carefully studied. Consequently these source documents should be constantly referred to for information on 'a need to know basis'. That need to know might be academic or a matter of stockmanship. Obviously a NACWO should not only be fully aware of the substances of these codes but should have a firm grasp of those details relevant to their duties. There follows merely an indication of the material that forms the scope of these two codes.

Code of Practice for the Housing and Care of Animals used in Scientific Procedures (1989) (COPHCASP)

The topics which define the scope of this code include:

- The animal house, its facilities, its staff and security.
- The environment provided within the unit.
- The sources, care and health of the animals.
- Transport, feeding, watering, handling and cleaning.
- The husbandry needs of certain species.
- The health status of the animals.
- Out-dated material on euthanasia in the light of the new 1997 Schedule 1 (a salutary lesson to be constantly aware of new legislation).
- Tables of requisite environmental data and cage sizes (the nightmare of examination candidates in this subject). These are liable to amendment, an acceptable excuse for not reproducing them here.

In 1993, the Inspectorate carried out an audit of non-academic user establishments for compliance with the published COPHCASP. A similar audit of academic establishments was carried out in 1996. (APC Report 1997 p. 14)

Code of Practice for the Housing and Care of Animals in Designated Breeding and Supplying Establishments

This code is more specific than the previous one, and is concerned only with those species listed in Schedule 2 before January 1999. They are mice, rats, hamsters, rabbits, guinea pigs, dogs, cats, non-human primates, and quail (*Coturnix coturnix*, the European quail). Eventually, special provisions may be inserted into this Code regarding the care of ferrets, gerbils, and genetically manipulated pigs and sheep.

It is probably within this context that we encounter the most restricted extension in law of the term 'animal'. The use of the word 'animal' in this code only applies to the species listed. Although restricted in respect to the species involved the scope of this code is the same as the COPHCASP, that is, standards of good husbandry. Because of the concentration on particular species the stipulations are more detailed. The first part of the this code deals with similar topics to those covered by COPHCASP. In the second part the more specific needs of Schedule 2 animals are stipulated.

Relevant comments on this code

The 1997 APC Report (p. 33) has a note relevant to breeding establishments:

> '16. The Committee accepts that some overbreeding of laboratory animals is unavoidable, but believes that it should be minimised and we have identified principles of good practice. These will be refined in the light of the outcome of the Laboratory Animal Science Association's current considerations of this issue with a view to inviting the Home Office to incorporate guidance in the code of practice for breeding establishments.

> 17. In order to be able to assess the total number of animals used or bred for use in scientific research, there is a case for collating and publishing data on over-breeding and animal use outside the Act. Whilst we believe that it would be possible to collate data on overbreeding for the most commonly used species, we accept that there are considerable practical difficulties on obtaining figures on the use of animals outside the controls of the Act (specifically, the use of tissue, blood or organs from animals which had been humanely killed). Thus, while we recommend that establishments be required to report to the Home Office figures for overbreeding, we shall need to discuss the matter of non-regulated use with the Home Office.'

Special provisions for dog welfare

Survey of Welfare Standards for Dogs Within Designated Establishments was published by the Home Office at the end of 1998. The study was a consequence of the Channel 4 *Countryside Undercover* programme, 'It's a Dog's Life' (March 1997). The resulting recommendations stemming from the study will be incorporated into the relevant Code of Practice when next revised.

Inspectors will be pursuing the implementation of these recommendations.

- Dogs should be housed in groups or pairs, unless persuasive veterinary, husbandry or scientific reasons can be provided for single housing. Socialisation programmes should be adopted for dogs held singly/in small groups.
- Pens should be cleaned daily with waste material being replaced with fresh bedding. Pen design must offer some environmental complexity and choice.
- Where restraint/confinement is required justification must be included in the project licence application with details of measures to provide high welfare standards.
- Staff training should completely cover welfare including housing, husbandry, handling, behaviour and health.
- Environmental enrichment and welfare as well as training and assessment of competency should be considered in the LERP.

(*RDS News*, Jan 99 and APC Report 1998 p. 19)

As an illustration of the constant need for awareness regarding new developments in this area, the attention of interested parties should be drawn to the prospect of another relevant and useful Code of Practice. A draft of a Home Office Code of Practice for the Housing and Care of Pigs Intended for use as Xenotransplants Source Animals is in circulation (September 1999).

Legal force of the codes

The legal basis for these codes of practice is s. 21 of the ASPA where the Secretary of State is encouraged to use his enabling powers to produce subordinate legislation in the form of codes of practice.

'21. (2) The Secretary of State shall issue codes of practice as to the care of protected animals and their use for regulated procedures and may approve such codes issued by other persons.'

Subsection (3) provides for consultation with the APC in respect to these codes. Subsections (5) and (6) give the details of the parliamentary process for bringing the codes into law.

It is only subsection (4) that has practical significance for those involved with animals in research:

'21. (4) A failure on the part of any person to comply with any provision of a code issued or approved under subsection (2) above shall not of itself render that person liable to criminal or civil proceedings but –
  (a) any such code shall be admissible in evidence in any such proceedings; and
  (b) if any of its provisions appears to the court conducting the proceedings to be relevant to any question arising in the proceedings it shall be taken into account in determining that question.'

In short one can not be prosecuted for breaching a stipulation of any of the codes. If, however, one were to be accused of an offence e.g. causing an animal unnecessary suffering, then any relevant provision of the codes would be considered. If any such provision has been flouted the burden of proof, usually borne solely by the prosecution would roll over partly on to the accused. He/she would now have to establish that the method of care he/she used was as good as if not better than the method of care proposed by the code. This would be a difficult proposition to establish to the satisfaction of any court.

Chapter 11

Re-use of Animals

This much debated issue is covered by s. 14 of ASPA and paras. 4.21–29 of HOG. From experience it appears that the issue of re-use is the most complex topic associated with the ASPA. It is obviously an aspect of animal use which could arouse great concern in the mind of the interested public. Consequently it is understandable that the legislation on the matter and commentary on that legislation is couched in cautious terms. Because of the delicate nature of this area of the law the official documentation (the Act and HOG) will be closely adhered to. The most telling sentence occurs in HOG 4.21.

> 'All re-use must therefore be specifically authorised in advance.'

This would usually imply discussion with the Inspector. Here, as in fact throughout the whole practical application of the ASPA; the key phrase – 'discussion with the Inspector' and compliance with proffered advice – is paramount.

The APC 1997 Report (p. 108) confirms the bewilderment experienced by some workers in the field.

> '4. Concerns were expressed that the criteria for and restrictions on re-use were confusing, difficult to interpret and unduly restrictive; and that, as a result, some animals that could be re-used had to be humanely killed – requiring additional animals to be used instead. We are aware that this is an issue which the Home Office has been looking at with a view to clarifying the position when it revises the guidance on the operation of the Act.'

The use of such terms as, 'repeated or continuous use' without clear definition of those words, has not helped to elucidate the concept involved.

Future guidance from the Home Office will, no doubt, clarify the notion of re-use, vary some of the text on the matter and should be consulted as soon as possible after publication. The pertinent extracts below from HOG are, however, still relevant. In the meantime, of course, the amended version of s. 14 of the ASPA is in place. This constituted one of the most drastic changes among the 1998 amendments.

Subsection 1 of the amended section replaces the previous subsection 1 and introduces a new and absolute prohibition of re-use:

'Where –
    (a) a protected animal has been subjected to a series of regulated procedures for a particular purpose; and
    (a) any of those procedures has caused severe pain or distress to that animal,
that animal shall not be used for any further regulated procedures which will entail severe pain or distress.'

The former subsection 1 has now been combined with the previous subsection 2 to read:

'Where a protected animal has been subjected to a series of regulated procedures for a particular purpose and has been given a general anaesthetic for any of those procedures and been allowed to recover consciousness, that animal shall not be used for any further regulated procedures unless the Secretary of State has given his consent to such further use and –
    (a) the procedure, or each procedure, for which the anaesthetic was given consisted only of surgical preparation essential for a subsequent procedure; or
    (b) the anaesthetic was administered solely to immobilise the animal; or
    (c) the animal will be under general anaesthesia throughout the further procedures and will not be allowed to recover consciousness.'

The previous subsection 3 has been slightly adjusted and abbreviated:

'Without prejudice to subsections (1) and (2) above, where a protected animal has been subjected to a series of regulated procedures for a particular purpose it shall not be used for any further regulated procedures except with the consent of the Secretary of State.'

The previous subsection 4 remains unchanged.

Section 14(4) sets the overall scene in respect to permission for re-use. 'Any consent for the purposes of this section may relate to a specified animal or to animals used in specified procedures or specified circumstances.' In other words, there is not going to be any general permission for re-use. Due authorisation for re-use should appear on Protocol Sheet 19b (continued) in the form of an 'x' in the appropriate one of three squares.

Home Office Guidance on re-use

'4.22. In general, if the same animal is being used as a matter of necessity, as in a series of regulated proedures for a particular purpose, this is not regarded as re-use. For example, where it is necessary to know how an animal responded to drugs A, B and C before interpreting its response to drug D, there is no choice and the successive use of the animal constitutes a single series of procedures without re-use.'

So if it is necessary from the nature of the series of procedures to use the same animal – it is not re-use in law. Usually the absence of re-use in the legal sense can be identified by the presence of a single purpose for the series. On the other hand if another animal can be used in a proposed procedure besides the one already used then it is a matter of re-use requiring permission.

> '4.23. By contrast, if the procedures are unrelated or a different animal could equally be chosen for the second or subsequent procedures, use of the same animal is regarded as re-use. For example if, by choice, repeated samples of normal blood were taken from a rabbit, but each sample could equally well have come from a fresh rabbit, this would count as re-use and would require specific authority.'

HOG 4.24 lists the circumstances in which permission can be given to re-use an animal that has been used in a series of regulated procedures involving a general anaesthetic (which would have been 'the first use'):

(i)   if the procedure, or each procedure, for which the anaesthetic was given consisted only of surgical preparation for a subsequent procedure; or

(ii) if the general anaesthetic was given solely to immobilise the animal, for instance, for the safety and/or comfort of the animal and/or the operator; or

(iii) if, during subsequent re-use, the animal is kept under general anaesthesia from which it is not allowed to recover consciousness.

HOG Appendix V 3(2) (h) refers to the need for a certificate from the NVS confirming the fitness of an animal for re-use after general anaesthesia. If the animal was not given an anaesthetic in the first use and the series of procedures in the first use, which was for a particular purpose, is complete, as long as the animal is fully recovered, it is possible for authority to be given to re-use the animal. (4.25.)

> '4.26. A series of regulated procedures for a particular purpose can normally be taken as corresponding to a single complete protocol (in section 19b of the project licence). It follows that any use of the animal on the same protocol again or on another protocol, whether on the same licence or on another licence, will constitute re-use and so would require specific authority in the project licence (section 19b).'

A specific example of permitted re-use is given in HOG 4.27 which effectively illustrates the working of the administration in practice of this area of the law:

> 'Section 14(2) (a) provides that surgically-prepared animals may (subject to permission) be re-used for subsequent procedures provided that the purpose remains the same and that the surgical preparation was essential for each of the subsequent uses. Thus, a dog which has been surgically prepared under general anaesthesia with a carotid loop to test cardiovascular drugs may (subject to

permission) be successively used for several such drugs, provided that the tests all require the carotid loop.

4.28. Since project licences are theme based, it follows that, with rare exceptions, movement of an animal from one project to another would involve some change of purpose, however subtle. This will generally preclude the movement between projects of an animal which has been subjected to regulated procedures under general anaesthetic. Exceptions will be animals prepared under a project licence where the declared purpose is to prepare animals for use under another project licence and animals re-used under terminal anaesthesia.

4.29. Because of section (14)(2)(b), an animal given a general anaesthetic solely to immobilise it may be re-used (subject to permission) in exactly the same way as an animal to which no anaesthetic has been administered. It is necessary to decide on a case by case basis [this is an important phrase indicating the flexibillity associated with the application of the ASPA and recalls the oft-recurring need to seek and accept inspectorial advice] as to whether the anaesthetic is given to prevent the animal feeling pain or to make the procedure easier for the operator or the animal by restraining or immobilising the animal. Implicit in the latter alternative is the assumption that the procedure is mild enough to be carried out without anaesthesia with a tractable, cooperative animal.'

Chapter 12

Records, Returns and Reports

Records

The 1998 amendment gives extra force within the ASPA itself to the stipulations in detail concerning identification of animals of particular species. Section 10 subsection (6)(b) (in the original and amended form) imposes a condition requiring the CH:

'to keep records as respects the source and disposal of and otherwise relating to the animals kept at the establishment for experimental or other scientific purposes or, as the case may be, bred or kept for breeding there or kept there for the purposes of being supplied for use in regulated procedures.'

Added to this is the new subsection (6A):

'The conditions of a certificate issued under section 6 or 7 above shall, if the certificate permits dogs, cats or primates to be kept or bred at the establishment in question, include conditions requiring the holder of the certificate to ensure –
  (a) that particulars of the identity and origin of each dog, cat or primate kept or bred at the establishment are entered in the records referred to in subsection (6) (b) above;
  (b) that before it is weaned, every dog, cat or primate in the establishment not falling within paragraph (c) above [sic] is provided with an individual identification mark in the least painful manner possible.
  (c) that where a dog, cat or primate is transferred from one establishment to another before it is weaned and it is not practicable to mark it beforehand, the records kept by the establishment receiving the animal identify that animal's mother until the animal is provided with an individual identification mark; and
  (d) that any unmarked dog, cat or primate which is taken into the establishment after being weaned is provided as soon as possible thereafter with an individual identification mark.'

Guidance on records

The CH should ensure that all records are properly maintained and preserved for a period of five years following the death of the animal or its release from the establishment. (HOG 1.2)

For regulated procedures involving immature forms different records are required according to the use of the animal. The Inspector may agree to allow the recording only of batches of such animals. (HOG 1.3)

'1.4. Adult fish, amphibians, reptiles, unweaned rodents and lagomorphs and non-adult birds may, with the agreement of the Inspector, be recorded in batches until they are used for regulated procedures.' (HOG 1.4)

The list of requisite records in Appendix V is not exhaustive, and there can be requests for other records in certain circumstances. (HOG 1.5)

Records associated with the establishment

'2.1. In the case of dogs, cats, equidae, primates, cattle and other farm animals and adult birds, each animal accomodated in the establishment must be readily identifiable. In the case of dogs, cats and primates this must be by a method of permanent marking agreed with the Inspector.

2.2. Each cage or confinement area holding protected animals not undergoing a regulated procedure should bear a label on which at least the following information is recorded;
  (i)   cage/area identification;
  (ii) identification of animals held (by individual or batch numbers as appropriate);
  (iii) date entry made.

2.3. The following information is to be recorded for all normal animals, pretreated animals or animals with harmful genetic defects;
  (i)   source (and name of breeder or supplier, if animal was bred elsewhere);
  (ii)   species;
  (iii) breed or strain;
  (iv)   identification (by individual or batch number as appropriate);
  (v)   date of arrival (or, if the animal was bred at the establishment, the date of transfer to holding unit or user unit);
  (vi)   approximate age on arrival;
  (vii) sex;
  (viii) if female, whether pregnant or not;
  (ix)   dates in and out of quarantine or isolation, if appropriate);
  (x)   microbiological status (gnotobiotic, SPF or conventional);
  (xi)   pretreatment, if any;
  (xii) harmful genetic defects, if any;
  (xiii) project licence to which allocated or other disposal.'

Health records of the animals must be kept under the supervision of the NVS. The form in which they are to be kept will be decided in consultation with the CH licensees and the Inspector. (HOG 2.4.)

There is a requirement to maintain records of the environmental conditions in each room. This ensures that if there are problems, they are picked up quickly and are dealt with swiftly. The environmental conditions vary depending on the species and the codes of practice state what they should be depending on the species housed. A certificate of designation will only be issued if the Inspector is satisfied that these conditions can be met by the establishment.

Records to be maintained under the control of project licence holders

Condition 9 on the project licence requires the project licence holder to keep records in a form agreed with the Inspector which will be open to her/his inspection at any time. (HOG 3.1)

'3.2. The record should include the following information:
   (i)   name of the project licence holder, deputy project licence holder (where applicable) and project licence number;
   (ii)   name(s) of personal licensees involved;
   (iii)   details of procedures to include;
      (a)   species of protected animal used;
      (b)   number of each species used (running tally);
      (c)   sex and approximate age at commencement of the regulated procedure;
      (d)   identification of protected animal (where appropriate);
      (e)   date of commencement of the regulated procedure;
      (f)   any unexpected morbidity or mortality;
      (g)   brief description of procedures used;
      (h)   re-use within the project (for re-use after general anaesthesia include certificate of fitness for re-use obtained from veterinary surgeon or other suitably qualified person if appointed);
      (j)   date of end of the regulated procedures;
   (iv)   fate of animals at the end of the regulated procedures, i.e. whether released to the wild; despatched to private care; released for slaughter; killed within the establishment; or if permission for re-use was granted, identification of the project to which the animal was allocated.'

Records to be maintained by personal licensee

Condition 11 on the personal licence imposes the obligation to ensure that all cages or enclosures are labelled. The Inspector should be able to identify (even when codes are used) – the project licence on which the animals are being used, the responsible personal licensee and the principal procedures involved. (HOG 4.1–3.) The introduction here of the adjectival phrase 'the responsible' qualifying 'personal licensee', is most welcome because in practice there may be more than one personal licensee dealing with a particular animal.

'4.4. Personal licensees should ensure that records are kept of all procedures performed and whether they were supervised.'

The above material is mainly a word-for-word reproduction of HOG Appendix V. Any attempt to summarise such essential information could easily distort it. Furthermore the details may prove of practical significance to persons in the animal room.

Annual returns

Obligation to complete a return

The general notes on the Return of Procedures Form plainly presents the obligations of the project licensee.

'1. It is a condition' (10) 'of every project licence that the project licence holder should make a return before 31 January of all regulated procedures on living animals commenced during each year. Only one reminder of this obligation will be sent.
Thereafter steps will be taken to revoke any licence for which a form has not been received.'

This is no idle threat. If a project licence holder has more than one project licence, a separate form will be sent for each project. Care must be taken to ensure that the work of personal licensees appears on the Return of Procedures Form carrying the correct number. It is the responsibility of project licence holders to ensure that the work of all personal licensees performing regulated procedures on their project is included in their returns.

This is not the place to reproduce the Return of Procedures Form since all interested parties will receive copies accompanied by full instructions on how the form should be completed. Another reason for not presenting too much detail in this context is that the required information may vary and some parts of the format might need adjustment, as it did in 1999 in order better to accomodate some requirements of the European Commission. Appropriate variations have also been introduced for the better assessment of re-use. Such variations in the form are bound to recur particularly in respect to the classification of countries as regards membership of the EU or the Council of Europe, etc.

Filling out a return

The instructions on the Return of Procedures Form clearly indicate the various codes to be used for; the types of animal, the stage of development of the animal, the source of the animal, types of anaesthetic, the types of procedure, reason for use, re-use, etc. Directions are also given on where these codes are to be inserted in the appropriate columns and rows. A special Annex A is devoted to the more complicated method of recording work involving genetic manipulation where caution is needed not to make a a double entry regarding these animals. The aim is that gentically manipulated animals should be recorded either as produced but not used or simply as used without a reference in the return to their production. The same genetically manipulated animals should not be entered under both categories of production and use.

Some of the bewilderment associated with the Return of Procedures Form may be alleviated if we consider that the questions are intended to produce a comprehensive picture of:

- the animals used and the number of animals used
- the source of the animals used
- the stage of development of the animals used
- the genetic status of the animals used
- the anaesthetics or neuromuscular blocking agents (if any) used
- the reason for animal use
- the nature of the procedures
- the number of procedures
- re–use.

It is important to realise that this exercise is purely for statistical purposes. The returns are dealt with by a Home Office group separate from the Inspectors. However:

- it is not another assessment of your project
- it is not a demand to describe your project so far
- it is merely a request to answer specific questions about your use of animals.

Ultimately it is the researcher herself or himself who is best equipped to answer each question. These questions cannot be answered, as it were, speculatively. They call for specific answers one by one, within the context of a particular project. In some cases, consultation with your Inspector is highly recommended, because she/he may have a special interpretation on the way a particular question should be answered, in the context of your project.

The end product

Valuable information an animal use in research can be gleaned from these returns. Although, perhaps, only of interest in 1999 this, the useful extracts from the *RDS News* (July 1999), shown in Table 12.1 and Figure 12.1, are an interesting portrayal of the extent of animal experimentation at the end of the twentieth century.

This article is only a fraction of the total amount of useful source material that is made available by the Research Defence Society, which stands out as a positive outspoken force in the controversy surrounding biological research.

Table 12.1   Statistics for scientific procedures on animals in 1998

Total number	2 659 662	(up 0.9% from 1997)
Purposes		
Biomedical research*	2 445 039	(92% of total, up 1% from 1997)
Other toxicology (not cosmetics)	154 111	(down 8% from 1997)
Direct diagnosis	51 976	(down 6% from 1997
Education/training	7887	(up 6% from 1997)
Testing cosmetics and toiletries	590	(down 55% from 1997)
Forensic enquiries	59	(down 4% from 1997)
Species used		
Rodents	2 259 792	(86%, 1997 = 86%)
Dogs	6828	(down 9% from 1997)
Cats	1261	(down 13% from 1997)
Primates	3635	(down 6% from 1997)
Numbers of procedures		
Conducted by universities	35%	(1997 = 33%)
Conducted by commercial concerns	43%	(1997 = 46%)
Numbers of project licence holders		
Universities	71%	(1997 = 68%)
Commercial concerns	13%	(1997 = 15%)

* Includes biological, medical and veterinary research, development, production of biological substances and pharmaceutical toxicology

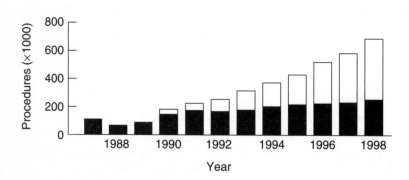

Fig. 12.1   Statistics for scientific procedures on animals in 1998. Procedures include breeding and genetic status (including animals bred, but not subsequently used in other regulated procedures). □, Transgenic/Knockouts; ■, harmful genetic defect. *Source:* Research Defence Society.

Reports

Condition 12 on the project licence states:

'The project licence holder shall submit such other reports as the Secretary of State may from time to time require'.

Condition 11 deals with a similar theme:

'The project licence holder shall maintain a list of publications resulting from the licensed programme of work and a copy of any such publication shall be made available to the Secretary of State on request, The list shall, on request, be submitted to the Secretary of State or made available to be seen by an Inspector, and it shall be submitted to the Secretary of State when the licence is returned to him on expiry or for revocation.'

A significant feature of both these conditions is the contingent terms in which they are couched. They come into operation only either on request or in stipulated circumstances.

Chapter 13

Offences, Penalties, Prosecutions, etc.

A quote from *Hansard* indicates a certain lack of clarity in official information on this topic.

> **'Mr. Baker:** To ask the Secretary of State for the Home Department how many prosecutions have been initiated in respect of cruelty inflicted on animals in the course of approved experiments for each year since 1980; and if he will make a statement.[33017]
>
> **Mr. George Howarth** *[holding answer 6 March 1998]:* Prosecutions for such an offence would be instigated under the Protection of Animals Act 1911 Offences of Cruelty to Animals. The Court Proceedings database, held centrally, can identify only the number of prosecutions brought under the Act irrespective of circumstances. However, further sources of information
>
> [*11 Mar 1998: Column: 203*]
> suggest that there have been no prosecutions, in England and Wales, for cruelty to animals during the course of approved experiments.'

In view of the complexity of the material I will adhere closely to authoritative sources on the subject in hand.

Offences

The Report of the Animal Procedures Committee for 1991 presents in a clear manner salient offences against the 1986 Act. The report precedes its outlining of these offences by a reference to the most important piece of legislation which protects animals:

> '9.2 The Act not only controls the way in which scientific procedures on living animals are regulated, but also provides some exemption from the Protection of Animals Act 1911 (1912 in Scotland) for licence holders who are performing authorised procedures under the 1986 Act. However, where unauthorised procedures are being conducted, this immunity is not conferred and it would be possible to bring charges under the 1911 or 1912 Acts.'

The report then indicates offences specific to the 1986 Act:

'9.3 The main criminal offences in the Act relating to the performance of animal procedures can be set out broadly as follows:

(i)   An offence is committed by anybody who carries out a regulated procedure on a protected animal if:

      (a)   he does not hold a personal licence authorising him to carry out that procedure on that animal;

      (b)   the procedure or species of animal used is not authorised by a project licence; and

      (c)   the procedure is carried out somewhere other than a place authorised both in the personal licence and in the project licence (this is normally an establishment covered by a certificate of designation).

    The person who carries out the procedure is not guilty of the offence of acting without the authority of a project licence if he can show that he reasonably believed, after making due enquiry, that he had proper authority.

(ii)   An offence is committed by any project licence holder who procures or knowingly permits anybody under his control to carry out a regulated procedure either not authorised by the project licence or outside the authority of that person's personal licence.

(iii)   No offence under paragraph (i) above is committed by a personal licensee's assistant if the assistant carries out, under the personal licensee's direction and if they are authorised by the personal licence, subordinate duties permitted by the Home Secretary, examples of which are listed in Appendix VII of the *Guidance*. The personal licence must contain specific authorisation for the use of assistants. A personal licensee cannot delegate the authority of his licence to anybody else, and anybody who carries out a procedure which somebody else, but not he, is allowed to do by a personal licence, commits the offence described in paragraph (i) above.

(iv)   It is an offence to re-use an animal if the animal has previously been used in a series or combination of procedures carried out for a different purpose and one or more of those procedures consisted of giving the animal a general anaesthetic. The exceptions to this general rule are if the animal is under a general anaesthetic throughout the further procedures and is not allowed to recover consciousness; or if the anaesthetic was given only for surgical preparation, or only to immobilise the animal. But in any such case, the re-use must have been authorised in advance. It is also an offence, except where specifically authorised, to re-use an animal if the animal has previously been used in a series of procedures for a different purpose, even when none of those procedures involved giving the animal a general anaesthetic. Paragraphs 4.21–4.29 of the *Guidance* set out the circumstances in which authority for re-use can be sought.'

There is also reference to previous material on re-use, particularly to the 1998 amendment to s. 14 of the ASPA which introduces an absolute prohibition of re-use if there is a double jeopardy of severe pain or distress.

'(v)   The Act requires that an animal which has been used in a series of procedures carried out for any one purpose, and which at the conclusion of the series is suffering or is likely to suffer adverse effects, must immediately be killed or caused to be killed by the personal licensee, either by a Schedule 1 method of humane killing, or by some other method authorised in the personal licence of the person who carries out the killing. A personal licensee who does not comply with this requirement commits an offence.

(vi)   It is an offence to use a neuromuscular blocking agent unless expressly authorised to do so by the personal and project licences under which the procedure is carried out, or to use a neuromuscular blocking agent instead of an anaesthetic. Should a neuromuscular blocking agent be used without authority the person who carried out the procedure is not guilty of the offence if he shows that he reasonably believed, after making due enquiry, that he had that authority.

(vii)   If an Inspector considers that a protected animal is undergoing excessive suffering, it is an offence to fail to comply with the Inspector's requirement that the animal must immediately be killed either by a Schedule 1 method of humane killing or by another method authorised in the personal licence held by a personal licensee.

(viii)   In addition, breaches of standard licence conditions 1 to 5 of a project licence (page 49 of the *Guidance*) and standard conditions 1 to 10 of a personal licence (page 54 of the *Guidance*) may also constitute criminal offences.'

The Act also prohibits wrongful disclosure of information.

'1)   Disclosure of information obtained in the exercise of functions under the Act otherwise than for the purpose of discharging those functions, providing there are reasonable grounds for believing that the information was given in confidence. This prohibition is not intended to interfere with the performance of proper duties under the Act, such as an inspector consulting another inspector about an application for a licence (s. 24).

2)   Running a breeding or supplying establishment for experimental animals without the necessary designation (s. 22 (3) (a) and refer to s. 7 (1) and (2)).

3)   Presenting a regulated procedure as an exhibition to the general public or for live showing on television for reception by the general public or advertising such a performance to the general public. It is not an offence to

allow otherwise authorised procedures to be included in pre-recorded programmes. Nor is it an offence to allow bona fide visitors to laboratories to witness the performance of procedures (s. 22 (3) (a) and refer to s. 16).

4) Giving, knowingly and recklessly, information known to be false for the purpose of obtaining or assisting another person to obtain a licence or certificate under the Act (s. 23)

5) Obstructing intentionally a constable or inspector if the constable has been granted a search warrant, or refusing on demand to give the constable or inspector his name and address or gives a false name and address (s. 25 (3) (a) and (b)).'

A Home Office Circular (CDP 9/98) is certainly pertinent to this topic:

'The guidance notes for completing licence and certificate application forms currently contain a commitment that applications will be treated in confidence at all stages. We have been notified that leave for a judicial review has been sought on the basis that this goes beyond the provisions of section 24 of the 1986 Act. It is also unlikely that such commitments can continue to be given in view of the proposed Freedom of Information legislation. We have therefore decided to delete these clauses from the guidance notes with immediate effect. We will, however, continue to abide by the terms of section 24 of the Act (unless and until it is repealed) – i.e. we will not disclose information given, or believed to have been given, in confidence.'

Although this threat did not have any concrete consequences, a certain amount of disquiet on this subject will persist. Anyone involved in correspondence on licences, etc., should clearly mark all relevant material as confidential.

Penalties

The Act itself is quite specific in the matter of penalties. The topic is fully dealt with in s. 22, 23, 24 and 25. A penalty not exceeding two years imprisonment or a fine or both on conviction on indictment, or not exceeding six months imprisonment or a fine not exceeding the statutory maximum or both on summary conviction may be incurred for:

- performing or being involved in unauthorised regulated procedures (refer s. 3);
- contravening s. 1 (causing unnecessary suffering) of the Protection of Animals Act 1911 in a designated establishment (refer s. 22 (5);
- breach of confidentiality (refer s. 24).

A penalty, on summary conviction, not exceeding three months imprisonment or a fine not exceeding the fourth level on the standard scale or both may be incurred for:

- breach of Schedule 2 (refer s. 7);
- re-use without the appropriate consent (refer s. 14);
- not providing authorised euthanasia at the conclusion of regulated procedures when an animal may suffer (refer s. 15);
- performing exhibitions of regulated procedures or advertising the same (refer s. 16);
- use of neuromuscular blocking agent without observing the relevant conditions (refer s. 17);
- refusing to comply with an Inspector's order concerning euthanasia (refer s. 18 (3));
- making false or misleading statements in order to obtain a licence or certificate (refer s. 23);
- obstructing or misleading a constable or Inspector acting under s. 25 (3).'

Prosecution under the Act

The process of prosecution for offences under the Act is set out in s. 26:

'(1) No proceedings for –
  (*a*) an offence under this Act; or
  (*b*) an offence under section 1 of the Protection of Animals. Act 1911 which is alleged to have been committed in respect of an animal at a designated establishment,
shall be brought in England and Wales except by or with the consent of the Director of Public Prosecutions.

(2) Summary proceedings for an offence under this Act may (without prejudice to any jurisdiction exercisable apart from this subsection) be taken against any person at any place at which he is for the time being.

(3) Notwithstanding anything in section 127(1) of the Magistrates' Courts Act 1980, an information relating to an offence under this Act which is triable by a magistrates' court in England and Wales may be so tried if it is laid at any time within three years after the commission of the offence and within six months after the date on which evidence sufficient in the opinion of the Director of Public Prosecutions to justify the proceedings comes to his knowledge.

(4) Notwithstanding anything in section 331 of the Criminal Procedure (Scotland) Act 1975, summary proceedings for an offence under this Act may be commenced in Scotland at any time within three years after the commission of the offence and within six months after the date on which evidence sufficient in the opinion of the Lord Advocate to justify the proceedings comes to his knowledge; and subsection (3) of that section shall apply for the purposes of this subsection as it applies for the purposes of that section.

(5) For the purposes of subsections (3) and (4) above a certificate of the Director of Public Prosecutions or, as the case may be, the Lord Advocate as to

the date on which such evidence as is there mentioned came to his knowledge shall be conclusive evidence of that fact.'

In s. 29 (7) it is pointed out that the words 'Northern Ireland' should, where appropriate be substituted for 'England and Wales'.

Prosecutions in practice

The APC in its 1991 Report (pp. 12–13) took the opportunity to highlight and comment, not only on the first prosecution under the ASPA but also to reflect on a near-prosecution and on a possible breach of the Act:

'3.8 1991 saw the first successful prosecution under the Act. During the course of a routine inspection of a user establishment, it came to light that a commercial rabbit breeding company, which was not designated under section 7 of the Act to supply animals for scientific use, had supplied rabbits for such use. The user establishment had been led to believe that the company was properly designated and indeed had itself drawn the matter to the attention of the Inspector. As the breeding and supplying company was not designated under the Animals (Scientific Procedures) Act 1986, the Home Office had no powers to investigate the matter itself. It therefore reported the matter to the police, who carried out an investigation and referred it for prosecution. The breeding and supplying company was subsequently convicted under the Act of breeding and supplying animals for use in scientific procedures while not being designated under section 7 of the Act.

Referral for possible prosecution under the Act
3.9 The Committee was most disturbed to learn the details of a very serious case involving a series of infringements in an institution. The infringements involved the application of unauthorised surgical procedures to pigs, including instances of unauthorised re-use, some of which could not have been authorised under the terms of the Act even if authority had been applied for. It was also clear that there had been a lack of post-operative care which had undoubtedly caused avoidable animal suffering. The Home Office referred the matter to the prosecuting authorities in view of the serious nature of the infringements revealed.
3.10 We fully supported this action in referring to the prosecuting authorities what was clearly a very serious series of infringements. While we recognise that decisions on whether or not to prosecute are properly the responsibility of the prosecuting authorities, it was a matter of considerable disappointment that, in the event, the prosecuting authorities decided not to bring charges against those involved. We made our concern known to the Home Office who were later able, with the agreement of the prosecuting authorities, to set out for the Committee the considerations which led to the decision. It was clear that there

were highly unusual evidential problems peculiar to this case which would have materially reduced the likelihood of a successful prosecution. We are keen to ensure that any general lessons from this case are learnt for the future and the Home Office has discussed these matters with the prosecuting authorities. It is our view that the failure to prosecute in this case does not reveal any deficiencies in the provisions of the Act itself.

3.11 Although criminal charges were not brought against the project licence holder and the personal licensee involved, it was still open to the Home Office subsequently to take administrative action. Having considered the details of the case, the Home Secretary decided to seek the revocation of all the project licences and the personal licence of the project licence holder, and the personal licence of the personal licensee. We fully support this tough administrative action. Discussions are continuing with the institution where the infringements took place to ensure that it has in place proper controls to avoid a recurrence.'

The possible breach considered in depth by the APC could prove of special interest to 'old timers;'.

'3.12 In our last report, we referred to the case of Professor W S Feldberg and Mr J P B Stean who had conducted procedures on apparently under-anaesthetised animals. The Committee considered the general lessons to be learnt from this case which led to the recommendations in paragraphs 2.28 and 2.33 of that report about the need to ensure the proper control of licence holders who are passed [sic] retirement age.

3.13 In considering the general lessons of this case, we took note of the report of the inquiry by a team led by Sir Brian Bailey established by the Medical Research Council. One outstanding matter from Sir Brian Bailey's report was the allegation that offences under the Act had been committed in that regulated procedures had been conducted before the appropriate project licence authority had been granted. Having considered the evidence available to the inquiry team the Government decided not to refer the case to the prosecuting authorities. In answer to a Parliamentary Question from Sir John Wheeler JP MP (Westminster North), the Rt Hon Mrs Angela Rumbold MP CBE said:

"... We have now completed consideration of the evidence of possible breaches of the 1986 Act, including Professor Feldberg's notebooks, which the MRC forwarded to the Home Office.

We do not consider that, in all the circumstances of the case, there are grounds to justify referring the matter to the Director of Public Prosecutions. As soon as it was clear that avoidable suffering had been caused to animals, the Home Office took action to remove the personal and project licences held by Professor Feldberg and Mr Stean, thus ensuring that they did no further scientific work involving the use of living animals. While there is prima facie evidence that there were breaches of the Animals (Scientific Procedures) Act 1986, we consider that, in the light of all the circumstances of the case, *including the effective administrative action already taken, no further purpose would be served by asking the Director of Public Prosecutions to consider prosecution"*

The Committee endorses this decision which brings to an end consideration of those matters particular to the Feldberg affair. The Committee will however continue to monitor whether the general lessons to be learnt from this serious case have been learnt and acted upon.'

1998 saw the first actual prosecution of a scientist under the ASPA. Details of the case appeared in the Scottish newspaper, *The Herald* in July 1998).

A 55 year old research fellow of the University of Glasgow Vet School, pleaded guilty to breaching the ASPA by applying doses of deadly parasites to a herd of Friesian cows without a proper government licence.

He also admitted carrying out the experiment without a relevant certificate of designation for the land on which the experiments were performed.

The court heard that 45 cows worth an estimated £35,000 died during his project. His plea of not guilty to wilfully injecting the beasts with an injurious substance was accepted. He did hold a Home Office licence for the study of parasites. It applied only to cattle on land owned by the university.

He had 90 cattle artificially infected with lung worm and gut worm parasites. It was claimed that his intent was not to cause disease, but to infect the ground to ensure sufficient naturally acquired parasites for later experiments.

When animals began to die no remedial action was taken, but other beasts were added to the project. The cause of death in most cases was acute bacterial pneumonia.

In passing a sentence of 120 hours of community service the Sheriff, John Fitzsimons stressed: 'I am not dealing with a case of deliberate cruelty to animals.' He added: 'What makes this such a serious case is the fact that he did not call in a vet when it became clear that something was wrong – and that even after the RSPCA had contacted the authorities, more cattle were introduced to the experiment.'

Even where there is doubt that an offence has been committed involving more than a technical breach, consideration will be given to referring the matter to the Crown Prosecution Service. While a decision to refer a case to the Crown Prosecution Service is made by the Home Office, the decision to prosecute is made by the Crown Prosecution Service alone, based on judgement of the merits of the case, the evidence available and other relevant factors, including whether a prosecution would be in the public interest. In Northern Ireland and Scotland this legal process varies as regards the governmental departments involved. With devolution very much to the fore in political circles, it might not be appropriate to give present details of these variations in this text.

Infringements and non-criminal sanctions

Most infringements which can vary from the merely technical to the very serious come to light through the vigilance of the Home Office Inspectors.

In deciding whether, and which, sanctions are appropriate, the Home Secretary will take into account the nature and circumstances of the breach of authority, the number and severity of the procedures performed, previous conduct of the licence or certificate holder, and the likelihood of her/his having been granted authority had she/he requested it. (HOG. 7.4–6)

Among the sanctions which the Home Office can use against a breach of a condition or any other lack of compliance with the Act or instructions given under its authority are refusal, variation, revocation or suspension of a licence or certificate (refer s. 10 (7), s. 11, s. 12 and s. 13). Other sanctions which can be used are: replacement of deputy project licence holders, imposition of more restrictive conditions, imposition of some form of supervision, or disqualification from supervising, sponsoring or assessing other licensees. In deciding on appropriate sanctions the Home Secretary will take into account the nature and circumstances of the breach, the number and severity of any procedures involved, previous conduct of a transgressor and whether authority would have been granted if requested.

Other, perhaps lesser but often very effective, methods of dealing with miscreants in this area are: verbal admonitions skilfully and effectively delivered, written admonitions and referral for re-training – a procedure of which the author has a fair amount of experience, but only as one who has had to accomodate the disgruntled.

No doubt the most drastic of these non-criminal sanctions is the revocation of a licence or certificate; careers can be damaged or destroyed. On a more technical note it must be stressed that the Inspector can only recommend suspension or revocation, the final authority is the Secretary of State. Immediate suspension of the licence may however be imposed for the protection of the animal. (APC 1997 Report, (n. 9.5)

With regard to possible penalties, it should be remembered that licences and certificates are issued to individuals. The individual, not the organisation, is accountable for ensuring compliance with conditions etc. Some allowance is made for authorities to be delegated, but responsibility and accountability is retained by the licence or certificate holder. (APC Report 1997 p. 89, n. 7)

The APC and infringements

Over the years the APC has paid careful attention to infringements and their treatment by the Inspectorate. Twenty three infringements were reported in the 1997 Report, an increase of three compared to 1996. Twenty occurred in academic establishments and three in commercial establishments. These figures did not include infringements associated with the *Countryside Undercover* television programme already referred to. The APC Report went on to expound on the topic on pp. 18–19:

'136. Fourteen were discovered by Inspectors (five during the course of unannounced visits and nine during announced visits) and one by another member of Home Office staff. Three had been brought to the attention of the Inspector by licensees, one by the Named Animal Care and Welfare Officer, one by a certificate of designation holder, one by a deputy chief technician, and one by a Home Office liaison officer. One infringement was discovered when a licensee applied for a continuation of his personal licence.

i) Nature of the infringements

137. As in previous years, the nature of the infringements varied from the relatively minor and technical to the more serious.

138. In six cases, regulated procedures were performed without appropriate personal licence authority in breach of section 3(a) of the 1986 Act; and in twelve cases, without appropriate project licence authority in breach of section 3(b). In two cases, animals had been acquired from non–designated sources and were used without Home Office authority. In one case, a licensee failed to supply, by the specified date, a report of work in progress as required by an additional condition placed on his project licence (a breach of section 10 of the Act). In another case, a licensee failed to provide accurate statistical reports of work performed under authority of his project licence. In the final case, rodents were killed by a method not listed in Schedule 1 of the Act or otherwise authorised by the Secretary of State.

139. In last year's report, we stated that it was essential that licence applications and new licences be checked very carefully on receipt from the Home Office, and regularly thereafter. It is disappointing that, as in previous years, many of these infringements could have been avoided if those involved had taken the time to check that appropriate project and personal licence authorities existed.

ii) Action taken

140. As a result of these infringements, seven project licences and four personal licences were revoked. Seventeen licence holders were required to undertake relevant modules from an accredited training course. Thirty–nine licensees and one certificate of designation holder were admonished. Those who received admonitions were advised that any further infringements may be dealt with more severely.

141. In one case, a project licence holder was requested to submit a report on how the record keeping system in his department had been revised to ensure that future annual statistical returns were accurate.

142. In another, a certificate of designation holder was required to relieve the Named Animal Care and Welfare Officer of his responsibilities and to appoint a suitable replacement within 28 days. Four certificate holders were asked to conduct internal reviews of their control mechanisms and submit reports detailing how these systems had been improved to prevent further breaches of the Act and, in one case, a certificate holder was asked to improve arrangements for supervision of licensees at his establishment.'

The 1998 APC Report continued the useful instructive practice of giving details of infringements on pp. 9–10:

'58. This section of the report summarises the infringements reported to the Committee during the year and what action was taken. Infringements are relatively rare events – there were 17 reported during 1998 but there were approximately 15,000 people who held personal project licences during the year. But they can provoke intense and lengthy discussions within the Committee. Concern over the observation of the controls of the Act is shared by all members and the Committee's aim is to use these discussions to look for common causes and problems, and possible solutions.

Summary of infringements reported in 1998
59. The 17 infringements reported to the Committee during 1998 represented a decrease of six compared to 1997. Fourteen occurred in academic establishments and three in commercial establishments.

60. Twelve were discovered by inspectors (nine during the course of routine visits and three during unannounced visits). Four had been brought to the attention of the inspector by licensees and one came to light when a licensee sought an annual return of procedures form for a project licence which had not been granted; the licensee mistook a draft project licence, returned by the Home Office for further amendments, for the actual project licence.

61. As in previous years, the nature of the infringements varied from the relatively minor and technical to the more serious. In three cases, regulated procedures were performed without appropriate personal licence authority in breach of Section 3(a) of the 1986 Act; in ten cases without appropriate project licence authority in breach of Section 3(b); and in two cases, without either authority. In one case, an animal was re-used without appropriate authority and in another a special condition requiring a licensee to complete an accredited training course by a specific date was not complied with.

62. Once again, many of these infringements could have been avoided if those involved had taken the time to check that appropriate project and personal licence authorities existed. The Education and Training Sub-Committee will take this issue forward in the coming year. Ethical review processes also have a part to play in addressing these problems.

(ii) Action taken
63. As a result of these infringements, one project licence was revoked and seven certificate of designation holders were requested to review, with their local inspector, the systems of controls at their establishments and to report on any additional controls which had been implemented to prevent recurrence. Five licence holders were required to undertake relevant modules from an accredited training course and twenty-six licensees were admonished. In one case a revised supervision order was included on a personal licence.

64. In another case, a personal licensee chose to make representations against the Secretary of State's decision to revoke the licence. The person appointed to consider the representation under Section 12 of the Act recommended that revocation was too severe and that the licensee should only receive a letter of admonition and be required successfully to complete a Module 1 course. After careful consideration of all the evidence, including the written representations received from the licensee, the Secretary of State accepted this recommendation.'

An outside description of Home Office action on infringements appeared in the *Guardian* (24 June 1993). It was reported that the Home Office investigated Wickam Laboratories following infiltration by a former policeman, Neil Fry, on behalf of the British Union for the Abolition of Vivisection (BUAV).

The Home Office reported that the major allegations made by the BUAV – that animals were used unnecessarily, that there was unauthorised re-use of animals and that inadequate caging led to animal suffering – were not substantiated, but did reveal a number of weaknesses in procedures and practices. The Home Office minister, Charles Wardle, announced that he was satisfied that 'all the work carried out by Wickham was properly licensed under the Act'.

The Home Office required a number of changes to be made at Wickham to strengthen perceived weaknesses in local management practices, which had led to 'a readiness to falsify' test data and 'one case of unnecessary animal use'. These changes included replacement of the named day-to-day care person, and removal of his personal licence and improvements to formal technical training and operational procedures. The Minister said that the Medicines Control Agency considered that the faults 'did not call in question the validity of the particular tests, nor did they raise doubts about Wickham's continued operation as a contract research establishment.

Prosecutions under the Protection of Animals Act 1911 involving research establishments

The British Union for the Abolition of Vivisection v. *The Royal College of Surgeons* (1985) was commented upon in Chapter 1.

The case in 1989 involving a company which supplied beagles for research but unfortunately lost 79 of them en route to Sweden because of lack of the provision of adequate ventilation was also dealt with in Chapter 1.

It would not be possible to improve upon the APC's reporting of a 1997 case associating a prosecution under the 1911 Act with a research establishment.

> '106. On 26 March, Channel 4 broadcast a programme entitled "It's a Dogs Life" as part of their "Countryside Undercover" series. The programme featured video material recorded in a dog toxicology unit by an undercover investigator who had worked at the establishment in the Autumn of 1996. The material showed dogs being physically abused and made other allegations about the operation of the Act at the establishment.
> 107. The Committee first discussed the implications of this programme at our April meeting. We were provided with an account of immediate Home Office actions. We strongly approved of the decisions to suspend immediately the personal licences of two persons shown in the film to be mistreating dogs and to refer the matter to local police to investigate possible offences under the Protection of Animals Act 1911. We unequivocally condemned the brutality that was shown in the film and noted that these two individuals were subsequently convicted of offences under the 1911 Act. Some members expressed

concern, however, about the sentences imposed by the court which they felt were too lenient.

108. At this very early point, although immediate action had been taken, the Home Office had not decided how the matter should be investigated, and indeed wished to take our views on this matter. One option put to us was that the Chief Inspector personally carry out the investigation, but we also considered an independent investigation. There were practical problems to an independent investigation: only inspectors (or the police, with a warrant) have a right of access to establishments; and it would take too long to arrange when speed of response was critical. The over-riding consideration was, however, that we had confidence in the chief Inspector carrying out a thorough and impartial investigation. We recommended, therefore, that he proceed.

109. The Inspectorate had attracted criticism for not identifying the problems shown in the broadcast. The Committee felt this to be unfair. Even if the Inspectorate was significantly enlarged, inspectors could not be present at an establishment all the time and the sort of actions shown in the programme would never have taken place in front of an inspector. Indeed, it is extremely unlikely that any third party inspection system would have picked up the physical abuses.

110. The Chief Inspector's final report was submitted to Ministers in July. Whilst it was clear that the certificate holder had no knowledge of the problems, he was ultimately responsible to the Home Office for conduct within the establishment. It was subsequently announced, through a Parliamentary Question, that the certificate of designation would be revoked but that, to avoid the destruction of animals, the proposed revocation would be delayed for 4 months. An application for a replacement certificate would only be considered if 16 stringent conditions designed to rectify the problems identified and to prevent recurrence, had been met. These conditions are attached at Appendix D to this report.'

Chapter 14

Officials, Bodies and Publications

Home Office Inspectors

The pivotal role of the Home Office Inspector in the application in practice of the ASPA is obvious from all that has already been written in this text.

The following extract from the APC 1992 Report (n. 19) epitomises the role of the Inspector.

> 'Inspectors consider in detail applications for licences and advise the Home Secretary how to ensure that only properly justified work is licensed. They carry out visits, mainly without notice, to establishments designated under the Act to ensure that its controls and the terms and the conditions of licences issued under it are being observed.'

It is obvious from the above that the role of the Inspector is multifarious. Besides other commitments e.g. dealing with correspondence from members of the public concerned about the use of animals in research, she/he:

- advises
- reviews
- inspects
- reports.

Visiting a designated establishment is therefore only one facet of the Inspector's duty and it is difficult to comment on it in isolation from other responsibilities. It would, consequently, be an inadequate presentation of the law on the crucial and all – pervading role of the Inspector in the administration of the ASPA, if one concentrated solely on the visiting activities of an Inspector. The other aspects of her/his work will also be considered along with 'visiting' which will be dealt with under the section entitled 'The Inspector inspects'.

Section 18 of the ASPA stipulates in detail the legal status and duties of the Inspector. It empowers the Home Secretary to appoint Inspectors; sets out their duties to visit establishments and advise and report to the Secretary of State; and empowers Inspectors to order the killing of an animal:

> 's. 18. (1) The Secretary of State shall, with the consent of the Treasury as to numbers and remuneration, appoint as inspectors for the purposes of this Act persons having such medical or veterinary qualifications as he thinks requisite.'

These Inspectors work from five regional offices in Cambridge, Dundee, London, Shrewsbury and Swindon.

The further two subsections and paragraphs of s. 18 list the specific duties of the Inspector which can be classified under the categories given above.

The Inspector advises

The inspector advises on the welfare of protected animals and offers advice to project and personal licensees on their applications, for example, on amendments of their licences. Consultation with the Inspector can prove to be a most fruitful source of direction in respect to animal experimentation. Such counselling may be the most beneficial result of an Inspector's visit. The Inspector's advice can be sought even by telephone in urgent cases and in emergencies. The Home Office website has a page ABCU at http://www.homeoffice.gov.uk/ccpd/abcu.htm

An advisory function of the inspector is referred to in subsection (7) of ss. 6 and 7 of the Act. There is provision for the NACWO or the NVS to notify the Inspector if they are concerned about the health or welfare of an animal. The implication is that they would be seeking advice on the matter.

The advisory function of the Inspector is by no means one-sided:

's. 18. (2)   It shall be the duy of an inspector-
   (a) to advise the Secretary of State on applications for personal and project licences, on requests for their variation or revocation and on their periodical review;
   (b) to advise him on applications for certificates under this Act and on requests for their variation or revocation;'

This advisory role of the Inspector is also mentioned in s. 9:

'(1) Before granting a licence or issuing a certificate under this Act the Secretary of State shall consult one of the inspectors appointed under this Act . . '

The Inspector reviews

The Inspector reviews applications for licences and certificates and may also review applicants for a personal licence.

From s. 18 (2)(a) it is obvious that the Inspector is officially involved in the periodic review of both personal and project licences.

The Inspector inspects

Most visits by an Inspector to a designated establishment are usually for the purpose of an inspection though, as indicated above, visits may be to advise licensees, named persons, certificate holders or other personnel.

The purposes for the visits of Inspectors are clearly laid down in law:

'S. 18. (2) It shall be the duty of an inspector –

(c) to visit places where regulated procedures are carried out for the purposes of determining whether those procedures are authorised by the requisite licences and whether the conditions of those licences are being complied with;

(d) to visit designated establishments for the purpose of determining whether the conditions of the certificates in respect of those establishments are being complied with;'

Both of these paragraphs indicate that the visiting Inspector would be concerned during the inspection with the welfare of the animals.

The Inspector should be given ready access to any area of a designated establishment. Section 25 of the Act stipulates the only circumstances in which there is an absolute legal right of entry to any animal unit.

'(1) If a justice of the peace or in Scotland a sheriff is satisfied by information on oath that there are reasonable grounds for believing that an offence under this Act has been or is being committed at any place, he may issue a warrant authorising a constable to enter that place if need be by such force as is reasonably necessary, to search it and to require any person found there to give his name and address.

(2) A warrant under this section may authorise a constable to be accompanied by an inspector appointed under this Act and shall require him to be accompanied by such an inspector if the place in question is a designated establishment.'

Subsection (3) stipulates a maximum penalty, on summary conviction, for an offence under this section, of three months imprisonment or a fourth level fine or both.

The Inspector reports

'S. 18. (2) It shall be the duty of an inspector –

(e) to report to the Secretary of State any case in which any provision of this Act or any condition of a licence or certificate under this Act has not been or is not being complied with and to advise him on the action to be taken in any such case.'

Other aspects of the inspectorial office

The Inspector has one absolute executive power.

'S. 18. (3) If an inspector considers that a protected animal is undergoing excessive suffering he may require it to be immediately killed by a method appropriate to the animal under Schedule 1 to this Act or by such other method as may be authorised by any personal licence held by the person to whom the requirement is addressed.'

In s. 24 the Act, under threat of a maximum of two years imprisonment and/or a fine, imposes a strict obligation of confidentiality. It is an offence for a person who knowingly receives confidential information in the exercise of her/his functions under the Act to disclose such information otherwise than in the course of her/his functions. Inspectors or members of the APC may communicate confidential material amongst themselves, to assessors or to the Home Secretary. The offence relates only to disclosures which are made with the knowledge that, or with reasonable grounds for believing that, the information was given in confidence. Care must therefore to be taken by those who provide sensitive information in the first place to indicate that they wish it to be treated in confidence.

The Inspectorate, since January 1994, works under an officially approved code of practice, the *Licensing and Inspection under the Animals (Scientific Procedures) Act 1986 – Code of Practice*. It sets out the objectives of the Inspectorate and outlines the modus operandi of the Home Office regarding the administration of the ASPA.

It is hardly necessary in this context to reproduce the details of this code of practice. It would, no doubt, be worth perusing by those interested in the more intricate working of the Inspectorate. On the other hand it would be remiss to pass over in silence the most salient topic of discussion concerning Inspectors at modules on the ASPA – variation in inspectorial decisions. As always, an APC Report (1997) deals admirably with this matter.

> 'Such is the variety of designated places and research proposals, however, that a flexible response is essential to match advice precisely to local circumstances. Thus it is consistency rather than uniformity which is sought.'
>
> (p. 63 n. 2)

'Similar' proposals and facilities are seldom identical in practice. It should not come as a surprise that similar applications, once all of the relevant factors are weighed (including the experience of the personnel involved, their track record, and the resources available), result in differing advice to the Secretary of State by the Inspectorate (p. 63. n. 5.3).

The Animal Procedures Committee (APC)

This legally constituted body has been referred to frequently throughout this book and the learned Reports of the Committee have proved to be a fruitful source for much of the information presented. Sections 19 and 20 of the ASPA clearly spell out the powers, membership and role of the APC:

> '19. (1)   There shall be a committee to be known as the Animal Procedures Committee.
>
> (2)   The Committee shall consist of a chairman and at least twelve other members appointed by the Secretary of State.

(3)   Of the members other than the chairman –
  (a)   at least two-thirds shall be persons having such a qualification as is mentioned in subsection (4) below; and
  (b)   at least one shall be a barrister, solicitor or advocate, but so that at least half of those members are persons who neither hold nor within the previous six years have held any licence under this Act or under the Cruelty to Animals Act 1876; and in making appointments to the Committee the Secretary of State shall have regard to the desirability of ensuring that the interests of animal welfare are adequately represented.

(4)   The qualifications referred to in subsection (3)(a) above are full registration as a medical practitioner, registration as a veterinary surgeon or qualifications or experience in a biological subject approved by the Secretary of State as relevant to the work of the Committee.

(5)   Members of the Committee shall be appointed for such periods as the Secretary of State may determine but no such period shall exceed four years and no person shall be reappointed more than once.

(6)   Any member may resign by notice in writing to the Secretary of State and the chairman may by such a notice resign his office as such.

(7)   The Secretary of State may terminate the appointment of a member if he is satisfied that-
  (a)   for a period of six months beginning not more than nine months previously he has, without the consent of the other members, failed to attend the meetings of the Committee;
  (b)   he is an undischarged bankrupt or has made an arrangement with his creditors;
  (c)   he is by reason of physical or mental illness, or for any other reason, incapable of carrying out his duties; or
  (d)   he has been convicted of such a criminal offence, or his conduct has been such, that it is not in the Secretary of State's opinion fitting that he should remain a member.

(8)   The Secretary of State may make payments to the chairman by way of remuneration and make payments to him and the other members in respect of expenses incurred by them in the performance of their duties.

(9)   The Secretary of State may also defray any other expenses of the Committee.

20. (1)   It shall be the duty of the Animal Procedures Committee to advise the Secretary of State on such matters concerned with this Act and his functions under it as the Committee may determine or as may be referred to the Committee by the Secretary of State.

  (2)   In its consideration of any matter the Committee shall have regard both to the legitimate requirements of science and industry and to the

protection of animals against avoidable suffering and unnecessary use in scientific procedures.

(3) The Committee may perform any of its functions by means of sub-committees and may co-opt as members of any sub-committee any persons considered by the Committee to be able to assist that sub-committee in its work.

(4) The Committee may promote research relevant to its functions and may obtain advice or assistance from other persons with knowledge or experience appearing to the Committee to be relevant to those functions.

(5) The Committee shall in each year make a report on its activities to the Secretary of State who shall lay copies of the report before Parliament.'

The role of the APC in the referral process

The APC 1996 Report states

'There are misconceptions in some quarters about our role in the licensing process, we see any applications for project licences which involve:
- the use of primates in procedures of substantial severity;
- the use of wild-caught primates;
- the testing of cosmetics or tobacco; or
- microsurgical training.

We may, however, also be asked for our advice by the Home Secretary on other applications where it is felt that this may be useful.'

(p. 3, n. 23)

'The Committee does not grant licences. Our role, in this area. is to advise the Secretary of State on whether the applications we see should be granted.'

(p. 3, n. 24)

'During 1996, the Committee recommended that one application to use animals for microsurgical training be granted, but no applications to test tobacco or tobacco products were considered.'

(p. ii, n. 5)

Because of the amount of concern expressed about the use of animals in the testing of cosmetics and tobacco products it would not be out of place at this juncture to present a review of the situation.

Testing of cosmetics etc.

The 1996 APC Report rightly deals with this topic at some length and justifiably comments:

'Consideration of applications to test cosmetic products or ingredients on animals is one of the most difficult aspects of our work and always provokes intense and wide ranging discussion.'

(p. 5. n. 43)

Other relevant extracts concerning cosmetics are:

'No new applications for cosmetics testing licences were considered during 1996.'

(p. 5. n. 45)

'... the 6th. Council Amendment to the European Cosmetic Directive which sought to ban the marketing of cosmetics tested on animals after 1 January 1998 (but only if validated alternative tests are in place). However, it was already clear in 1996 that validated alternatives for tests would not be in place and that the proposed ban would, therefore, be postponed by the European Union.'

(p. 5. n. 47)

There is an intriguing comment in n. 48 on the same page which refers to controversy concerning the testing of other products which could be considered to be 'unnecessary'. No details are given.

'The Act requires that programmes of work are authorised on a case-by-case basis. The Act itself prohibits no particular type of procedures – such as the use of animals in the testing of cosmetic products. This is a disappointment to many critics but it exemplifies the point made in the Committee's report that the law provides a framework in which to balance the likely costs to animals against the benefits to man, animals or the environment.'

(p. 36. n. 8.)

The sensitive nature and importance of this topic is apparent from the serious comment on the above material which appeared in the *LASA Newsletter* (Winter 1997).

'A further response was issued by the Home Office on 6 November 1997 to announce that it had made further progress on the matter. It said that an end to cosmetic products testing, which was being sought when the Home Secretary's response was published had now been secured. The three companies undertaking this type of work in the UK had voluntarily agreed to stop cosmetic products testing. Current licences were being amended to prohibit such testing.

Legal advice had been taken and confirmed that revocation of current licences was not possible under the Animals (Scientific Procedures) Act 1986. A voluntary agreement was therefore the quickest way to achieve the cessation of cosmetics testing. An outright ban is not possible without primary legislation (this would seem to be beyond the scope of the enabling process associated with the ASPA, allowing for secondary legislation through Statutory Instruments)., but the Government will issue no new licences for the testing of finished cosmetic products on animals.

The Government also stated that it wished to see an end to the testing of ingredients used in certain forms of cosmetics which can be called vanity products. The definition of these products and the differentiation of their ingredients from others will need the advice of the APC and consultation with interest groups and industry. The difficulties arise because the ingredients of some vanity products are also used in a variety of other commodities where safety testing is regarded as essential including some pharmaceutical products.'

It is important to recall the official definition of 'cosmetic' contained in a former European Community Directive (76/768) on this subject:

'Any substance or preparation intended for placing in contact with the various parts of the human body (epidermis, hair system, nails, lips and external genital organs) or with the teeth and mucous membranes of the oral cavity with a view exclusively or principally to cleaning them, perfuming them or protecting them, in order to keep them in good condition change their appearance or correct body odours.'

It is this definition which is followed for the purposes of the Act. (cf. former edition of HOG Q. 17) It is obvious that in this context 'cosmetic' is not just the latest perfumery accessory but includes 'down to earth' soap.

The *LASA Newsletter* (Winter 1997) adds a further significant comment:

'The Government will also take the opportunity to explore, at the same time, the feasibility of a ban on testing finished household products on animals'

The definitive statement on animal use in the testing of cosmetics aptly appeared among other important material in the APC 1998 Report (p. 2):

'16. The Government made some significant announcements in November. These included
- an end to the use of animals in the testing of cosmetics ingredients, secured through a voluntary agreement with the companies carrying out this type of work in the UK – this was in addition to the end to finished cosmetics product testing announced in 1997;
- agreement that this Committee should be, and be seen to be, more independent and proactive. This would be facilitated by the setting up of a dedicated secretariat; and
- the appointment of new members to the Committee.

17. At the same time the Government announced the results of a survey of dog accommodation and care, included at Appendix D.'

The Winter 1997 *LASA Newsletter* also indicated the trend as regards other tests using animals:

'The Government will not allow tests which involve animals in the development and testing of alcohol or tobacco products. At present no such licences exist and none will be authorised in the future.'

Cloning

In keeping with its more proactive role which has evolved, especially during the 1990s, the APC produced an interesting commentary on the development of cloning, with particular reference to the ovine milestone, Dolly.

'115. In February 1997, articles appeared in the press announcing that scientists at the Roslin Institute had bred a lamb called Dolly, produced through a revolutionary cloning process.

116. In part, the cloning process had followed a well-established method whereby the nucleus of an egg cell is removed. The distinctive aspect of the new process that led to Dolly was that the replacement nucleus (to form the embryo) was that of specialised cell from an adult animal. The specialised cell had been persuaded to return to a state of quiescence in which it could function as a stem cell. In the past, while nuclear transfer had been commonly used, the nuclear material had always been derived from non-specialised tissue.

117. Much of the work carried out at the Roslin Institute did not need licence authority under the Animals (Scientific Procedures) Act 1986. The production of a living animal (or a foetus which was to be allowed to survive past the half-gestation period) does, however, require such authorities. The objectives of the programme, as identified in the project licence, were to create a better understanding of the biology of embryonic maturation and development, to use that knowledge to solve current welfare problems associated with established artificial breeding techniques, and to develop new and improved methods of artificial breeding applicable to agricultural animals. Other objectives included the production and rapid multiplication of transgenic agricultural animals as sources of pharmaceutical proteins and models of disease.

118. We had the opportunity to discuss this work at the March meeting of the Committee. We agreed that there were animal welfare implications to be considered as well as the wider implications, and that both of these could be considered in principle under the cost/benefit assessment. But the work also fell within the remit of other Government Departments, such as the Ministry of Agriculture, Fisheries and Food (which funded some of the work at Roslin). The regulatory implications of human cloning fell to the Human Fertility and

Embryology Authority and the Human Genetics Advisory Committee to consider, who were clear that human cloning was forbidden in the UK.

119. There was some concern, nevertheless, that the possibility of human cloning should have been considered when the project licence had been assessed and granted. It was apparent, however, that the scientific focus had been on the immediate achievement of the study objectives. The longer term consequences and benefits had been seen as agricultural or pharmaceutical. Some members were nevertheless concerned that a potential disbenefit, of which human cloning was a good example, should be taken into account when considering costs and benefits.'

(1997 APC Report p. 16)

Note that in the 1998 Report the APC produced a Code of Conduct for members. (cf. p. 14)

Other bodies associated with the ASPA

Among bodies having an impact on the application of the ASPA are, since April 1999, LERPs – local ethical review processes – which have already been commented upon in a special section.

Bodies having the most direct legal status under the ASPA would be tribunals constituted to deal with appeals against decisions of the Secretary of State.

Procedures for making representations

The Statutory Instrument 1986 No. 1911 (Animals) laid down the Rules for appeal against a decision of the Secretary of State involving the use of animals in research e.g. revocation or varying of conditions on a licence or certificate. The details of the order are couched in legal jargon but are expounded fully in HOG Appendix VIII accompanied by the text of the Statutory Instrument in Appendix IX. If one decides to appeal, the following procedure applies:

- One should notify the Secretary of State of his/her intention to make representation.
- A legally qualified person will be appointed to consider any such representation.
- The Secretary of State will send lists and copies of all relevant documents to him/her and to the person considering the case.
- One has the right to opt for an oral or written form of representation and even for a public hearing.
- One may call witnesses, address the person appointed and be represented at the hearing by a lawyer or other person.
- If an Inspector's report is involved one may question the Inspector who made the report.

Before embarking on such a process of appeal one should refer to HOG Appendix VIII and preferably seek the advice of a legal expert in the field.

Relevant official publications

Examples of such publications are HOG – the useful comprehensive commentary on the operation of the ASPA, official instructions in detail on some aspect of the ASPA such as the use of neuromuscular blocking agents, specimen forms of application concerning the transfer of protected animals or for licences and certificates as well as the accompanying documents giving the appropriate instructions in each case, and numerous shorter communications from the Inspectorate (PCD circulars). There was an important series of this latter type of letters on the topic of local ethical review processes between 1996 and 1999. Many of these documents have been referred to in the text. Reference to some can be found in the index under the heading of the topic involved.

Home Office Guidance on the operation of the Animals Scientific Procedures Act

This useful body of information and apt commentary on the application of the ASPA was issued following consultation with the APC under s. 21 of the Act. Much of the material contained in HOG has already appeared in this text.

In the text of HOG (n. 1.3) it is clearly indicated what the purpose of the document is:

'(i) To set out how applications for licences and certificates are considered.'

Clear definitions are presented of both 'protected animal' and 'regulated procedure'. Non-regulated procedures are described and the the exclusion of Schedule 1 killing from the concept of a 'regulated procedure' is indicated:

'(ii) The terms and conditions under which licences and certificates are granted.'

The validity and amendments of licences and certificates are explained:

'(iii) The arrangement for referral of applications to external assessors and/or the Animal Procedures Committee.

Under section 9(1), all applications for certificates and licences are assessed by one or more Inspectors. In certain cases, before a licence or certificate is granted, it may be referred to an external assessor, the Animal Procedures Committee or to both. The Animal Procedures Committee considered all project licence applications involving cosmetics; tobacco products (except where the animals are terminally anaesthetised); work of substantial severity in primates' (cf. APC Report 1996 p. 3. n. 23,); 'and the acquisition or maintenance of manual skills for microsurgery.'

(HOG 4.30)

'The Committee will not usually consider other individual applications unless a general question about the permissibility of a certain type of procedure is at issue.'

(HOG 4.31)

Referral to an external assessor may occur in cases, when, for example, there is a need to seek expert advice regarding a novel project or a complicated new technique. In such cases the applicant will be informed of the identity of the assessor and is given the opportunity, if they so wish, to object to the use of the particular expert chosen.

In section (iv) 'The responsibilities of certificate holders, licensees and named persons', the need to observe the Codes of practice are referred to and matters of concern in designated establishments are mentioned. Attention is drawn to the presence of levels of severity, humane endpoints and requirements as regards deputies, records, re-use and training.

Section (v) covers how ASPA is enforced, and pertains to both prosecution and non-criminal sanctions.

The final section (vi) describes the procedures for making representations under the Act.

Unfortunately, at the time of writing this book, HOG is undergoing revision. The best advice in the circumstances is to consult the new edition of HOG as soon as it is published and make note of any changes.

A final note

A recent welcome development in bringing the working of the ASPA before the public was announced in the Home Office PCD circular 2/99:

'A Forum is being organised at which scientists, animal welfarists, anti-vivisectionists and representatives of Government can discuss issues surrounding the use of animals in scientific procedures. (Those who seek to further their aims by violence, intimidation or other such activities have not been invited.) It will take place on 9 July at a central London location. The objective of the event is:

"For the Minister [on behalf of the Home Office and his colleagues] to hear the range of views, to encourage open and constructive dialogue, and to identify common ground concerning the use of animals in scientific procedures."

This is intended to be a one-off event in the first instance, but it could be repeated if judged to be successful.

The Forum is not designed to marginalise the Animal Procedures Committee and its statutory role: to provide independent and informed advice to the Secretary of State. Its chairman – the Reverend Professor Michael Banner – and members have been invited to hear the debate, along with the Minister.

Nor is the Forum set up to compete with the continuing work and role of the Boyd Group in seeking consensus on the way forward amongst the range of views concerning the use of animals in scientific procedures. All the Boyd Group members have been invited to the Forum.'

Part III

Other Relevant Legislation

Chapter 15

The Law on Veterinary Surgery

The Veterinary Surgeons Act 1966

The Act restricts the practice of veterinary surgery to specifically qualified individuals. Those permitted by law to practise veterinary surgery are persons registered as members of the Royal College of Veterinary Surgeons (RCVS). There is a closed list of qualified individuals who are entitled to practise by virtue of experience as veterinary practitioners. Apart from veterinary degrees from UK universities holders of certain Commonwealth and South African veterinary degrees are recognised for registration. The Veterinary Surgeons Qualifications (EEC Recognition Order) 1980 recognises EEC veterinary qualifications as sufficient for the practice of veterinary surgery in this country. Other veterinary qualified persons can sit an examination by the RCVS to obtain the necessary qualification to practise here.

Another important role of the RCVS in respect to veterinary medicine is monitoring the supply and administration of drugs by veterinary surgeons. This it does efficiently and strictly.

A veterinary surgeon may need an owner's consent to treat an animal in order to avoid an action for trespass to goods. In case of an accident or when an animal is suffering excessively a police constable, in keeping with the Protection of Animals Act 1911 may authorise a veterinary surgeon to kill the animal without the consent of the owner. The constable's decision will be taken on the basis of a veterinary surgeon's certificate.

Veterinary surgery

The Act defines the work which is restricted to veterinary surgeons as the art and science of veterinary surgery and medicine. This definition extends to:

(a)   the diagnosis of diseases in, and injuries to, animals including tests performed on animals for diagnostic purposes
(b)   the giving of advice based upon such diagnosis
(c)   the medical and surgical treatment of animals
(d)   the performance of surgical operations on animals.

Anaesthesia prior to veterinary treatment is covered by the Veterinary Surgeons Act 1966, whereas that used solely for management or handling is not considered veterinary surgery and such anaesthesia may be carried out by a non–veterinarian. A veterinary surgeon carrying out anaesthesia as a regulated procedure must be authorised under the ASPA 1986.

Permitted treatment of animals by a lay person

(a) Any treatment given to an animal by its owner or his employee, a member of the owner's household or his employee.

It is worth noting that the Act refers to 'any treatment' which it might be argued, refers to item (c) above in connection with the definition of veterinary surgery and does not extend to other aspects of the definition such as diagnosis and surgical operations.

An organisation which owns its animals, such as a research institution, may use its own non-veterinary staff to treat its animals. Care must be taken not to allow lay staff to treat animals which, although part of a research programme, do not belong to the institution.

Difficulties may arise in the care of sick or injured free-living wild animals found by non-veterinarians. They may give emergency first aid but unless the animal is taken into captivity for further attention (in the case of protected species, in accordance with the Wildlife and Countryside Act 1981) then the restrictions of the Veterinary Surgeons Act 1966 must be observed. If the animal is in fact legally taken into captivity then the owner may, of course, treat it. If the owner seeks the services of an non-veterinarian, e.g. an animal shelter, ownership must be given to the shelter if it is to provide the necessary treatment. Brief and temporary restraint of a wild animal does not render it captive in the legal sense, Refer to *Rowley* v. *Murphy* (1964).

(b) First aid measures taken by any person in an emergency to save life or relieve pain.

(c) Anything except a laparotomy, done other than for reward, to an animal used in agriculture by its owner or a person employed or engaged in caring for such animals.

(d) The castration of very young animals; the docking of a lamb's tail by a rubber ring within the first week of life. Debeaking, dubbing and desnooding by a person who is 18 years old (or 17 if participating in animal husbandry training under the direct personal supervision of a veterinary surgeon or at a recognised institution under the direct personal supervision of an appointed instructor).

Aspects of veterinary surgery which certain non-veterinarians may perform

(a) A person carrying out a regulated procedure under the 1986 Act.

(b) Doctors and dental surgeons carrying out treatment, tests and operations, and persons giving treatment by physiotherapy to an animal at the request of a veterinary surgeon. Doctors may remove organs and tissues from an animal for the treatment of human beings.

(c)   Those authorised to take blood samples from farm animals and poultry under the Veterinary Surgery (Blood Sampling) Order 1983.

Non-veterinarians may carry out laboratory tests on material taken from animals by veterinary surgeons but care must be taken that any diagnosis or advice which is based on the results is given by a veterinary surgeon. It might be acceptable under the 1966 Act to state a treatment for a given condition as part of a discussion on remedies as long as no diagnosis is offered by the non-veterinarian.

Certain latitude is allowed as regards treatment of animals in agriculture but the involvement of a veterinary surgeon is always required in the following circumstances.

(a)   A boar over six months must not only not be castrated without an anaesthetic, but the operation must be carried out by a veterinary surgeon.
(b)   De-beaking, by whomsoever carried out, must be performed as prescribed in the Veterinary Surgery (Exemptions) Order 1962.
(c)   Dubbing (trimming of the comb) of older birds should be done only on veterinary advice and by a skilled operator.
(d)   Docking of the tails of pigs over seven days old is forbidden unless done by a veterinary surgeon on health grounds or to prevent injury from tail-biting (Welfare of Livestock (Docking of Pigs) Regulations 1974).

Veterinary nurses, qualified under the RCVS Veterinary Nursing Bye-laws, do not have any special authority and are subject to the same restrictions in respect of veterinary surgery as other lay people.

If wildlife is temporarily caught for scientific purposes e.g. to apply superficial monitoring devices or using painless methods of identification as long as no diagnosis, treatment or surgical intervention is involved, the activity is not governed by the 1966 Act. If veterinary procedures are involved they should be performed by a veterinary surgeon unless it is a matter of first aid or they are being performed as regulated procedures authorised under the ASPA.

A veterinary surgeon giving an anaesthetic in a regulated procedure must be authorised under the ASPA. The complex legal situation of veterinary surgeons operating as named veterinary surgeons or licensees under the ASPA has been discussed already in the appropriate chapter. A letter in September 1998 from the Assistant Registrar and Head of Professional Conduct at the Royal College of Veterinary Surgeons drew attention to the intricate relationship between the ASPA and the Veterinary Surgeons Act 1966. A statement on the legal position of veterinary surgeons involved with both Acts accompanied this letter. In this statement issued by BLAVA (British Laboratory Animal Veterinary Association) six principles of good practice in confronting conflicting legislative requirements were presented. These recommendations are relevant to veterinary surgeons involved with designated establishments.

'Animal' in the 1966 Act

In the 1966 Act 'animal' includes birds and reptiles as well as mammals. Fish and invertebrates are excluded. Amphibians as such are not mentioned so in keeping with the dictum, *Expressio unius, exclusio alterius* (what is expressed excludes others) it would appear amphibians do not come under the 1966 Act at least until there is an authoritative decision to the contrary. Marine mammals are within the scope of the Act.

Statutory orders associated with the 1966 Act

The following is a list of the most important statutory orders relevant to the 1966 Act.

Veterinary Surgeons (Practice by Students) Regulations Order in Council 1981.

The Veterinary Surgery (Exemptions) (Amendments) Order 1982 restricts the removal of deer antlers in velvet to veterinary surgeons.

The Veterinary Surgery (Blood Sampling) (Amendment) Order 1988/1090.

The Veterinary Surgery (Blood Sampling) (Amendment) Order 1990/2217 permits non-veterinarians to take blood from badgers.

Chapter 16

Drugs in Research

The salient pieces of legislation relevant to the use of drugs in research are:

- the Medicines Act 1968
- the Misuse of Drugs Act 1971

Many of the complex regulations associated with the two Acts referred to are outside the scope of this book. Most of the material, even regarding animals, is more relevant to a specialised work on veterinary medicine, particularly in regard to the 'cascade system'. This controls the dispensing practices of veterinary surgeons as regards the use, with the assent of the owner of the animal, of veterinary medicines not specific to the type of animal being treated, human medicines or a proprietary brand made up on a one-off basis. Since the main concern underlying these stipulations is in respect to possible hazards arising from pharmacologically active ingredients in the human food chain, it suffices, I think, merely to refer interested parties to the Medicines (Restrictions on the Administration of Veterinary Medicinal Products) Regulations 1994. These Regulations express in UK Law EC Directive 81/851 and the amendment to Directive 90/696. The Veterinary Medicines Directorate issued a clarification of these Regulations in a Guidance Note.

The Medicines Act 1968

The influence of this Act through various statutory instruments is ubiquitous throughout the field of animal health. The Act controls the sale and use of medicinal products – that is any material which given to a person or animal which it is expected will be of benefit to them. It also controls other substances and articles through a comprehensive system of licences and certificates e.g. the Animal Test Certificate which permits the use of animals for the clinical testing of veterinary medicines without the need for either a Home Office Project or Personal Licence. (ASPA s. 2(6) and the Medicines Act 1968 s. 32(6) and s. 35(8)(b))

Misuse of Drugs Act 1971

The Misuse of Drugs Act 1971 lists and classifies controlled drugs and lays down restrictions on the importation, production, supply and possession of such drugs.

The Act provides strict and concise guidelines as to the storage of the drugs which it seeks to control the use of. In particular any room, cabinet or safe in which drugs are stored must only be accessible to a person licensed to handle or prescribe them. If controlled drugs are not so stored, the Act provides that 'as far as circumstances permit' they should be kept in a locked receptacle which can only be opened by authorised persons.

The Misuse of Drugs Regulations 1973, Part III, specifies the requirements for documentation and record-keeping. A record must be kept of drug use. Entries must be made in chronological sequence as set out in the Schedules. Each quantity of controlled drugs either obtained or supplied by a department must be entered in the register. A separate register or part of a register must be kept for entries of each class of drug and each of the individual drugs within that class, together with its salts. Any preparation or other product containing it or any of its salts must be treated as a separate class. Any stereoisomeric forms of a drug or its salts should be classed with that drug.

Registers

Regulation 19 sets out the following rules.

(1) The class of drugs to which the entries on each page of a register relate must be specified at the head of that page.
(2) Every entry in the register must be made on the day on which the drug is obtained or supplied.
(3) No amendment or deletion of an entry must be made. Corrections must be by a marginal note or footnote and specify the date on which the correction was made.
(4) Every entry and correction must be made in ink or other indelible material.
(5) The register must be used only for entries concerning drugs.
(6) Anyone required to keep a register must, on demand from the Secretary of State's inspectors, furnish particulars of drugs specified in Schedule 2 and obtained or supplied by him or in his possession. He must be able to produce proper documentation.
(7) Every register in which entries are currently being made should be kept at the premises to which it relates
(8) All registers and books shall be kept for two years from the date on which the last entry is made.

Purchase and supply of veterinary medicines and drugs

The supply of medicinal products is regulated according to the category to which they have been assigned in regulations. Those on the General Sale List, for example, flea powders, may be obtained without prescription and some of them may be sold elsewhere than in a pharmacy. Pharmacy drugs marked 'P' are not on prescription but are obtainable only from a registered pharmacy or a veterinary surgeon. A special category of medicinal products – PML (pharmacy and merchant list) medicines – are available not only from pharmacists and veterinarians but also from agricultural merchants without prescription provided that the buyer is a farmer or other person who has in his charge or maintains animals for business purposes; such 'other person' could be involved in using or supplying experimental animals. The incorporation of PML or POM (prescription only medicines) in animal feeds must be authorised by the written direction of a veterinary surgeon. Codes of Conduct on these matters have been issued by MAFF.

Drugs marked POM on the Prescription Only List of the Medicines (Veterinary Drugs) (Prescription Only) Order 1985 may be sold or supplied by a pharmacist on the authority of a prescription issued by a veterinary surgeon. The prescription must state that the drug is to be supplied to animals under the prescribing veterinary surgeon's care. (Medicines Act 1968 s. 58(2)(a).

Impact of medicine legislation on research

A person in charge of a laboratory the recognised activities of which include the conduct of scientific education or research and which is attached to a university or hospital maintained out of public funds or by a charity or other institution approved by the Home Secretary may possess or supply controlled drugs listed in Schedule 2 and 3 of the Regulations already referred to. Supply must be to a person legally entitled to have the drug in his possession.

POM may be supplied to institutions of research or higher education on the production of an order signed by a principal or head of department in charge of a specified course of research. The order must state the name of the institution, the quantity of the medicine required and the purpose for which it is required (Medicines (Veterinary Drugs) (Prescription Only) Order 1985, schedule 3, Part 1).

Veterinary prescription only medicines may be administered only by a veterinary surgeon or a person acting in accordance with the direction of a veterinary surgeon, whether they are required to be obtained on prescription from a pharmacy or through a veterinary surgeon or by a scientific establishment. The phrase 'in accordance with directions' has not been defined by the courts but it is considered that a veterinary surgeon has discretion as to what degree of direction, from verbal guidance to the actual overseeing of its use, which he should give to a client. It must, however, be in accordance with the circumstances of the case because there may be the possibility of civil liability for negligent advice or supervision.

The controlled drugs most commonly administered to animals are contained in Schedules 2 and 3 of the Regulations. Those listed in Schedule 3, including barbiturates are not subject to the requirements for record-keeping nor is the strict standard set for the safe custody of other listed drugs demanded. These Schedules (which are liable to be added to or amended) can be obtained with a copy of the

Misuse of Drugs Regulations 1973. Persons directly involved in these matters should consult this source material if they wish for clarification on the subject.

The Medicines (Exemptions from Restrictions on the Retail Sale or Supply of Veterinary Drugs) Order 1977 (SI 2167) allows the sale of certain veterinary preparations containing materials, otherwise only available on prescription, to persons 'known to have animals in their care'. This allows the person in charge of an animal unit to order such products without a countersignature.

Under the Control of Substances Hazardous to Health Regulations (COSHH) 1994, medicines are only exempt from the relevant stipulations of the Regulations in the hands of the patient. Pharmacists, doctors and nurses are bound by the COSHH Regulations regarding the control and use of these medicines, and likewise, veterinary surgeons and those in research institutes acting under their directions are similarly bound.

Poisonous substances which are not medicines are controlled by the Poisons Act 1972 and the Poisons Rules 1982 which restrict the supply of substances listed in the Poisons Lists Order 1978. Poisons must be sold through pharmacies except for Part II poisons which may be supplied by listed sellers to a person or institute concerned with education or research.

Chapter 17

Liability in the Animal Unit

Liability in respect of the hazards arising from animals' aggressive behaviour, condition, or even presence is also a matter for consideration within the scope of animal law as well as the more discussed liability to animals in respect to the responsibility for their care. Most animal legislation, such as the ASPA and the 1911 Act, is of its nature concerned usually with offences involving cruelty or neglect, and so falls within the realm of criminal law. One piece of animal legislation, called simply the Animals Act 1971, does however belong within the range of civil law. This Act is mainly concerned with liability arising from the commission of various torts.

A tort, a civil wrong, is an unlawful act arising primarily from the operation of law. A tort gives rise to a civil action for unliquidated (a sum of money to be awarded by a court) damages e.g. compensation to a person injured by an animal, or some other remedy e.g. an injunction may be issued in a *quia timet* (because one fears) action, where imminent danger is reasonably anticipated from the escape of a dangerous or infected animal. Such a mandatory injunction could impose strict conditions of containment. Non-compliance could result in being held in contempt of court. In cases concerned with tort the defendant is sued by a claimant (previously known as a plaintiff); he is not prosecuted by the Crown. Redress is being sought for an injury through a decision from a judge adjudicating in a civil court. The Crown is present rather in the role of arbitrator than in the capacity of administering retributive justice, its prominent function in criminal courts. There is a significant distinction in civil cases as regards the burden of proof. The claimant is only required to establish his claim on 'a balance of probabilities' not beyond 'reasonable doubt'.

A person may be liable for damage done by animals either in accordance with the Animals Act 1971 or on general principles in tort e.g. strict liability, negligence, nuisance, and trespass. There may be, in some cases liability arising from a breach of a statutory duty. The legal action for injuries arising from these sources will be duly considered.

The Animals Act 1971

Following review by the Law Commission the Animals Act came into force in 1971 and replaced the previously highly complex existing common law rules. One of the complexities of the common law had been the notion of 'scienter liability'. Animals had been considered in law as either *ferae naturae* (fierce by nature) or *mansuetae naturae* (tame by nature). The classification was a matter of law and was judicially noticed. In *McQuaker* v. *Goddard* (1940) it was judicially noted that a camel is a domestic animal and therefore *mansuetae naturae*.

Liability depended on knowledge (scienter) of the dangerous propensities of an animal by the one in charge of them. The owner of a *ferae naturae* animal was presumed to know it was dangerous. A claimant suing on account of injury from a *mansuetae naturae* animal had to prove 'scienter' – knowledge on the part of the owner that the animal was dangerous. Previous indication of a merely general vicious tendency of the wayward animal sufficed.

The new Act clarified this area of liability. It imposed strict liability (a topic which will be dealt with later) for damage done by dangerous animals. It defined dangerous animals as those species which are not commonly domesticated in the British Isles or those fully grown animals which normally have such characteristics that they are likely, unless restrained, to cause severe damage or that any damage they may cause is likely to be severe (s. 6(2)).

Where damage is caused by an animal which does not belong to a dangerous species the keeper is liable if:

'(a) the damage is of a kind which the animal, unless restrained, was likely to cause or which, if caused by the animal, was likely to be severe, and

(b) the likelihood of the damage or of its being severe was due to characteristics of the animal which are not normally found in animals of the same species or are not normally so found except at particular times or in particular circumstances: and

(c) those characteristics were known to that keeper or were at any time known to a person who at that time had charge of the animal as that keeper's servant ...'

(s. 2(2))

All this may seem far removed from research institutes but not all laboratory animals are little mice well tucked away in cages. I have known a worrying experience of a frisky experimental goat escaping on to a suburban road just when nearby schools were closing and numerous drivers had hazardous close encounters with the creature.

In spite of the reform of the law some features of the present legislation may seem a little strange.

'A keeper is not liable for damage caused by his animal kept on any premises to a person trespassing there, if it is proved either:-
(a) that the animal was not kept there for the protection of person or property; or
(b) (if the animal was kept there for the protection of persons or property) that keeping it there for that purpose was not unreasonable.'

(s. 5(3))

Liability of the staff of animal units

The Code of Practice of the ASPA draws attention to specific hazards associated with animals.

> 'Precautions should be taken in animal rooms to minimise the exposure of personnel to hazards which may arise from the incorrect handling of animals e.g. bites, scratches, allergens and infections and to prevent exposure to hazardous treatments intended for or applied to animals.'

This warning aptly applies to dangers in an animal unit from toxic substances, biological hazards and radiation. There are strict and detailed regulations covering the use of biological and radioactive material. This literature is referred to in the bibliography. It suffices here to mention COSHH 1994, particularly Regulation 10. Further guidance is given in *Surveillance of the People Exposed to Health Risks at Work* (Health and Safety Publication (HS(G) 61).

The supply by the employer to the employee of necessary and appropriate personal protective equipment is mandatory under the Personal Protective Equipment at Work Regulations 1992 (SI 2966). These Regulations give effect to the Directive (89/656/EEC) on the minimum health and safety requirements with regard to the use by workers of personal protective equipment at work.

The Regulations require employers to:

- provide personal protective equipment (PPE) where risks to health and safety cannot be controlled adequately by other means
- select PPE that is suitable for the risks to be protected against (This could imply the need to provide protective gloves for the handling of primates)
- maintain PPE to acceptable standards and provide storage space
- ensure that the PPE provided is properly used
- ensure employees are given information on and instruction in the use of PPE supplied.

Monitoring of exposures and provision of health surveillance should continue, where appropriate, alongside the use of PPE.

Risk assessment

The likelihood of damage of any sort arising from dealing with the animals should be considered as part of the overall risk assessment of the animal facility. 'Risk' should not be confused with 'hazard' which is a potential danger, avoidable or unavoidable in certain circumstances. A 'risk' means that there is a reasonable probability of an unfavourable outcome. Risk assessment should contain an element of quantification, a probability measurement. Consequent on such an assessment there should be an agreed system of work and availibility, if need be, of protective clothing as well as equipment and drugs for restraining purposes. Handling methods should balance minimum effective restraint and minimum risk. All those involved with animals must be trained in methods of handling and right use of methods of restraint. Licensee training in keeping with the Directive (86/609/EEC) and associated with the ASPA provides for this type of instruction.

In-house rules should be drawn up for dealing with large and dangerous animals. Particular attention should be given to the handling of infected animals as well as monkeys and venomous snakes. Any injury by an animal however slight, must be reported immediately and appropriate action taken. Even the fluffy bunny can pack a good kick with resulting deep scratches.

Two exceptions to liability appear in the Animals Act.

> 'Where a person employed as a servant by a keeper of an animal incurs a risk incidental to his employment he shall not be treated as accepting it voluntarily.'
>
> (s. 6(5))

This means that an employer cannot use a standard defence in tort cases *volenti non fit injuria* – the claim that one who takes on a risk voluntarily cannot be injured in law.

However no one can be liable for injury to a person who is completely to blame for the injury he has suffered. (s. 5(1))

If injury to the plaintiff takes the form of nervous shock, such damage is actionable under s. 2(1). This section also gives grounds for claims for infection from a diseased animal.

Employees must take care of their own health and that of others with whom they are involved. They must not recklessly interfere with anything provided in the interest of health and safety. (Health and Safety at Work etc. Act (s. 7)). Supervisors need to be alert. Allowing a new young technician to go unattended among housed cattle would be irresponsible. Even experienced stockmen have been fatally injured in such circumstances. (*Health and Safety Commission Newsletter*, Oct. 1995 p. 10).

Zoonoses Orders

The Agriculture (Miscellaneous Provisions) Act 1972 is concerned with the control of zoonoses. It is intended to reduce the risk to human health from any disease of, or organism carried in, animals. The minister (within MAFF) may by order designate any such disease or organism which in his or her opinion constitutes such a risk. There is a general directive providing the minister with contingent powers to deal with special cases. For this reason the list of zoonotic diseases, transferable from animals to man, and recognised in law, needs to be and is constantly updated. The Zoonoses Order of 1975 exempted those involved in research from the requirement to report occurrences of brucellosis and salmonellosis (reportable diseases as distinct from notifiable diseases) in food animals. The Zoonoses Order of 1989 updated the list of dangerous organisms. Information of changes in the Schedule of the Zoonoses Order can be obtained from the MAFF.

The Code of Practice of the ASPA appropriately refers to this matter:

'Animals that may harbour zoonotic agents should be caged, managed and handled in such a way as to minimise any risk of infection being transmitted.'

COSHH assessment should take account of all possible zoonotic hazards resulting from the presence of microorganisms hazardous to health. The consequences of the assessment should be strict control of contacts with possibly infected animals, prophylactic procedures where possible e.g. vaccination and strict adherence to quarantine rules. Regular checks must be available to endangered staff e.g. for TB where staff are in contact with primates from the wild.

Industrial diseases

Some animal diseases are referred to in the Industrial Diseases Act 1981. Under the Social Security (Industrial Diseases) Prescribed Diseases Regulations 1985 (SI 967) there are prescribed occupational conditions or diseases which will qualify claimants to receive benefits. The list includes:

Anthrax
Avian chlamydiosis
Hydatidosis
Leptospirosis
Brucella infections
Streptococcus suis infection
Ovine chlamydiosis
Tuberculosis.

Amendments to this list can be ascertained from the appropriate department of Social Services.

Biological hazards

The Biological Agents Directive (90/679/EEC) defined 'biological agents' as micro-organisms including genetically modified organisms and cell cultures, and applies to work activities where employees may be exposed to such agents. The COSHH Regulations 1994 (SI 3247) and subsequent amendments thereof implement the European directives on the subject. The COSHH Regulations control the use of 'biological agents' in the workplace, and define more clearly the following terms:

Biological agent – any micro-organism, cell culture, or human endoparasite, including any which have been genetically modified, which may cause any infection, allergy, toxicity or otherwise create a hazard to human health.

Micro-organism – a microbiological entity, cellular or non-cellular, which is capable of replication or of transferring genetic material.

The classification and additions of newly recognised 'biological agents' is an on-going process. The Amendment of the Classification of Biological Agents Directive (93/88/EEC) was discussed by the EC Technical Adaptation meeting (June 1997). Any proposed changes will duly appear in amended COSHH Regulations.

Employer's duties regarding biological hazards

There must be an assessment of the risks of any work with biological agents likely to be hazardous to the health of employees. A distinction is made between workers who work directly with biological agents and workers where exposure may be incidental, e.g. maintenance staff.

Hazards may be prevented by substituting a non-pathogenic organism for a harmful one or treating organisms in such a way as to render them harmless. Control of exposure should be secured, where reasonably practicable, by means other than by personal protective equipment. The use of safety cabinets and isolators will sometimes be necessary. Specific guidance is given in the *Code of Practice for the Prevention of Infection in Clinical Laboratories and Post-mortem Rooms*, issued by the Department of Health. Four levels of laboratory containment are described corresponding to the four hazard groups. In future, of course, these may be added to or altered.

Employers are required to take all reasonable steps to ensure that control measures are complied with and that equipment is examined and maintained in an efficient state. Records of examinations and tests must be kept for at least five years. Employees are required to make use of control measures and report any defects. (Health and Safety at Work Act (s. 7)).

Exposure of employees to biological hazards must be monitored. There are no occupational exposure limits for work with micro-organisms. Records of monitoring of exposure of identified employees must be kept for 40 years. Health surveillance must be provided where:

(a)   an identifiable disease may be related to exposure
(b)   there is a reasonable likelihood that the disease will occur under conditions of work
(c)   there are valid techniques for detecting disease.

The Reporting of Injuries, Diseases and Dangerous Occurences Regulations 1995 (RIDDOR) require reports to be made to the Health and Safety Executive (HSE) of the death of any person as a result of exposure to biological hazards arising out of or connected with work and any potentially serious accident or incident e.g. needle-stick injury where a pathogen is involved. There should be emergency plans for dealing with accidents with microbiological hazards. A Code of Practice has been issued by the Health and Safety Commission in connection with the COSHH Regulations 1994.

The Rabies Virus Order 1979 permits the importation, use and keeping of rabies virus only under licence.

All pathogens must be stored safely and securely with adequate labelling. Incineration, after autoclaving, is the preferred mode of disposal. Guidance from the HSE appears in *Safe working and the prevention of infection in clinical laboratories*.

Analogous regulations exist as regards exposure to radioactive hazards in the animal house. Naturally such regulations are stricter and vary as regards disposal of such hazardous material as isotopes. This subject is a very specialised area, it is not so relevant to most animal work and the legal scene is due to change. Council Directive (96/29/Euratom) revised the Basic Safety Standards Directive (80/836/Euratom) as amended by (84/467/Euratom). This new Directive was adopted in May 1996. The date for implementation is 13 May 2000. Regulations based on this Directive will be duly issued. Details will be available in publications by the Health and Safety Commission.

Allergies

Laboratory Animal Allergy (LAA), a recognised clinical syndrome, can render a person unfit for work with animals. Since 1981 it has been a recognised industrial disease.

Occupational asthma from exposure to animals in laboratories was also recognised as an industrial disease in 1981. Cases of LAA requiring medical treatment and an absence from work must be reported to the HSE under the Reporting of Injuries, Diseases and Dangerous Occurences Regulations 1995 (RIDDOR). The date of diagnosis, the nature of the disease and occupation of the person affected should be recorded.

The COSHH Regulations 1994 require employers to assess risks of work with potential hazards e.g. animals, dust, disinfectants, etc., control exposure, monitor control measures and provide health surveillance. This surveillance should identify symptoms of an allergy at an early stage. There must be provision of adequate ventilation and personal protective equipment, though the latter must be regarded as a second line of defence.

Relevant torts

1   The rule in *Rylands* v. *Fletcher*

In *Rylands* v. *Fletcher* (Court of Exchequer Chamber 1866) Blackburn J. formulated the underlying principle: 'The person who for his own purposes brings on to his land and collects and keeps there anything likely to cause mischief if it escapes, must keep it in at his peril and if he does not do so, is prima facie answerable for all the damage which is the natural consequences of its escape.' This means that no negligence on the part of the defendant need be proved in a claim for damages caused on the land of the plaintiff which could be the expected result of the activity of an escaped animal.

A horsey story, albeit not very research orientated, illustrates a possible association of animals with this rule. However, in view of the comments of Mr Justice Widgery in *Weller & Co* v. *Foot and Mouth Disease Research Institute* (1965), below, it is hard to see how a motorist could be said to have any proprietary interest in the highway. In *Jaundrill* v. *Gillett* (1996), a keeper of horses which had been maliciously released on to the road, where they panicked and galloped into an oncoming car, was not liable to a driver who collided with the horses. The Court of Appeal so held allowing an appeal by the defendant against a decision in the County Court in favour of the plaintiff Jaundrill. Section 2 of the Animals Act (as presented in the early part of this chapter) was considered by the court.

The horses had escaped from a field where they were kept by Gillett. It was common ground. Some malicious intruder had opened a gate and driven the horses on to the highway. The only issue in the County Court had been whether the plaintiff was entitled to rely on what was basically the strict or absolute liability of the keeper of an animal other than a dangerous species. The plaintiff had relied on evidence of a veterinary surgeon that a group of horses when moved from their accustomed environment did tend to behave abnormally, and that horses removed from their field on to the road with other horses in the dark would tend to panic and gallop aimlessly in any direction. Mr. Recorder Hussain in the County Court had found that the plaintiff had satisfied s. 2(2)(b) of the Animals Act. In the Court of Appeal however, there were grave reservations whether a horse which galloped on a highway and panicked was displaying a characteristic under s. 2 of the Act.

Section 8 of the Act made express provision for the liability of a keeper whose animal escaped on to the highway through his own negligence. It was unnecessary to come to a conclusion under that aspect of the case. There had to be a causal link between the animal's characteristic under section 2 of the Act and the damage done. In Lord Justice Russell's view, the real cause of the accident was the release of the animals on to the highway. Gillett's appeal was allowed and he was not liable for the damage.

2   Negligence

Negligence is the omission to do something which a reasonable man would do or doing something which a prudent and reasonable man would not do (Baron Alderson in *Blyth* v. *Birmingham Waterworks Co.* (1856)). Lord Atkin elaborated on this in *Donoghue* v. *Stevenson* (1932) (the case of the snail in the ginger-beer bottle): 'You must take reasonable care to avoid acts or omissions which you can reasonably foresee would be likely to injure your neighbour'.

Weller and Co. v. *Foot and Mouth Disease Research Institute* (1965) was a case where a research institute carried out experiments on their land concerning foot and mouth disease. They imported an African virus which escaped and infected cattle in the vicinity. Damages were paid to local farmers but in this case it was auctioneers who sued for loss of business because as a consequence of the calamity two cattle markets in the vicinity had to be closed. It was held by Mr Justice Widgery; that as far as negligence was concerned the defendants owed no duty of care to the plaintiffs who were not cattle owners, and had no proprietary interest in anything which could be damaged by the virus. Furthermore, the defendants owed no absolute duty to the plaintiffs under *Rylands* v. *Fletcher* (1866), because the plaintiffs had no interest in any land to which the virus could have escaped.

3   Nuisance

Perhaps this tort is less relevant to research establishments though in the past debarking of experimental dogs had been considered so as not to incur liability for causing a nuisance to neighbours.

The tort of nuisance is based on the common law maxim; *sic utere tuo ut alienum non laedas* – so use your own property so as not to injure your neighbour's. There have been numerous cases of nuisance involving animals as regards noise – cocks crowing (*Leeman* v. *Montague* (1936)), destruction of property by animals (*Farrer* v. *Nelson* (1885)) and smell (*Benjamin* v. *Storr* (1874)) – Benjamin claimed that the smell from the excreta of Storr's horses outside his coffee house deterred customers).

4   Trespass

This tort is hardly likely to be of interest to research workers unless they are dealing with cattle. The Animals Act (s. 4) imposes strict liability for trespassing cattle, so no fault need be proved. The tort however is not actionable *per se* as it was in common law because consequent damage must be proved.

5   Breach of statutory duty

This tort is relevant to all the various COSHH Regulations referred to earlier and the following section on waste disposal.

To succeed in a claim in a case of breach of statutory duty the plaintiff must prove that:

(a)   the statute was breached
(b)   the breach caused the injury
(c)   the plaintiff was a person the statute was intended to protect
(d)   the injury was one the statute was intended to prevent.

A case which could be analogous to situations involving a duty to provide services such as adequate ventilation in animal units was *Bonnington Castings Ltd.* v. *Wardlaw* (1956). The plaintiff was injured by inhaling silica dust because of the defendant's breach of the Factories Acts with respect to ventilation. Bonnington admitted the breach but denied it caused Wardlaw's injury. The House of Lords rejected this plea. Circumstances such as occurred in this case now come within the wider range covered by the Health and Safety at work etc. Act 1974 and obligations are more clearly defined under the Workplace (Health, Safety and Welfare) Regulations stemming from the European Workplace Directive (89/654/EEC).

There was litigation concerning a university animal facility in which four technicians were awarded a total of £200,000 in out of court settlements after they developed asthma. Their complaint was that their asthma was due to working in animal rooms in which their employers, although obliged to do so, had not installed adequate ventilation. (*The Times* 21 November 1995)

Disposal of waste

The Code of Practice of the ASPA prescribes:

> 'A vermin-free collection area should be provided for waste, prior to its disposal. Special arrangements should be made for handling carcasses and radioactive or other hazardous material. ... infected. toxic or radioactive carcasses must be disposed of so as not to present a hazard.'
>
> (2.33 and 4.17)

Animal house waste disposal may be subject to specific regulations and codes of such bodies as the Advisory Committee on Dangerous Pathogens and the Health Services Advisory Committee. Animal carcasses from animal facilities are classified as 'clinical waste' in the Health Services Advisory Committee's guidance booklet.

The safety policy should cover arrangements for colour coding, segregation, storage, transportation and disposal of waste. Records of the disposal of radioactive material must be kept.

Local authorities may impose specific control on waste disposal. The Association of London Boroughs has issued: 'Guidelines for the Segregation, Handling and Transport of Clinical Waste (1989).

Non-domesticated animals

The Dangerous Wild Animals Act 1976, as amended, lists in a Schedule (which may vary in the future) non-domesticated animals which are considered capable of causing greater injury than could a domesticated animal. A licence is needed for the possession of these animals. Circuses, zoos, pet shops and designated establishments under the ASPA are exempt from the need to have a licence.

Chapter 18

Ecological Aspects of Animal Legislation

There is an abundance of legal material concerned with conservation. Most of such legislation is beyond the scope of this book. There is, however, some intrusion of this area of law into research. Ecologists holding project licences under the ASPA are not unknown, in my experience, either on remote Scottish isles or in wild areas of Wessex. Their targets of research are not within the confines of an animal unit. They may enjoy a free life closely associated with a PODE (place outside a designated establishment).

Categories of legal protection of non-domestic animals

There are several district categories of protection offered by the law.

(1) Conservation in general of wild animals. In law 'wild animal' is defined as any animal (other than a bird) which is or (before it was taken or killed) was living wild. (Wildlife and Countryside Act 1981 s. 27(1)). There is a presumption that an animal is a wild one, so the burden of proof falls on the person alleging captive breeding.
(2) Close season protection.
(3) Control of pests.
(4) Trade control. In this context 'sale' includes hire, barter, exchange and offering for sale. Restrictions imposed apply to parts of and products derived from the animal.

The Wildlife and Countryside Act 1981 (WCA)

This is the main piece of legislation on conservation. It has been amended (1985 and 1991) and numerous statutory orders have been issued under it e.g. the updating of Schedules which by their very nature require review.

The WCA makes it an offence:

- to take, kill or injure a wild animal (within the terms of this Act – those named in the Schedules)
- to have possession or control, or to sell or advertise for sale a live or dead wild animal (again within the terms of the WCA)

- to disturb, damage or destroy any structure or place used for the shelter or protection of wild animals (again within the terms of the WCA).

The WCA does protect birds in their own right. In s. 8, for example, it stipulates that birds can only be kept in cages of sufficient dimensions which would enable birds to stretch their wings freely. Section 8 does not apply to a bird being examined by a veterinary surgeon, a bird being transported, or a bird being shown at exhibition, nor does it apply to poultry. It might seem that relief is given least where the shoe pinches most: Schedule 3 Parts I, II and III of the WCA deals with the sale of wild birds.

The strictness with which the WCA is applied is illustrated by the fact that legal possession is deemed to arise independently of any intention on the part of the accused thus creating an offence of strict liability.

Enforcement of the WCA

The Department of the Environment, Transport and the Regions (DETR) is responsible for enforcement through its Chief Wildlife Inspector. Persons authorised by the DETR have a right of entry to inspect premises, at reasonable times. Local authorities play a part in enforcing the WCA (s. 250).

Exemptions are allowed in respect to regulations under the WCA; for the benefit of animals e.g. if an injured animal is painlessly killed, or to prevent serious damage to stock or crops (s. 10 and s. 16).

The sale of legally protected species must be authorised by a DETR licence under the WCA or in the case of badgers by the National Conservancy Council. Legislation protective of Brock and even his abode has been consolidated in the Protection of Badgers Act 1992. It would seem that the badger is the most protected of animals. This may alter in the wake of concern about bovine TB in 1999. On the other hand it would seem that the mole is the least protected of our mammals (cf. Pests Act 1954).

Licences regarding wildlife may be issued to an individual authorising one or more transactions or may be an open general licence (OGL) which enables a person to sell within the scope and conditions of the OGL.

Licences relaxing restrictions imposed by the WCA may be issued for scientific, educational or other purposes accepted as justified by MAFF on the advice of such bodies as the Nature Conservancy Council.

Schedules of the WCA

The schedules of the WCA list conserve and protect species (Table 18.1). However, conservation law is by no means static. For example, the 1985 Amendment of the WCA was repealed by the Wildlife and Countryside (Service of Notices) Act 1985.

In 1998, regulations added some species of animals to Schedule 5 and there were some deletions e.g. the carthusian snail and the Chequered Skipper butterfly. The WCA (Variation of Schedule) Order 1989/906 added 22 butterfly species. Examples of other Orders are those concerning coypus and seals. Obviously details such as these

Table 18.1   Schedules of the Wildlife and Countryside Act 1981 (WCA)

Schedule	Details
Sch. 1	Lists the birds protected by special penalties.
Sch. 2	Lists the species of birds which may be killed or taken outside close season.
Sch. 3	Lists birds which may be sold.
Sch. 4	Lists birds which must be registered and ringed if captured.
Sch. 5	Lists the species of animals which are protected. These include: some mammals some reptiles some amphibia some insects some spiders

are only of interest to specialists in the field, but they illustrate the nature of the legislation.

The 1991 Amendment of the WCA varied permitted methods of killing.

CITES

The Convention on International Trade in Endangered Species 1973 (CITES) was enacted as law in the UK in the form of the Endangered Species (Import and Export) Act 1976 (ESA). The species protected fall into several categories (Table 18.2).

Table 18.2   Categories of endangered species defined by the Convention on International Trade in Endangered Species 1973 (CITES)

Category	Classification
A(1)	Endangered species (CITES Appendix I) No trading in these animals is allowed. There are exceptions made for captive-bred specimens and non-commercial dealing between scientific institutes. The DETR will take scientific advice before granting a licence. The imported animal must be kept at specified premises and be subject to inspection. Corresponding export documents are required.
A(2)	Threatened species (CITES Appendix II) These animals can be traded if it is not detrimental to conservation. There must be evidence of country of origin, compliance with its laws and corresponding export documents
B1	Vulnerable species (CITES Appendix III) Licences are normally available for trade in these species if their conservation status is satisfactory.
Other species	HM Customs may require an importer to declare on the arrival of an animal that there is no legal restriction on its importation.

If an ESA animal is to be released, a licence authorising the release under the WCA must be obtained before an ESA licence can be issued.

EU regulation provides for the recognition of CITES licences issued by member countries. ESA animals taken from the wild within the EU and moved between EU countries require a certificate of origin. Specimens imported from outside the EU do not normally require additional permits on movements between member countries. There may, however, be specific national legislation on this matter which will need to be considered. Our own UK law is liable to be more demanding in this area of importation of animals.

Violation of the licensing provisions of the ESA may involve prosecution. A person in possession of an ESA animal must be able to prove permission under the Act. A power of entry exists to ascertain whether animals have been imported legally (ESA s. 1(10)). Further provisions occur in the Trade in Endangered Species (Enforcement) Regulations 1985.

The European legal dimension has had an impact on the use of ESA animals in research. Council Regulation (EEC) 3626/82 on the implementation in the Community of the Convention on International Trade in Endangered Species of Wild Fauna and Flora required UK law to provide that endangered species must not be used for regulated procedures unless:

(1)   the animals are in conformity with the Regulations
(2)   the *research* is aimed at the preservation of the species used or
(3)   for a biomedical purpose, and the species is the only species suitable for the research involved.

The Control of Trade in Endangered Species (Fees) Regulations 1997 introduced fees for CITES import/export permits in respect to non-European Union Member States. Information on the application of CITES in the UK is available from the Department of the Environment, Transport and the Regions (tel: 0117 987 8168 with regard to mammals and 0117 987 8691 for other animals).

Chapter 19

Some Relevant Regulations and the Impact of European Legislation

Genetic manipulation

The EEC has issued Directives on the matter of genetic manipulation and, of course, will continue to do so. The principal instruments in this area have been Directive 90/219/EEC, On the Contained Use of Genetically Modified Organisms and 90/220/EEC, On the Deliberate Release in the Environment of Genetically Altered Organisms (*Official Journal of the European Communities* No L 117 8.5.90. pp. 1 & 15).

These Directives have been translated into UK law by the following Statutory Instruments:

- The Genetically Modified Organisms (Contained Use) Regulations 1992 [under the Health and Safety at Work etc. Act 1974]
- The Genetically Modified Organisms (Deliberate Release) Regulations 1992 [under the Environmental Protection Act 1990]

These basic regulations on genetic modification have been altered and added to in keeping with later European Directives. New regulations on deliberate release were issued as the Genetically Modified Organisms (Deliberate Release) Regulations 1993. The Regulations on Contained Use were amended by the Genetically Modified Organisms (Contained Use) (Amendment) Regulations 1996. The Council Directive of 26 October 1998 (98/81/EC) amended the original Directive (On the Contained Use of Genetically Modified Organisms (90/219/EEC)). The UK Government agreed that Regulations would be issued in the UK in 2000 to implement this new Council Directive (98/81/EC).

The Animal Procedures Committee (APC 1997 Report p. 34) has concerned itself with the regulatory control of the genetic modification and cloning of animals. It intends to:

'(i)   consider the adequacy and appropriateness of the present regulatory regime under the ASPA in relation to transgenic and cloned animals,
(ii)   take note of the Farm Animal Welfare Council's recent report on cloning,
(iii) take evidence, as appropriate, including from regulators, researchers and welfarists.'

This is an indication of further legal control in this area so it is a matter of 'watch this space.'

Transplantation

This area of advanced research became the special concern of the Kennedy Committee which recommended the establishment of the UKXIRA (United Kingdom Xenotransplantation Interim Regulatory Authority). The relationship between the Home Office's operation of the ASPA and the scope of the UKXIRA has been considered. The Home Office is responsible for any animals used but not for determining or checking whether the quality of the animals was acceptable for use as a source of organs for clinical use. The Home Office is producing a new code of practice for the housing of high health status source animals for transplantation. It was agreed that the Home Office would not consider project licence applications to use animals in clinical trials unless these had been endorsed by the Department of Health and UKXIRA. (APC Report 1997 p. 14)

Regulatory toxicology

This is an area strewn with an abundance of regulations often of Byzantine complexity. Knowledge of their details and observance of their rules is vital to those working in this field but it would need volumes to do justice to this vast literature. Those involved should consult the specific material of concern to them. Anticipation of variation in regulations is certainly justified particularly in the light of the intention of the APC to review progress and developments in the area of regulatory testing. (APC Report 1997 p. 35)

Examples of the regulatory authorities responsible for this type of regulation are:

> The Veterinary Medicines Directorate
> The Health and Safety Executive
> The Ministry of Agriculture, Fisheries and Foods
> The Department of Health
> The Medicines Control Agency
> The Department of Trade and Industry
> The Pesticide Safety Directorate
> The Medical Devices Agency
> The Department of the Environment, Transport and the Regions

Good laboratory practice

Although somewhat on the periphery of legal control of animal use in research, good laboratory practice (GLP) is a very important issue in the pharmaceutical industry, especially in the field of toxicology. Although GLP is not law *per se*, its requirements are often backed by such sanctions as non-acceptance of products, which render GLP obligatory in some situations.

For many years GLP was the direct responsibility of the Department of Health; now the Medicines Control Agency deals with the observance of GLP.

The purpose of GLP is to control processes and conditions under which laboratory studies are planned, performed, monitored, recorded and reported. Adherence by laboratories to GLP ensures the proper planning of studies and the provision of adequate means to carry them out. GLP facilitates the proper conduct of studies, promotes their full and accurate reporting, and provides a means whereby the integrity of the studies can be verified. The application of GLP to studies assures the quality and integrity of the data generated and so qualifies for approval of the ensuing results by government regulatory bodies. Once approved by UK regulatory bodies such data may be accepted by foreign regulatory bodies. This is of special significance in hazard and risk assessments of chemicals.

UK GLP conforms with the European Directives 87/18/EEC and 88/320/EEC. Even in a wider field UK GLP is in accordance with the standard set by the Organisation for Economic Co-operation and Development (OECD). (*GLP in the Testing of Chemicals, Final Report of the OECD, Expert Group on GLP* 1982.)

Details of GLP

The details of GLP are presented in *Good Laboratory Practice: the United Kingdom Compliance Programme* published in 1989 by the Department of Health in London. Some details of GLP may be of special interest, particularly items of animal husbandry.

The application of GLP to the animal unit is concerned with:

(a) animal room preparation
(b) environmental monitoring of animal rooms
(c) animal care
(d) handling of animals found moribund or dead on test
(e) identification of animals on test and correct allocation of cages
(f) cleaning of cages, racks and accessory equipment
(g) monitoring of food for analysis and shelf life
(h) monitoring of drinking water
(i) monitoring of bedding materials
(j) adequate documentation of all relevant observations.

Several developments have arisen out of GLP, notably SOPs (standard operating procedures). SOPs are written procedures which describe how routine operations, normally not specified in a study plan, are to be performed. The imposition of an extra condition on a certificate of designation is referred to in the APC Report 1997 (p. 24) and illustrates well the nature of SOPs.

'(xiv) That the applicant submits Standard Operating Procedures and protocols for the dog facilities relating to the housing, husbandry, care, restraint and performance of regulated procedures, with evidence that staff have successfully completed appropriate structured training. This should include:

(a)   a protocol for the group-exercising of dogs which specifies the minimum daily exercise period per dog, defines the minimum amount of staff time to be used to socialise with the dogs, and identifies the type of area for the exercise to take place;

(b)   protocols for the restraint of dogs to enable intravenous dosing and sampling and the proper production of haemostasis thereafter. Evidence should be supplied that animal care staff have been appropriately trained or re-trained.'

The legal status of GLP

Joint arrangments exist between the Medicines Control Agency (MCA) and the Health and Safety Executive which could lead to legal action in respect to lack of GLP compliance. GLP Inspectors will not enter laboratories or attempt to gain access to data without permission. Should access be refused, however, the MCA may inform any regulatory authority about a refusal and that the compliance with GLP by that laboratory cannot be established.

Inspections are carried out in accordance with internationally agreed principles. They ascertain that laboratories have implemented GLP principles for the proper conduct of laboratory health and environmental safety studies on chemical substances where the results are to be submitted to regulatory authorities. It examines the systems set up to comply with GLP. The wide diversity of studies means that not all GLP principles will be relevant in each case.

Inspection does not involve the formal approval of laboratories. Effective compliance with the requirements of GLP is secured by the need for laboratories to satisfy the monitoring body. Failure to satisfy the monitoring body may result in the fact that testing which is being carried out by a laboratory would not be accepted by a regulatory authority.

US Food and Drug Administration regulations

The USA Federal Register (Part II) is the source material for the FDA's GLP Regulations. These Regulations were instituted to assure quality and integrity of data submitted to non-clinical laboratory studies in support of applications to carry out clinical trials and the marketing of new drugs in the USA. They are, therefore, of great relevance to pharmaceutical companies involved in export of products to the USA. The sanction for observance of these GLP Regulations is the possible disqualification of the testing facility. Disqualification may be disclosed to the public. The FDA may inspect foreign (that is to the USA) facilities that seek a USA marketing permit.

European legislation

The more important and relevant pieces of European legislation have been referred to throughout this work where appropriate. This seems to be the best approach to this intricate topic. One cynic in the early balmy days of the EEC noted that while the textual bases for morality for millenia fitted upon two stone tablets, a European missive on duck eggs occupied 52 pages of close print. It is crucial to realise that the majority of laws coming from Brussels do not directly bind us as citizens of the European Union. We are not directly concerned with most of this legislation until it has gone through the UK legislative system either as an Act such as ASPA, or secondary legislation such as regulations and orders.

The regulations of the kind referred to above result from European Directives which direct the governments of the member states to produce appropriate legislation on the matter covered by the Directive. Directives differ from European Regulations coming from Brussels in two important ways: they can be addressed to any one member state and do not have to be directed at all members of the EU; and they are binding as to the end to be achieved while leaving some choice as to form and method to the member state. Those Directives which apply to all member states have to be published in the *Official Journal of the European Communities* (now the European Union).

Regulations coming directly from Europe are binding upon all the member states and are regarded as directly applicable within all such states. Regulations have to be published in the *Official Journal* and come into force on the date specified in the Regulation. Regulations in this European sense are rare and are usually not directly relevant to animal legislation.

Finally, decisions are commonly responses from the Commission to specific requests and are binding in their entirety on those to whom they are addressed.

Our concern in the UK, therefore, is with European Directives which will eventually result in regulations from the UK government. Such Directives are already woven within this text.

A good illustration of how the process works is found in Directive 98/58/EEC concerning the protection of animals kept for farming purposes. The Council of Agriculture Ministers agreed a final text in June 1998 and the Directive was formally adopted in July 1998. This Directive sets minimum standards for welfare of livestock throughout the EU and a framework for adoption of more detailed standards for individual farm species. Article 3 requires that owners or keepers of any vertebrate animals kept for these purposes

> '. . . take all reasonable steps to ensure the welfare of animals under their care and to ensure that those animals are not caused any unnecessary suffering or injury'.

Eventually regulations will be issued on this material in the UK. The exact nature of such regulations cannot be predicted for two reasons. Article 4 seems a little imprecise on the definition of 'animal' and we already have in place detailed regulations (The Welfare of Livestock Regulations 1994 as amended) stemming from the Agriculture (Miscellaneous Provisions) Act 1968. (*Veterinary Record* August 14 1999 p. 178)

A new version of a 1988 Directive on the patenting of biotechnology inventions appeared in 1993. This new version stated that patents could not be granted on processes for modifying the genetic identity of animals which are likely to inflict suffering or physical handicaps without benefit to man or animal. The EPO (European Patent Office) granted a patent on the onco-mouse (carrying an implanted human oncogene) after initially rejecting it. In its final decision, it ruled that the benefit to humans of fighting cancer outweighed the suffering of an animal designed to develop cancer. This is an ideal example of official cost/benefit assessment. The decision opened the door to European patents on transgenic animals. (*LASA Newsletter*, Spring 1993 and *New Scientist* 16 January 1993)

Enforcement of European law

The Commission can refer cases of non-compliance with European legislation to the European Court. A complaint of the RSPCA was upheld by the EEC Commission which then referred the UK to the European Court for its failure to enforce, and in the case of France, for its failure to implement, the EEC Directive on animal transportation in 1977 and 1981.

Sources of information on European law

European Information Office (London) tel: 020 7222 8122
British Library of Political and Economic Science, Portugal Street, London, tel: 020 7955 7273.
Many large local libraries stock some of European documentation
Office for Official Publications of the European Union, 2 Rue Mercier L-2985, Luxembourg
CELEX (Communitatis Europaeae Lex) available on CD-ROM
    This covers a compendium of European legislation
    Hosts: Eurobases; Contex Limited/Justis: Profile Information
ECLAS (European Commission's Library Automated System)
    Hosts: Eurobases. Commission of the EU, Rue de Loi 200, B-1049, Brussels.
A note of caution – some of these details may change.

The Council of Europe

The Council of Europe, based in Strasbourg, is a supernational body supported by agreement between national governments throughout Europe. Its influence is wider than that of the European Union, affecting states such as Switzerland, but it lacks direct legislative power. It considers the need to issue Conventions which serve as prototypes of relevant legislation in member countries (e.g. those in Table 19.1).

Table 19.1   Council of Europe Conventions on Protected Animals

Convention for the Protection of Animals during International Transport 1968
Convention for the Protection of Animals for Slaughter 1972
Convention for the Protection of Animals kept for Farming Purposes 1976
Convention on the Conservation of European Wildlife and Natural Habitats 1979 (The Berne
   Convention)
Convention for the Protection of Vertebrate Animals used for Experimental and other
   Scientific Purposes 1986

The UK's ASPA stems directly from the last named Convention which was adopted by the Council in May 1985, was opened for signatures in March 1986 and within two weeks had received the signatures of sufficient member states, including the UK, to bring it into force in October 1986, prior to ratification by individual countries. In fact some have still not ratified it. As often happens with such Conventions, the EEC adopted a Directive (Council Directive 86/609/EEC) on the subject requiring member states to comply with the provisions of the Convention within three years. This gives the Convention legal bite on the European Union level. Further European Directives can be expected to be followed by UK regulations on material within the scope of this Convention. In January 1999 the first meeting was held in Strasbourg of the working party for the preparation of the fourth multilateral consultation of parties to the European Convention for the Protection of Animals used for Experimental and Other Scientific Purposes.

The boundaries of Europe no longer set the limits of the area which can influence our legislation. A parliamentary question to President of the Board of Trade if she would raise the issue of the effect of GATT on EU Animal Welfare Directives during the World Trade Organisation in Geneva in May 1998 elicited the reply that the European Community's final position for the World Trade Organisation Ministerial Conference in May was still under internal EU discussion (*Hansard* 24/3/1998; Column 111).

The further broader legal dimension of international law is not usually of direct concern to the law abiding citizen. In the area of animal legislation one international convention is relevant in animal experimentation. The Convention on International Trade in Endangered Species of Wild Fauna and Flora 1973 (Washington Convention: CITES) was expressed in UK law as the Endangered Species (Import and Export) Act 1976. This matter has been referred to in Chapter 18.

Table 19.2   Some international conventions on wildlife

Migratory Birds Treaties 1916–1976
International Convention for the Regulation of Whaling 1946
Convention on Wetlands of International Importance especially as Waterfowl Habitat 1971
Convention for the Conservation of the Vicuna 1969
Convention for the Conservation of Antarctic Seals 1972
Convention on the Conservation of Migratory Species of Wild Animals 1979

Other examples, possibly of some interest, from the corpus of international law are shown in Table 19.2. Unfortunately it is not unknown for some states to honour such international ideals in the breach.

Chapter 20

Animal Welfare in Law

Animal welfare may be defined as the maintenance of animals under conditions of space environment, nutrition, etc., consistent with the physiological and social needs of the species. This welfare is best achieved by good husbandry within the framework of the Five Freedoms.

Husbandry was defined by the Littlewood Committee (1965) as: 'Routine application of sensible methods of animal care based on experience – a natural gift refined by study and improved by experience' (Littlewood Report n. 201), in short, good stockmanship. An acceptable approach to animal welfare is ideally made through the practical expression of the five freedoms:

(1)   Freedom from thirst, hunger and malnutrition
(2)   Freedom from discomfort
(3)   Freedom from pain, injury and disease
(4)   Freedom to express normal behaviour
(5)   Freedom from fear and distress.

The concept of animal welfare is a relative latecomer to legislation. The Animal Health Act 1981 was a more positive approach to the care of animals than the previous basic Act in this area, the Diseases of Animals Act 1950. Even more positive was the further development, expressed in the title of the next Act, the Animal Health and Welfare Act 1984.

The early legislation on this topic was inspired usually by economic interests and so was concerned mostly with farm animals, with 'livestock' defined as animals kept for production of food, wool, skin or fur on agricultural land. The last term 'fur' may eventually be dropped from this definition. A private members bill, with the blessing of the government, intended to outlaw fur farming was talked out of time in Parliament in May 1999. It could be back. The definition of 'livestock' applies to horses or dogs when being kept for the farming of land. Agricultural land is land used for the purpose of an agricultural trade or business. This legislation then is not applicable if the produce such as meat, milk or eggs are purely for private consumption (Agricultural (Miscellaneous Provisions) Act 1968).

There are traces of earlier legislation concerning animal health than the Diseases of Animals Act 1950. Various pieces of legislation such as Statutory Orders concerned with particular diseases e.g. of cattle – Cattle Plague Order 1928. There was a long tradition of this type of ad hoc law making. An outbreak of disease among the cattle of Islington was met after consultation with cow-doctors in 1714 by destruction and burning – by order.

By 1960 public concern was beginning to form about intensive farming and so there were motives, other than purely economic ones, to propose legislation concerning animals. The Brambell Committee (1965) examined the conditions in which livestock were kept and advised on standards of welfare. New legislation was the product of these deliberations. After the Farm Animal Welfare Advisory Committee (FAWAC) had been set up in 1967 the Agricultural (Miscellaneous Provisions) Act 1968 (A(MP)A) was passed to implement the findings of the Brambell Committee. This law made it an offence to cause or allow livestock on agricultural land to suffer unnecessary pain or distress. These terms were more clear and more embracing than the mere 'unnecessary suffering' of the Protection of Animals Act 1911. Detailed and practical Codes of Recommendation stemmed from the A(MP)A. The work of Professor Brambell continued and bore fruit in the formulation of the Five Freedoms in 1979 when the FAWAC became the Farm Animal Welfare Council (FAWC). The FAWC review the welfare of farm animals on agricultural land, at market, in transit and also at places of slaughter. The FAWC also advises the agriculture minister on any changes necessary to legislation. Various orders and regulations (the 1994 Regulations will be dealt with in detail) flowed from the A(MP)A.

Animal Health Act 1981 and Animal Health and Welfare Act 1984

The Animal Health Act 1981 was amended (particularly as regards animal breeding, medicines in foodstuffs and veterinary drugs) by the Animal Health and Welfare Act 1984.

Under this legislation MAFF acts through the MAFF Veterinary Service (Animal Health Division) with enforcement by local authorities as regards:

- diseases designated as notifiable, e.g. anthrax and foot and mouth disease
- the eradication of such diseases as tuberculosis, (hence the concern with badgers in 1999 in the West Country)
- the control of zoonoses and the institution of reportable diseases (zoonoses orders)
- the provision of a veterinary service
- the cleansing and disinfection of premises and vehicles (there are stipulations of great detail, e.g. types of disinfectants, under this heading)
- the slaughter and disposal of animals infected with notifiable diseases and compensation for their destruction
- the destruction of wildlife, e.g. in an outbreak of rabies
- the welfare of imported animals.

Disease orders

These are a major legal expression of the effect of the Animal Health Act and the Animal Health and Welfare Act though many such orders have a longer history than either Act e.g. Pleuro-Pneumonia Order 1928 (Contagious bovine pleuro-pneumonia).

There is neither the space nor the need to deal in detail with the plethora of diseases orders in this book. In general the orders:

- limit outbreaks of disease
- promote the eradication of disease

by supervision of farms, markets, the movement of animals (often in great detail particularly in the case of pigs) and by the supervision of animal importation.

Most of these orders are extremely specific and may change frequently. They are usually only of interest to those directly involved, important though they are to those affected by them.

Up-to-date information on this legal material can be obtained from MAFF. Suffice it here to refer to some significant ones to illustrate the pattern of this type of legislation.

The Psittacosis and Ornithosis Order 1953 introduced a category of scheduled diseases, such as chlamydiosis, as distinct from 'notifiable'. This Order was concerned not only with fowl but also such birds as parrots.

The Rabies (Importation of Dogs, Cats and Other Mammals) Order 1974 was within the enabling powers of the Diseases of Animals Act 1950. It is now within the scope of the Animal Health Act 1981. 'Animal' is defined to cover most warm blooded animals – an animal (except man) belonging to the six orders of mammals in Schedule 1. Importation of such an animal is prohibited without a licence, a condition of which is isolation in quarantine for life if the animal is a vampire bat or for six months if it is an animal specified in Scheduled I part II (the effect of the European Belai Directive will be referred to later).

The Rabies Control Order 1974 was concerned with Schedule 1 of the 1974 Order. The Rabies Virus Order 1979 prohibited the importation of the Lyssa virus of the family Rhabdoviridae (other than when contained in a medicinal product). Under this Order it is an offence to keep the rabies virus or to deliberately introduce the virus into an animal. The specific Rabies Act 1974 provides for the prevention and control of rabies.

The Zoonoses Order 1975 established a category of reportable disease. The duty to report is restricted to cattle, sheep, goats, pigs, rabbits, fowls, turkeys, geese, ducks, guinea-fowl, pheasants, partridges and quails. (Art. 7) Outbreaks of salmonellosis and brucellosis in animals produced for human consumption must be reported to MAFF which has powers to investigate an outbreak. Occurrences in other species need not be reported but MAFF may investigate an outbreak which comes to its notice, e.g. through a veterinary investigation laboratory. There is no requirement to report the introduction of the disease into an animal for research purposes. Such animals must, of course, be disposed of without risk to human health. The Zoonoses Order of 1989 amended and added to the list of dangerous organisms.

Medicines (Hormone Growth Promoters) (Prohibition of Use) Regulations were passed in 1988. Some exceptions are allowed under the European Communities Act 1972.

The Artificial Insemination (Cattle and Pigs) (Fees) Regulations 1989/390 are concerned with the need for official approval and an appropriate licence.

The Bovine Spongiform Encephalopathy (No. 2) Amendment Order 1990/1930 prohibits the use of specified offal in animal food.

These and other orders can be found in full with their amendments in *Halsbury's Statutory Instruments.*

Other disease legislation

A new and growing area of law covering animal disease has developed since the introduction of the Diseases of Fish Act 1983. The Act gave MAFF powers to deal with outbreaks of notifiable diseases in fish. It requires the registration of fish farms and stipulates that a licence from MAFF is needed for the importation of salmonid fish.

The Diseases of Fish (Definition of 'Infected') Order 1984 deisgnates the following as notifiable diseases:

- bacterial kidney disease
- infectious pancreatic necrosis (IPN)
- viral haemorrhagic septicaemia (VHS or Egtved Disease)
- myxosoma cerebalis (whirling disease)
- infectious haematopoietic necrosis (IHN)
- ulcerative dermal necrosis (UDN)
- spring viremia of carp (SVC)
- furunculosis of salmon.

This Order applies to fish of any kind. Notification must be made to the Fisheries Department of MAFF if it is suspected that fish at fish farms or elsewhere are infected with these diseases. MAFF has powers to designate areas where there is an outbreak and to regulate the movement into and out of the area of live fish. The registration of inland and marine fish farms and shellfish farms carries the obligation to maintain appropriate records.

The Diseases of Fish Regulations 1984 define further the conditions on licences in respect to the provisions as to disposal, transport, inspection, cleaning and disinfection of fish or their eggs, their containers, the means of transport and any other conditions to prevent the spread of disease.

European legislative activity is developing in reference to infectious salmon anaemia (MAFF can supply information on this).

There is a Bees Act 1980 which empowers MAFF to make provision for the control of disease in bees. The Bee Diseases Control Order 1982 makes notifiable American foul brood, European foul brood and varroasis diseases.

The above material is merely a taste of the complexities of the legislative attempt to control disease. I am sure it is enough for any reader apart from those with an avid interest in the topic.

Welfare regulations

Specific legal material concerned with the welfare of experimental animals has been noted in Chapter 10 in the context of the codes of practice and reference has been made to the role played as regards animal welfare by the local ethical review process in Chapter 8. Here, we are concerned with the wider demand in law for the care, particularly, of farm animals. Here it is not merely a matter of codes of practice but much more legally enforceable regulations. In practice, it is the Welfare of Livestock (Amendment) Regulations 1994 and the Welfare of Livestock (Amendment) Regulations 1998 that strictly and comprehensively control the welfare of farm animals.

Welfare of Livestock Regulations 1994

These Regulations were made through the enabling powers of the Agricultural (Miscellaneous Provisions) Act 1968 so terms used in the Regulations have the same meaning as in that Act unless otherwise stated. The Regulations fully implement numerous relevant European Directives and the European Convention for the Protection of Animals kept for Farming Purposes 1976. There are four Schedules in the Regulations:

Schedule 1   Conditions under which laying hens in battery cages must be kept
Schedule 2   Calves
Schedule 3   Pigs
Schedule 4   Part I   General conditions under which livestock must be kept
             Part II   Additional conditions for intensive systems

The Regulations give prominence to any associated welfare codes:

'4–(1) Any person who employs or engages persons to attend to livestock shall ensure that the person attending to the livestock –
   (a)   is acquainted with the provisions of all relevant welfare codes relating to the livestock being attended;
   (b)   has access to a copy of those codes while he is attending the livestock; and
   (c)   has received instruction and guidance on them.
   (2) Any person who keeps livestock, or who causes or knowingly permits livestock to be kept, shall not attend the livestock unless he has access to all welfare codes relating to that livestock while he is attending to them, and is acquainted with the provisions of those codes.
   (3) In this regulation 'welfare code' means a current code issued under section 3 of the Agriculture (Miscellaneous Provisions) Act 1968.'

There is little doubt about the legal force of these Regulations:

'7. A person who contravenes or fails to comply with any provisions of these Regulations other than regulation 5 (concerned with automatic equipment and alarm systems) shall be guilty of an offence under section 2 of the Agriculture (Miscellaneous Provisions) Act 1968.'

The 1994 Regulations lay down requirements for the prevention of injury, inspection, provision of feed and water, space, the provision of testing alarms on automated equipment. For further details one should consult the Regulations if there is a special interest in them. They are not applicable to animals under the ASPA (cf. s. 1(2) of the Agriculture Miscellaneous) Provisions Act nor do they apply to shellfish, crustaceans or molluscs.

A 1998 amendment to the 1994 Regulations tightened up the existing Regulations considerably, particularly as regards environmental conditions, tethers, daily checks and space. The full force of the Amendment will not apply until 1/1/2004.

For more details on this area of legislation refer to MAFF's website www.maff.gov.uk/animal/welfare/default.htm.

Law and the killing of animals

Although the killing of animals is not *per se* illegal, this unfortunate procedure is hedged around by various laws prohibiting the killing of specific animals, e.g. the Protection of Badgers Act 1973, or concerned with the methods of killing, e.g. the Firearms Act 1968, or even the time of killing, e.g. the numerous and ancient Game Acts. The law may permit the killing of animals under licence e.g. the Wildlife and Countryside Act 1981 or may require the killing of animals e.g. the Pest Act 1954 or under the Protection of Animals Act 1911, on the order of a constable with the advice of a veterinary surgeon if an animal is seriously injured (in such a case overriding even the property rights of the owner).

This topic as regards laboratory animals has been covered in the appropriate chapter under the heading of Schedule 1 of the ASPA.

It may be noted, however, in passing that the Slaughterhouses Act 1974 deals with the commercial killing of animals. The Welfare of Animals (Slaughter or Killing) Regulations 1995 spells out the details of this legislation. These Regulations stipulate the methods for the humane treatment of the animals and require that a person in authority be available to take action necessary to safeguard the welfare of live animals in slaughterhouses and knackers' yards (Regulation 5). There are now also the Welfare of Animals (Slaughter or Killing) (Amendment) Regulations 1999. These confine the slaughter of animals for religious reasons to slaughterhouses.

Chapter 21

Legal Aspects of the Transport of Animals

Correct transport of animals is an important feature of animal welfare. Many laboratory animals may never leave the animal unit where they were born and even if they do, the time spent in transport will be a very small fragment of their total life. Nevertheless such transportation may prove to be the most traumatic experience of their whole life, particularly at times of loading and unloading. The legislation concerning the transit of animals is perhaps the most complex, extensive and detailed area of animal law, especially as regards pigs. The difficulty here has been trying to avoid referring to endless minutiae. Such fascinating detail, as the permitted method of sending leeches by post, would no doubt be of great importance to some specialists but of little interest to most technicians, scientists or farmers working with animals. The control of the transport of animals is considered here within the context of the laboratory, but there is a need to consider the recent and crucial relevant legislation and its amendments – the Welfare of Animals (Transport) Order 1997.

The development of the law on the transport of animals

There have been numerous transit orders regarding animals in the past e.g. the Transit of Animals Order 1927. Some referred to particular species of animals e.g. the Conveyance of Live Poultry Order 1919, or were concerned with specific forms of transport – the Transport of Animals (Road and Rail) Order 1975. The Transit of Animals (General) Order 1973 was a milestone in animal transport law. Such orders e.g. the Transport of Animals (Cleaning and Disinfection) Order 1999 (implementing European Directives 91/628/EEC, 92/65/EEC, and 97/12/EC on cleansing and disinfection in animal transport) will continue to be issued in the future. It will be the business of those involved in moving animals around to keep abreast of developing legislation through contact with MAFF.

Apart from legislation there are other rules governing the correct transport of animals. The International Air Transport Association (IATA) issue annually the standards of packaging etc. which they demand before they will accept animals for air transport. These stipulations are mandatory on member airlines. MAFF has produced a code of practice for the air carriage of farm animals and recommended conditions applicable particularly to endangered species (CITES Guidelines 1980). The railways have regulations regarding the carriage of animals. In literature issued on this matter, the need to care for all animals in transit was emphasised with the slogan: 'Animals can't complain'. So solicitous was British Rail for animal travellers that they would not transport mice on high speed trains. They were aware of the deleterious effect on mice of excessive noise or vibration. The Post Office stipulates its own requirements on the mailing of invertebrates.

The various transit orders may have been detailed, but in the context of law they have been relatively clear. In practice, however, some cases resulting from this form of legislation may seem a little bewildering to the layperson. *British Airways Board* v. *Wiggins* (1977) involved two crates of tortoises transported from Amsterdam to Heathrow. Although British Airways staff did not load the crates it was held that the airline was guilty of an offence under the Transit of Animals (General) Order 1973. The magistrates decided that even from a glimpse at the crates it should have been obvious that the receptacles were unsuitable. The tortoises were stacked in columns of six, one on top of the other. In some cases their bodies were protruding through the slats in the side of the boxes.

British Airways appealed on the grounds that the offence was committed outside UK jurisdiction. The Lord Chief Justice, Lord Widgery dismissed the appeal in the Divisional Court. There had been a continuing duty on the carrier to ensure that the containers would be adequate. The offence was committed on landing just as much as on taking off.

This case established that the carrier or any other person having charge of an animal is responsible throughout its journey for the provision of a suitable receptacle for it.

The House of Lords decided in *Air India* v. *Wiggins* (1980) that a carrier would be in breach of the Transit of Animals (General) Order 1973 if it carried animals in unsuitable containers or in conditions which caused unnecessary suffering when entering British territory. The carrier could be prosecuted even if it was not based in the UK and even if the journey commenced abroad. Air India, however, won its appeal against conviction. On appeal Lord Scarman decided that no crime had been committed in the UK against the 2031 dead parakeets out of the 2120 parakeets transported from India to Heathrow. Engine trouble had delayed the aircraft for 31 hours in Kuwait. The 2031 dead birds had never been landed in the UK, only their carcasses. The charge in respect to the 89 living birds which had been landed and had also been exposed to the gruelling journey with insufficient ventilation was also quashed at the appeal. The legal reason for the dismissal of this part of the prosecution was that it was impossible to identify which crates contained the live birds. It seems Air India had no liability for a cargo of unidentified live birds nor for birds already deceased outside the UK.

The movement of laboratory animals

This topic has been referred to in the context of the ASPA but some further notes on the subject will not be out of place here. The Code of Practice for the Housing and Care of Animals used in Scientific Procedures has a section on the topic on p. 13:

'3.11. Stress during transport should be minimised by making animals as comfortable as possible in their containers and, if confinement is to be prolonged, by providing food and water. Time in transit should be kept to a minimum. Animals that are incompatible should not be transported together. 3.12. The sender should ensure that the animals to be transported are in good health and that their containers are adequately labelled. Sick or injured animals should be transported only for purposes of treatment, diagnosis or emergency slaughter.
3.13. Pregnant animals need special care. Farm animals should not normally be transported during the last week of pregnancy and small animals in the last fifth of pregnancy.
3.14. Where animals are subject to control under the Act, it is necessary to consult the Inspector about authority to transfer them to other designated premises.'

[There is a special form associated with the project licence for application for permission to transfer animals between project licences. Certification by a veterinary surgeon of the fitness of the animal for any associated travel must be provided with such an application.]

'3.15. The advice of the DoE [now the DETR] should be sought about the transport of wild animals. Special considerations apply to the transport of fish. Farm animal transport is regulated by various orders under the Animal Health Act 1981 and details should be obtained from MAFF.'

A useful source of relevant details on this subject was published in 'Guidelines for the care of laboratory animals in transit', *Laboratory Animals* (1993) **27**, 93–107. Various interested groups cooperated in this production which is attributed to the Laboratory Animal Breeders Association of Great Britain Ltd. (LABA) and the Laboratory Animal Science Association (LASA).

The Welfare of Animals (Transport) Order 1997

Background of the 1997 Order

Only some indication of the contents of this piece of legislation can be given here and much of the peripheral documentation such as applications for licences, certificates e.g. of competency are omitted. Further information if required can be got from MAFF. The special telephone number for communications in connection with this 1997 Order is 020 8330 8787 (MAFF). A database has been set up to maximise the effectiveness of the transport authorisation scheme. It is called TRADE.

This 1997 Order modifies the Welfare of Animals during Transport Order 1994 and its 1995 amendment. It implements the European Council Directive 91/628/EEC on the protection of animals during transport and its amendment Directive 95/29/EEC. The Order requires compliance with CITES and with the standards set by the International Air Transport Association (IATA). The 25th Edition (October

1998) of the IATA Live Animals Regulations (LAR) contains the latest approved changes.

The 1997 Order applies to all journeys regardless of distance. There are some exemptions for journeys of less than 50 km as in the case of farmers transporting their own animals.

'Animal' has a wider meaning under this Order than in the parent Act – the Animal Health Act (s. 87(1)). The term 'animal' includes all vertebrate animals other than man and other cold blooded animals. The Order does not, however, apply to animals which are not of a commercial nature e.g. pets travelling with their owners.

The 1997 Order strengthened enforcement powers through authorisation of transporters. Transporters of cattle, sheep, goats, pigs and horses for journeys of over eight hours in road vehicles and for all journeys by sea or air will need to hold specific authorisations. All relevant information on this 1997 Order can be obtained from MAFF's Divisional and Regional Offices.

Food, water and rest

Requirements for food, water and rest under the 1997 order are shown in Table 21.1. For other species suitable food and water must be supplied and adequate rest periods must be taken at approved staging posts. During transport dogs and cats should be fed at least every 24 hours and given liquid every 12 hours.

Table 21.1   Requirements for food, water and rest under the welfare of Animals (Transport) Order 1997

Species	Food requirements	Water requirements	Rest period (basic vehicles)	Rest period (high standard vehicles)
Pigs	Every 8 hours	Continuous access	24 hours (after 8 hour journey)	Maximum journey of 24 hours (no rest)
Cattle, sheep and goats	Every 8 hours (care needed to prevent dehydration)	Every 8 hours	As above	1 hour for 14 hour journey, then max. 14 hour journey
Horses (excl. Registered)	Every 8 hours	Every 8 hours	As above	Maximum journey of 24 hours (no rest)
Unweaned calves, lambs, kids, pigs and foals	May not be appropriate	Provide electrolyte solution	As above	Max. 9 hour journey, 1 hour rest, then a further max. of 9 hours.
Poultry, domestic birds and rabbits	Every 8 hours	Every 8 hours	As above	No listing

Rules on stocking

Animals should have enough space to lie down and to stand in a natural position. Exemption from this requirement is allowed for where IATA rules apply. In the case of some smaller animals small containers may be more appropriate for their protection. Birds should not be able to protrude heads, legs or wings nor should they be carried in sacks. There are special provisions regarding day old chicks.

Where animals are understocked, partitions should be placed and used correctly. Compartments need direct access to allow for the animals to be cared for. Provisions must be made for the segregation of animals to prevent fighting.

There should be enough litter on the floor to absorb urine and droppings. Soiled bedding and dead animals should be removed as soon as possible.

Animals needing special care

Under certain conditions, animals are deemed unfit to be transported (unless for veterinary treatment or to slaughter. In such circumstances it is forbidden to push, drag or lift the animal by mechanical means except under veterinary supervision) if they are:

(i)   ill, injured, infirm or fatigued
(ii)   mammals likely to give birth during transport or have given birth during the previous 48 hours or are newly born and the navel has not completely healed, or
(iii)   infant animals or birds (other than poultry and domestic birds), domestic rabbits, dogs and cats not accompanied by their mother and incapable of feeding themselves. This prohibition does not apply to the young of farm livestock and horses.

Provision should be provided for isolation of sick or injured animals and first aid should be available. Animals in milk should be milked at the appropriate times. Females should travel with their young when suckling.

Vessels and aircraft should carry the means to effect the humane slaughter of an animal.

Vehicles and containers

All vehicles used to transport animals must comply with basic standards set out in Schedules 1 and 2 of the 1997 Order (additional requirements are found in Schedules 3–5 as appropriate to the species). In Schedule 7 there are additional requirements as regards farm livestock and horses for journeys longer than 8 hours:

(i)   the vehicle must carry sufficient food for the journey
(ii)   there must be adjustable ventilation
(iii)   vehicles are equipped for a connection to a water supply.

Containers and vehicles should be easy to clean. They should be cleaned and disinfected before the animals are loaded. Excessive noise or vibration must be avoided. Floors and ramps should be strong and slip resistant. Lighting should be adequate especially for loading and unloading. These requirements also apply where appropriate to containers being transported by sea or air.

The journey plan

Journey times must be considered to include the period from loading of the first animal to unloading of the last and should be planned accordingly.

Journeys should not exceed eight hours unless the vehicle is equipped with bedding and the means to inspect, feed and water without unloading. Young animals that are unweaned need one hour of rest after a nine hour journey. Horses can travel for 24 hours if they can be fed and watered in transit. All other cattle, sheep and goats need to have a 1 hour rest after 14 hours travelling. They can then travel for another 14 hours. After the journey they must be unloaded and rested for 24 hours. These journey times can be extended if the vehicle is weatherproof.

Responsibilities and competency of the carrier

The transporter is responsible for the requisite documentation for the whole journey and for the transport, rest, feed and water throughout the journey.

On all journeys of more than 50 km involving vertebrates, the animals must be accompanied by an attendant who has the knowledge and ability to look after them. Animals being transported in secured receptacles which contain food and liquid in dispensers which cannot be tipped over and in sufficient quantity for twice the anticipated journey length may not require an attendant.

Carriers should entrust their animals only to the care of staff who have demonstrated that they are qualified to handle, transport, care for and safeguard the welfare of animals in the context of the certificate of competence referred to in Schedule 8 of the 1997 Order. The details of what is required from an attendant is to be found on the certificate of competence.

Some further points

Fixtures and fittings of the means of transport must be suitably constructed and undue exposure to the weather must be avoided. There should be side protection on ramps. Small animals can be loaded by carrying. 'Small' is defined as 'being carried by not more than 2 persons'. There must be provision for emergency unloading.

If necessary provision must be made for tethering. The tethers must be adjusted for the comfort of the animal. If animals are wild or timid, warning should be fixed to the container. Containers such as boxes must be properly ventilated and constructed so as air holes are not blocked. They should be secure. Sedation of an animal can only be used under veterinary supervision. Details of sedation must accompany the animal to the destination.

Enforcement

Inspectors are appointed under MAFF to enforce the Order. Inspectors may issue a warning for minor infringements. A notice may be issued requiring the carrier:

- not to transport a particular group of animals
- to fulfil special conditions for transport
- to complete a journey or return animals to their place of departure
- to hold animals pending the resolution of a problem
- to have an animal humanely slaughtered.

Inspectors may decide to prosecute if a situation is serious. As a source of help, MAFF have issued *Guidance Notes 1998 on the Welfare of Animals (Transport) Order 1997*.

The APC (1998 Report, p. 7) published a pertinent and topical news item on the transport of laboratory animals:

'34. During 1998, the Animal Procedures Committee was extremely concerned to learn of the deaths of three primates in transit to the UK. The Home Office took immediate action, suspending authority to acquire animals from the source involved while the causes were investigated. Later, it emerged that it had not been possible to ascertain the causes of death. But it is likely that they were due to a combination of factors:

(i) the animals concerned were larger than normal;

(ii) although International Air Transport Association minimum dimensions were not breached, the containers were not large enough for these particular animals – they did not allow the animals to stand up and turn around freely; and

(iii) all the dead animals had been in central compartments, which were less well ventilated.

35. The Committee understands that the breeding establishment co-operated fully and immediately redesigned the containers to improve ventilation and to increase their size, and that the Home Office has now renewed authority to acquire animals from this source, subject to there being no further problems.'

Chapter 22

Law on The Import and Export of Animals

Introduction

Even the complexities of legislation already encountered come nowhere near the convolutions of legal detail associated with the import and export of animals. It would be impossible to do full justice to this area of law in a book such as this. Much of the material is hardly relevant to those who deal with laboratory animals e.g. the niceties of the legality of importing bees from Fiji (*Implementation of the Balai Directive (92/65) in Great Britain*, paragraph 11; an annex from the Animal Health and Veterinary Group, August 1993). Other examples of the minutiae from regulations concerning animals imported into the UK are found in the Animals and Animal Products (Import and Export) Regulations 1993:

> 'Schedule 5
> 3 (a) The official health certification accompanying all cattle imported into Great Britain from Canada must state the animals do not originate from herds in the geographic region of the Okanagan Valley in British Columbia as defined by Commission Decision 88/212/EEC on health protection measures concerning bluetongue in respect of Canada (OJ No. L95, 13/4/88 p. 21). Cattle imported from Canada may only land in Great Britain between 1st February and 15th of April inclusive.'

or

> '11 (b) The official health certificate accompanying all swine imported into Great Britain from Bulgaria must state that the animals comply with the requirements of Commission Decision 93/24/EEC of 11th December 1992 concerning additional guarantees relating to Aujesky's disease for pigs destined to member states or regions free of the disease (OJ No. L16 25.1.93 p. 16).'

Such examples serve to make the point that in this chapter we will be merely viewing the very tip of the iceberg and that indeed from afar. A reader might rightly argue that it is hardly worth doing, but there may be some who are interested in this arcane subject and some laboratory animals do come from or go abroad. In fact the above information could easily now be obsolete. This legislation is extremely fluid depending on the vagaries of politics, the variable interests of commerce and the ever changing pattern of animal health. In the context of the Balai Directive there are continuous negotiations on animal trade between the EU and so-called third countries (listed countries outside the EU) which affect all member states within the Union such as the Irish Republic and the UK. Special concessions for example may be granted to Latvia by Brussels as regards goats or a special concession may be granted as regards mules from Moldavia. Such obscure agreements may have implications for an Irish purchaser of a goat or a horse dealer in Devon.

There is only one practical answer in the presence of such a plethora (the unkind might say quagmire) of regulatory material – availability of an authoritative source or an appropriate address (see Appendix of Useful Addresses).

In Northern Ireland, relevant information should be available from the Northern Ireland Office at Stormont. This may vary a little from mainland legislation. Crown dependencies, such as Jersey or the Isle of Man usually have comparable legislation to England and Wales.

Again of course, the times are changing and devolution marches on. Some of the addresses in the Appendix may be altered. Indeed, an official Notice issued by the Department of the Environment Wildlife Trade Licensing Branch (as revised May 1995) on Import and Export Controls passes the buck, stating:

> '2. Although care has been taken in the preparation of this Notice, it is intended for guidance only and is not an authoritative interpretation of the law. On points of law, applicants should obtain their own independent legal advice.'

However, even in what rightly could be regarded as the appropriate professional circles the law is not always as crystal clear as we might hope. Expert lawyers can come up with wrong answers. Solicitors have in fact been found guilty of negligence when following counsel's advice. The courts have held that a solicitor ought to have realised that the advice given by counsel was wrong or that the solicitor has chosen the wrong barrister for the job (*Law Notes*, Sept 1992 col. 1 p. 23. Butterworth, London).

Quarantine

Quarantine may be described as the isolation of individuals suspected of possibly carrying infectious material, for a period that is reckoned to be longer than the supposed period of incubation of the feared disease. Pieces of legislation appearing to tackle the problem directly are such Orders as:

- Rabies Virus Order 1979
- Specified Animal Pathogen Order 1993

The Rabies Virus Order applies to lyssa virus of the family Rhabdoviridae (other than that contained in a medicinal product which may be imported under the Medicines Act 1968). It is even an offence to keep or use the rabies virus. Both are modern examples of a long line of orders stretching back to the reign of King John (1199–1216) which were intended to protect a farmer's property from destruction by disease.

The salient piece of legislation in the twentieth century was the Rabies (Importation of Dogs, Cats and Other Mammals) Order 1974 with its various amendments in 1984, 1986 and the important 1994 amendment taking into account the Balai Directive. The Balai Directive allows for commercial importation of cats and dogs under stringent conditions of place of origin and certainty of vaccination. The Rabies Act of 1974 was mainly concerned with the control of a possible outbreak of rabies in this country.

UK quarantine laws still apply in respect to animals coming from countries outside the European Union. There may be some specific regulations regarding such matters as certification if, as already mentioned, the EU has specific agreements with the third country from which the animals are obtained. If such agreements exist there could also be European stipulations as regards the export of animals or particular species to that country.

UK quarantine regulations still apply to any animals coming from another member state of the EU if the animal does not conform with exemptions allowed for under the Balai Directive (see below), or if the animal is a pet, or if the animal is not being transferred in the course of trade.

The detailed provisions of UK quarantine law come from the Rabies (Importation of Dogs, Cats and Other Mammals) Order 1974 and its amendments. This legislation controls not only the movement of imported animals, but also contacts with imported animals, vaccination of dogs and cats, action to be taken regarding illegally landed animals or stray animals in ports and airports as listed in Schedule 2 of the Order. There are strict provisions to prevent animals on board boats in British harbours from coming into contact with animals ashore. Offences against the Rabies Order carry heavy penalties including the destruction of the animal. Special arrangements may be made for animals travelling to and from the UK for the purposes of sport, entertainment or breeding.

The term of quarantine for most species is six months. In the case of the vampire bat it is perpetual. For most birds it is 37 days. In some cases the period of quarantine may be specified in the import licence.

The landing of imported animals into the UK is supervised by Customs & Excise. Quarantine must be spent at MAFF approved premises. There must be regular veterinary inspection. Vehicles for the transport of quarantine animals must be MAFF approved.

Some orders on importation are still made independently of EU Directives. The Importation of Animals Order 1977 was amended by the Importation of Animals (Amendment) Order 1996. It was short and consisted only of an extension of the definition of 'animals':

> 'In the definition of "animals" in article 2(1) of the Importation of Animals Order 1977(b), for the words "ruminating animals and swine", there shall be substituted the words "ruminating animals, swine and elephants".'

The importation of invertebrates is covered by UK law. A plant health import legislation guide for importers enitled *Importing Invertebrates* was published by MAFF in 1988. The most important sentence in the guide is: 'If in doubt seek help from the Department concerned.'

It is forbidden to import plant and tree pests. The DETR controls apply both to import and export of listed invertebrate pests. It is an offence to knowingly keep, release, sell, exchange or give away any live invertebrate that is a plant or tree pest.

There is always the possibility that even in respect to invertebrates there may be a need to consider law originating outside the UK. The European Commission Regulations 3626/82 and 3418/83 give the provisions of CITES legal force throughout the European Community and set out the rules for importing species into and exporting species from the Union. For some species, CITES Regulations also impose strict trade controls and restrictions on sale and display. The Endangered Species (Import and Export) Act 1976 has largely been superseded by the EC CITES Regulations. The DETR will provide details and lists of animals which cannot be imported or are protected by European or international conservation controls. This data is regularly revised. Relevant information can be obtained from the Department of the Environment, Transport and the Regions, Endangered Species Branch (see Appendix of Useful Addresses).

Useful quick guides to the Endangered Species Import and Export Controls in line with the demands of European legislation have been issued by the Department of the Environment:

- guide to the endangered species import and export controls
- guide to the controls that apply to the parts or derivatives of species
- guide to species not normally permitted in trade
- guide to which application form to use
- guide to documentation: imports
- guide to documentation: exports
- guide to importing live specimens through airports and ports.

If required, licences can be issued by the DETR to allow importation. Thirteen detailed conditions, including the names of approved Airports and Ports, are attached to the import licence.

Whither quarantine?

In October 1997 the Government set up an Advisory Group on Quarantine. It was chaired by Professor Ian Kennedy, The group was intended to provide an independent risk assessment of the introduction of rabies into the UK under present legislation of quarantine for pet animals compared with possible less stringent alternatives.

Among the recommendations of the Group's 1998 report was that pet dogs and cats would be allowed to travel into the UK from other EU member states and specified rabies-free countries, as long as the animals:

- had been protected against rabies by vaccination;
- were identified by microchips;
- had been blood tested to check that the vaccine had proved effective;
- carried appropriate certificates to prove this;
- carried recent certificates of freedom from parasites

The report proposed that pet cats and dogs (and seemingly other susceptible pet animals from elsewhere) from countries not conceded the above exemption would still be subject to a six month period in quarantine. The supposition that other susceptible pet animals from anywhere else would be subject to quarantine could be based on the legal dictum *expressio unius est exclusio alterius* (when something is clearly expressed it excludes all else).

A Swedish style scheme similar to the above proposals was introduced as a pilot in March 2000 to come into full operation in 2001 according to an announcement by the agriculture minister, Elliot Morley, made in August 1999.

It is obviously a matter of 'watch this space'. Relevant future information will be available from the MAFF website (http://www.maff.gov.uk).

The Balai [catch-all] Directive

'Balai' (from the French) well merits the translation 'catch-all' for it truly affects all aspects of free trade within and into the the European Union. The movement of animals, if involved in commerce, is directly affected by the Regulations stemming from this Directive (92/65/EEC). UK regulations on the import and export of animals have been moulded by this Directive. The comprehensive Animals and Animal Products (Import and Export) Regulations 1993 implemented the Council Directive 90/425/EEC concerning veterinary and zootechnical checks applicable in intra-Community trade in certain live animals and products with a view to completion of the single market; and Council Directive 91/496/EEC laid down principles governing the organisation of veterinary checks on animals entering the Community from third countries. The Animals and Animal Products (Import and Export) Regulations 1995 were written in the light of the Balai Directive (refer to Article 11 of these Regulations). Various other Directives and Decisions of the European Commission have influenced the formation of these Regulations e.g. Sch. 3 (I) of the 1995 Regulations:

> '(i) In accordance with Commission Decision 95/108/EC the importation into Great Britain from the Italian region of Sardinia of animals of the suidae family [pigs] is prohibited.'

Among all this array of legal technicalities one salient piece of legislation must be stressed and clearly presented. Because of an opt-out obtained by the UK government, part of the quarantine legislation remains intact in Sch. 6 of the Animals and Animal Products (Import and Export) Regulations 1995:

'The Rabies (Importation of Dogs, Cats and Other Mammals) Order 1974 shall continue to apply to all carnivores, primates and bats. It shall continue to apply to the importation of all other animals unless such animals are imported by way of trade and can be shown to have been born on the holding of origin and kept in captivity since birth.'

Schedule 6 lists other minor opt-outs from the Balai Directive as regards birds, fish, embryos, ova and semen. It should be consulted by interested parties. It is the clearest official source material in the whole of this legislative maze.

Significant points from the Balai Directive

The scope of the Directive

The Balai Directive lays down specific rules and conditions for:

- apes
- ungulates (including zoo ruminants, deer and suidae)
- birds (other than poultry)
- bees
- rabbits and hares
- ferrets, mink and foxes
- cats and dogs
- other rabies-susceptible species (a true 'catch-all' Directive)
- semen, ova and embryos of the ovine, caprine and equine species and ova and embryos of swine (Articles 5–11).

The Directive lays down the animal health requirements governing intra-community trade in, and imports into the Community of, animals, semen, ova and embryos not subject to animal health requirements laid down elsewhere in specific Community rules.

It does not cover movements of animals or genetic material inside a member state or the movement of pet animals. Any animals such as reptiles, amphibians, and insects (other than bees) not subject to specific rules or animal health rules laid down in other EC Directives, may be traded freely within the Community. In fact, as a general rule, member states are not permitted to prohibit or restrict trade in animals within the Community not covered by Community rules (Articles 3–4). However, in case of imports from third countries, all consignments must be accompanied by approved certification.

A statement in Article 10 is crucial:

'The United Kingdom and Ireland can maintain their quarantine regulations for all carnivores (without prejudice to the provisions for cats and dogs (referred to below in reference to cats and dogs), primates, bats and other rabies-susceptible species covered by the Directive which have not been born on the holding of origin and kept in captivity since birth.'

The Directive was published in the *Official Journal of the European Communities* No. L268 pp. 54–72 (14/9/1992). Copies are obtainable from the Stationery Office.

Special provisions regarding various groups of animals

(i)   Apes
Intra-community trade in apes will be generally confined to animals consigned to and from bodies, institutes and centres approved by the competent authorities of member states in accordance with criteria laid down in the Directive. However, by way of derogation member states may authorise acquisition of apes belonging to an individual. All consignments will have to be accompanied by a health certificate corresponding to the model laid down in the Directive (Article 5).

Imports of apes into Great Britain from other member states will be permitted without the animals going into quarantine if they are consigned from and to an approved body, institute or centre.

(ii)   Cats and dogs
When cats and dogs which have been born, and have remained, in a single rabies-free premises, have been vaccinated, and where the subsequent blood test has proved that vaccination has been effective, such animals may be exported to the UK without quarantine. They must be identified in accordance with detailed rules and have full veterinary records, and be carried in an approved manner (Article 10).

(iii)   Birds
In the case of the importation of birds, it would seem that it would be possible to obtain permission to bring them into the UK without quarantine if the birds have been resident in the member state or in quarantine in that member state for a period of at least 35 days and are accompanied by full health certification (Article 7).

(iv)   Lagomorphs
Lagomorphs born on the holding of origin and kept in captivity since birth may be imported into Great Britain from another member state, providing that they are accompanied on importation by all the appropriate certification (e.g. that the holding of origin has been free from rabies for at least one month (Article 9)).

(v)   Other rabies-susceptible animals (e.g. rats and mice)
If they can be shown to have been born on the holding of origin and kept in captivity since birth, these animals may be imported into Great Britain from another member state providing that they are accompanied on importation by a certificate completed by the exporter confirming that status, that the animals do not show any obvious signs of disease at the time of export, and that the premises of origin are not subject to any animal health restrictions (Article 10).

(vi)   Genetic material
Intra-community trade in semen, ova and embryos of the ovine, caprine and equine

species and ova and embryos of swine is permitted subject to collection and processing in approved centres or by approved teams, under conditions laid down in the Directive. Consignments must be accompanied by a health certificate (Article 11).

Balai approval

The Directive provides for the approval of bodies, institutes or centres where animals are kept:

- for display and the education of the public or
- for conservation of the species or scientific research and which intend either to export to or import from other member states any animal covered by the Directive.

From personal contact with those involved in the importation of laboratory animals, it appears that Balai approved establishments are not only thin on the ground, but difficult to locate (Articles 14–15).

Third countries

Animals, semen, ova and embryos may only be imported from approved third countries whose name appears on a list drawn up by the Community. All such consignments must be accompanied by a health certificate agreed by Standing Veterinary Committee procedure confirming that the animals or genetic material meet any specific animal health requirements laid down by the Community. Outside the scope of this list of third countries, existing national import rules apply (Articles 17–18).

Balai and animal exportation

The main concern of the Directive is the promotion of free trade without let or hindrance, so its controls on export are less severe than its stipulations on importation of animals. This aspect is not of so much concern to us because animals are going out of this country and our quarantine laws are not involved. Here the emphasis of the Directive is on export into member states either from other member states, from third countries with agreement or from any other states. The rules of the Directive stress the importance of the provision of extensive certification which must be bilingual in nature.

Export of animals in UK law

The Animal Health Act 1981 restricts the export of horses and other animals and makes provision for those which are exported. A Department of Trade Order may be required for the export of certain farm animals.

The Animal Health Act stipulates that proper arrangements for conveying animals to their destination must be made. A route plan should be provided, with, if appropriate, details of the air waybill on the route plan. There should be out-of-hours emergency contact numbers of at least two people to avoid animals being left waiting too long before being collected from the point of arrival.

It must be realised when exporting animals that most countries in the world have a substantial network of import restrictions. Very few species of animals, their products or parts can be exported without passing through government control of the country of destination. These often include an importation licence, comprehensive health certification, maybe quarantine in the country of departure and subsequent quarantine in the country of destination and customs procedures on arrival.

ASPA and importation

The Animal Procedures Committee expressed their concern about importation of animals within the context of ASPA. In their 1997 Report (p. 35, vii) they express their intention to:

> 'Investigate what can be done to ensure that, when animals are acquired from overseas, they are obtained from suitable sources and journey times are minimised;'

The Home Office Inspectorate is therefore involved with the importation of laboratory animals, particularly primates. In the case of Schedule 2 animals, it is obvious that special permission must be obtained from the Secretary of State to acquire such animals because from the very fact that they originate outside the UK, they could not have come from a designated establishment.

Appendix 1

Nine official appendices were included in the Guidance on the Operation of the Animals (Scientific Procedures) Act 1986 (HOG). The four which would most likely need to be consulted in detail are reproduced in the following pages. They are:

Appendix II	Standard Conditions: Designated Scientific Procedure Establishments
Appendix III	Standard Conditions: Designated Breeding and Supplying Establishments
Appendix IV	Standard Conditions: Project Licences
Appendix VI	Standard Conditions: Personal Licences

The material from the other appendices of the Act is covered as follows:

Appendix I	The section titles and the text of the Act. For the summary of each section refer to p. 15.
Appendix V	Record Keeping in Designated Scientific Procedure Establishments, and by Project and Personal Licence Holders. For this material refer to pp. 109–14.
Appendix VII	Examples of the Kind of Procedure which may with Permission be delegated to Non-Licensed Assistants. For this material refer to pp. 38–39.
Appendix VIII	Procedure for Representations under the Animals (Scientific Procedures) Act 1986. For comment on this and the following appendix refer to p. 138.
Appendix IX	Statutory Instrument, 1986 No. 1911, The Animals (Scientific Procedures) (Procedure for Representations) Rules 1986.

Appendix II: Standard conditions: designated scientific procedure establishments

The authority conferred by this certificate is subject to the following conditions. Certificates may be revoked or varied for a breach of conditions.

For the purpose of these conditions, "Inspector" means a person appointed under the terms of section 18 of the Animals (Scientific Procedures) Act 1986.

1. The areas within the establishment approved by the Secretary of State for the housing of protected animals or the performance of regulated procedures shall be maintained to at least the standards set out in the Home Office Code of Practice for the Housing and Care of Animals used in Scientific Procedures, except where variations are authorised by the Secretary of State.

2. Unless authorised by the Secretary of State, there shall be no variation of the use of the approved areas of the designated establishment that may have adverse consequences for the welfare of the protected animals held.

3. Unless otherwise authorised by the Secretary of State:

    (i)   only the types of protected animals specified in the certificate may be kept in the establishment for use in experimental or other scientific purposes; and

    (ii) these animals may only be kept and used in the areas listed in the schedule to the certificate.

4. The establishment shall be appropriately staffed at all times to ensure the well-being of the protected animals.

5. Unless otherwise authorised in a project licence, regulated procedures shall not be carried out on any of the types of animal listed in schedule 2 of the Animals (Scientific Procedures) Act 1986 (as amended) unless the animals have been bred at or obtained from an establishment designated by a certificate issued under section 7 of that Act.

    Furthermore, unless otherwise authorised in a project licence, regulated procedures shall not be carried out on cats or dogs unless the animals have been bred at and obtained from a breeding establishment designated by a certificate issued under section 7 of the Animals (Scientific Procedures) Act 1986.

6. Records shall be maintained, in a format acceptable to the Secretary of State, of the source, use and final disposal of all protected animals accommodated in the establishment for experimental or other scientific purposes. Such records shall, on request, be submitted to the Secretary of State or made available to an Inspector. The certificate holder shall, on request, submit to the Secretary of State a summary report, in a form specified by the Secretary of State, of the source, use and disposal of all protected animals accommodated in the establishment for experimental or other scientific purposes.

7. Records shall be maintained, in a format acceptable to the Secretary of State and under the supervision of the Named Veterinary Surgeon, relating to the health of all protected animals kept for experimental or other scientific purposes and accommodated or used in the establishment. These records shall be readily available, on request, for examination by an Inspector.

8. For the purpose of this condition, "marked" means clearly identifiable by a method acceptable to the Secretary of State.

    (i)   Each cat, dog and non-human primate in the establishment which is used, or intended for use, in regulated procedures shall be marked, and particulars of the identity and origin of all such animals shall be entered into the records referred to in 6 above.

    (ii) Every cat, dog and non-human primate in the establishment which is used, or intended for use, in regulated procedures shall be marked before it is weaned except where:

          (a)   the animal is transferred from one establishment to another before it is weaned; and

          (b)   it is not practicable to mark it beforehand,

          in which case, the receiving establishment shall maintain records attesting the identity and origin of the animal's mother until the animal is marked.

(iii)   Any unmarked cat, dog or non-human primate which is taken into the establishment after weaning shall be marked as soon as possible.

9.   In accordance with the Code of Practice for the Housing and Care of Animals used in Scientific Procedures, all protected animals must at all times be provided with adequate care and accommodation appropriate to their type or species. Any restrictions on the extent to which such an animal can satisfy its physiological and ethological needs shall be kept to the absolute minimum; and the health and well-being of protected animals, and the environmental conditions in all parts of the establishment where protected animals are kept, shall be checked at least once daily by competent persons. Arrangements shall be made to ensure that any suffering or defect discovered is remedied as quickly as possible.

9A.   The certificate holder shall nominate and be responsible for the performance of named persons, acceptable to the Secretary of State, as required by section 6(5) of the Animals (Scientific Procedures) Act 1986.

10.   The person(s) named in the certificate as responsible for the day-to-day care of animals (the Named Animal Care and Welfare Officer(s)) shall ensure that any protected animal which is not the immediate responsibility of any personal licensee and which is found to be in severe pain or severe distress which cannot be alleviated shall be promptly and humanely killed by a competent person using an appropriate method under Schedule 1 to the Act or another method authorised in the certificate of designation.

11.   In any case where it appears to the Named Veterinary Surgeon(s) or to the Named Animal Care and Welfare Officer(s) responsible for the day-to-day care of the animals that the health or the welfare of a protected animal kept for experimental or other scientific purposes at the establishment gives rise to concern, he or she shall notify the personal licensee responsible for the animal. If there are no such licensees or if one is not available, the Named Veterinary Surgeon or the Named Animal Care and Welfare Officer responsible for the day-to-day care of the animal shall take steps to ensure that the animal is cared for or, if necessary, humanely killed by a competent person using an appropriate method under Schedule 1 to the Act or another method authorised in the certificate of designation.

12.   Arrangements to ensure that animals are given adequate care must be made in the event that the Named Persons referred to in 9A above are not available for any reason.

13.   Adequate security measures shall be maintained to prevent the escape of protected animals and to prevent intrusions by unauthorised persons.

14.   Quarantine and acclimatisation facilities shall be provided and used as necessary.

15.   Adequate precautions against fire shall be maintained at all times.

16.   The certificate holder shall take all reasonable steps to prevent the performance of unauthorised procedures in the establishment, and make adequate and effective provision for regular and effective liaison with and between those entrusted with responsibilities under the Act and with others who have responsibility for the welfare of the protected animals kept there.

17.   In any case where it is intended to kill a protected animal that has been kept at the establishment for scientific purposes but is not required to be killed under the terms of a project licence, the method of killing employed must be one that is appropriate under Schedule 1 to the Act or otherwise authorised in the certificate. The certificate holder

shall ensure that a person competent to kill animals in accordance with this condition is available at all times. A register shall be maintained of those deemed by the certificate holder to be competent to kill by Schedule 1 methods and by any other method specified in the certificate; these methods of killing shall only be entrusted to and performed by such people. The register shall, on request, be submitted to the Secretary of State or made available to an Inspector.

18. Inspectors shall be provided with access at all reasonable times to all parts of the establishment which are concerned with the use, holding or care of protected animals.

19. The certificate holder shall take steps to provide such education and training as is necessary for all licensees and others responsible for the welfare and care of protected animals at the establishment.

20. The certificate holder shall notify the Secretary of State of any proposed change in:

   (i)   the title of the designated establishment; or

   (ii)   the full name of the certificate holder; or

   (iii)   the full name(s) and qualifications of the Named Animal Care and Welfare Officer(s) responsible for the day-to-day care of the protected animals; or

   (iv)   the full name(s) and qualifications of the Named Veterinary Surgeon(s); or

   (v)   the areas appearing on the Schedule of Premises for the designated establishment or the class of use within those areas; or

   (vi)   the types of protected animals to be used, or kept for use, in regulated procedures.

21. The certificate holder shall notify the Secretary of State of the death of a project licence holder within seven days of its coming to his or her knowledge when, unless the Secretary of State directs otherwise, the project licence shall continue in force for 28 days from the date of notification. The certificate holder will, during that period, assume responsibility for ensuring compliance with the terms and conditions of the project licence.

22. A protected animal which, having been subjected to a completed series of regulated procedures, is kept alive shall continue to be kept at the designated establishment under the supervision of a veterinary surgeon or other suitably qualified person unless:

   (i)   it is moved, with the authority of the Secretary of State, to another designated establishment;

   (ii)   a veterinary surgeon certifies, and the Secretary of State accepts, that it will not suffer if it ceases to be kept at the designated establishment; or

   (iii)   its re-use in another procedure is authorised by the Secretary of State.

23. The certificate holder is required to have instituted, and to maintain, local ethical review processes acceptable to the Secretary of State. Details of the processes and records of the outputs from the processes shall, on request, be submitted to the Secretary of State or made available to an Inspector. Any substantial changes to the processes that are proposed must be submitted to the Secretary of State for approval.

24. A copy of these conditions shall be readily available for consultation by all licensees and named persons in the establishment.

25. The certificate holder shall pay such periodical fees to the Secretary of State as may be prescribed by or determined in accordance with an Order made by him.

26. The certificate remains the property of the Secretary of State, and shall be surrendered to him on request.

Appendix III: Standard conditions: designated breeding and supplying establishments

The authority conferred by this certificate is subject to the following conditions. Certificates may be revoked or varied for a breach of conditions.

For the purpose of these conditions, "Inspector" means a person appointed under the terms of section 18 of the Animals (Scientific Procedures) Act 1986.

1.   In these conditions the word "animal" means any of the species listed in Schedule 2 to the Act (as amended).

1A. Unless otherwise authorised by the Secretary of State, only those types of animal specified in the certificate, and intended for use in experimental or other scientific procedures, may be bred or kept at the establishment. Furthermore, they may only be bred and kept in the areas listed in the schedule to the certificate.

2.   The areas of the establishment approved by the Secretary of State for the housing of protected animals shall be maintained to at least the standards set out in the Home Office Code of Practice for the Housing and Care of Animals in Designated Breeding and Supplying Establishments, except where variations are authorised by the Secretary of State.

3.   Unless authorised by the Secretary of State, there shall be no variation of the use of the approved areas of the designated establishment which may have adverse consequences for the welfare of the protected animals held.

4.   The establishment shall be appropriately staffed at all times to ensure the well-being of the animals.

5.   Records shall be maintained, in a format acceptable to the Secretary of State, of the source, use and final disposal of all protected animals bred, kept for breeding or kept for subsequent supply for use for experimental or other scientific purposes. These shall, on request, be submitted to the Secretary of State or made available to an Inspector. The certificate holder shall, on request, submit to the Secretary of State a summary report, in a form specified by the Secretary of State, of the source, use and disposal all protected animals bred, kept for breeding or kept for subsequent supply for use for experimental or other scientific purposes.

6.   A health record relating to all protected animals bred, kept for breeding or kept for subsequent supply for use for experimental or other scientific purposes and accommodated in the establishment, shall be maintained in a format acceptable to the Secretary of State and under the supervision of the Named Veterinary Surgeon. This record shall, on request, be submitted to the Secretary of State or made available to an Inspector.

7. For the purpose of this condition, "marked" means clearly identifiable by a method acceptable to the Secretary of State.

   (i) Each cat, dog and non-human primate in the establishment which is intended for use in regulated procedures shall be marked, and particulars of the identity and origin of all such animals shall be entered into the records referred to in 5 above.

   (ii) Every cat, dog and non-human primate kept in the establishment which is intended for use in regulated procedures shall be marked before it is weaned except where:

   (a) the animal is transferred from one establishment to another before it is weaned; and

   (b) it is not practicable to mark it beforehand,

   in which case, the receiving establishment shall maintain records attesting the identity and origin of the animal's mother until the animal is marked.

   (iii) Any unmarked cat, dog or non-human primate which is taken into the establishment after weaning shall be marked as soon as possible.

8. Unless otherwise authorised by the Secretary of State, animals must be obtained from establishments designated under section 7 of the Animals (Scientific Procedures) Act 1986.

9. In accordance with the Code of Practice for the Housing and Care of Animals in Designated Breeding and Supplying Establishments, all protected animals must at all times be provided with adequate care and accommodation appropriate to their type or species. Any restrictions on the extent to which such an animal can satisfy its physiological and ethological needs shall be kept to a minimum; and the health and well-being of protected animals and the environmental conditions in all parts of the establishment where protected animals are kept shall be checked at least once daily by competent persons and arrangements made to ensure that any suffering or defect discovered is remedied as quickly as possible.

9A. The certificate holder shall nominate and be responsible for the performance of named persons, acceptable to the Secretary of State, as required by section 7(5) of the Animals (Scientific Procedures) Act 1986.

10. The person named in the certificate as responsible for the day-to-day care of animals (the Named Animal Care and Welfare Officer) shall ensure that any animal which is found to be in severe pain or severe distress which cannot be alleviated shall be promptly and humanely killed by a competent person using an appropriate method under Schedule 1 to the Act or another method authorised in the certificate of designation.

11. In any case where it appears to the Named Veterinary Surgeon or to the Named Animal Care and Welfare Officer responsible for the day-to-day care of the animals that the health or the welfare of an animal at the establishment gives rise to concern, he or she shall take steps to ensure that the animal is either cared for or, if necessary, humanely killed by a competent person using an appropriate method under Schedule 1 to the Act or another method authorised in the certificate of designation.

12. Arrangements to ensure that animals are given adequate care must be made in the event that the named persons referred to in condition 9A above are not available for any reason.

13. Adequate security measures shall be maintained to prevent the escape of protected animals and to prevent intrusions by unauthorised persons.

14. Quarantine and acclimatisation facilities shall be provided and used as necessary.

15. Adequate precautions against fire shall be maintained at all times.

16. In any case where it is intended to kill a protected animal which has been bred, kept for breeding or kept for subsequent supply for use for experimental or other scientific purposes then the method of killing employed must be one which is appropriate under Schedule 1 to the Act or otherwise authorised in the certificate. The certificate holder shall ensure that a person competent to kill animals in accordance with this condition is available at all times. A register shall be maintained of those deemed by the certificate holder to be competent to kill by Schedule 1 methods and by any other method specified in the certificate; these methods of killing shall only be entrusted to and performed by such people. The register shall, on request, be submitted to the Secretary of State or made available to an Inspector.

17. Inspectors shall be provided with access at all reasonable times to all parts of the establishment relating to the holding or care of protected animals.

18. The certificate holder shall notify the Secretary of State of any proposed change in:

    (i)   the title of the designated establishment; or

    (ii) the full name of the certificate holder; or

    (iii) the full name(s) and qualifications of the Named Animal Care and Welfare Officer(s) responsible for the day-to-day care of the protected animals; or

    (iv) the full name(s) and qualifications of the Named Veterinary Surgeon(s); or

    (v)   the areas appearing on the Schedule of Premises for the designated establishment; or

    (vi) the types of protected animal to be bred or kept for use on regulated procedures.

19. The certificate holder shall take steps to provide such education and training as is necessary to those entrusted with the care and welfare of protected animals at the establishment and to ensure that adequate and effective provision is made for regular and effective communication with and between those entrusted with responsibilities under the Act and with others who have responsibility for the welfare of the animals kept there.

20. The certificate holder is required to have instituted, and to maintain, local ethical review processes acceptable to the Secretary of State. Details of the processes and records of the outputs from the processes shall, on request, be submitted to the Secretary of State or made available to an Inspector. Any substantial changes to the processes must be submitted to the Secretary of State for approval.

21. A copy of these conditions shall be readily available for consultation by all persons in the establishment responsible for the health, care and welfare of animals.

22. The certificate holder shall pay such periodical fees to the Secretary of State as may be prescribed by or determined in accordance with an Order made by him.

23. The certificate remains the property of the Secretary of State and shall be surrendered to him on request.

Appendix IV: Standard conditions: project licences

The authority conferred by this licence is subject to the following conditions. Licences may be revoked or varied for a breach of conditions.

In addition, breaches of conditions 1 to 5 may be criminal offences under the Act.

For the purposes of these conditions, "Inspector" means a person appointed under the terms of section 18 of the Animals (Scientific Procedures) Act 1986.

1. The project licence holder shall not, in pursuit of this programme of work, procure or knowingly permit any person under his or her control to carry out regulated procedures otherwise than in accordance with:

    (i)   the programme of work specified in this licence; and

    (ii)   that person's personal licence.

2. Procedures under the authority of the project licence shall be carried out only at the place or places specified in the licence, unless their performance elsewhere is authorised by the Secretary of State.

3. No person working under the authority of the project licence shall use any neuro-muscular blocking agent in place of an anaesthetic.

4. No person working under the authority of the project licence shall use any neuro-muscular blocking agent without express authority from the Secretary of State, which must be contained in both the project and personal licences.

5. No animal which has completed a series of regulated procedures for a particular purpose may be used again on the same procedure/protocol, or on another procedure/protocol whether on the same licence or another, without express authority in this project licence.

6. For any procedure, the degree of severity imposed shall be the minimum consistent with the attainment of the objectives of the procedure, and this shall not exceed the severity limit attached to the procedure. The minimum number of animals of the lowest neurophysiological sensitivity shall be used in procedures causing the least pain, suffering, distress or lasting harm.

6A. All authorised procedures shall be carried out under general, regional or local anaes-thesia unless:

    (i)   anaesthesia would be incompatible with the purposes of the procedures; or

    (ii)   anaesthesia would be more traumatic to the animal concerned than the pro-cedures themselves.

6B. Except where incompatible with the purposes of the procedures, when an anaesthetised animal suffers considerable pain once the anaesthesia has worn off that animal shall be given pain-relieving treatment in good time or, if this is not possible, it shall be promptly killed by a competent person using an appropriate method under Schedule 1 to the Act or another method authorised in the certificate of designation.

6C. Where, in accordance with 6A above, anaesthesia is not used, analgesics or other appropriate methods must be used appropriately in order to ensure, as far as possible, that pain, suffering, distress and harm are minimised and that, in any event, the animal is not subject to severe pain, distress or suffering.

7. Except with the authorisation of the Secretary of State:

 (a) regulated procedures shall not be carried out on any of the animals listed in Schedule 2 to the Animals (Scientific Procedures) Act 1986 (as amended) unless they have been bred at *or* obtained from a breeding or supplying establishment designated by a certificate issued under section 7 of that Act;

 (b) furthermore, regulated procedures shall not be carried out on cats and dogs unless they have been bred at and obtained from a breeding establishment designated by a certificate issued under section 7 of the Animals (Scientific Procedures) Act 1986; and

 (c) regulated procedures shall not be carried out on protected animals taken from the wild.

7A. Animals may only be set free into the wild during the course of a procedure with the authority of the Secretary of State. Animals shall not be set free into the wild as part of programmes of work for education and training.

8. It is the responsibility of the project licence holder to ensure adherence to the severity limits as shown in the listing of procedures/protocols (section 19a) and observance of any other controls described in the procedure/protocol sheets (section 19b). If these constraints appear to have been, or are likely to be, breached, the project licence holder shall ensure that the Secretary of State is notified as soon as possible.

9. It is the responsibility of the project licence holder to maintain a contemporaneous record of all animals on which procedures have been carried out under the authority of the project licence. This record shall show the procedures used and the names of personal licensees who have carried out the procedures. The record shall, on request, be submitted to the Secretary of State or made available to an Inspector.

10. The project licence holder shall send to the Secretary of State, before 31 January each year (and within 28 days of the licence having expired or been revoked), a report in a form specified by the Secretary of State, giving details of the number of procedures and animals used, and the nature and purpose of the procedures performed under the authority of the project licence during the calendar year.

11. The project licence holder shall maintain a list of publications resulting from the licensed programme of work and a copy of any such publication shall be made available to the Secretary of State on request. The list shall, on request, be submitted to the Secretary of State or made available to an Inspector, and it shall be submitted to the Secretary of State when the licence is returned to him on expiry or for revocation.

12. The project licence holder shall submit such other reports as the Secretary of State may from time to time require.

13. The project licence holder shall ensure that details of the plan of work and procedures described in section 18 and 19 of the schedule of this licence, and any additional conditions imposed on those procedures, are known to:

 (i) all personal licensees performing those procedures;

   (ii)   the Named Animal Care and Welfare Officers responsible for the day-to-day care of the animals; and

   (iii)   the Named Veterinary Surgeon, on request.

14.   The project licence holder shall ensure that the appropriate level of supervision is provided for all personal licensees carrying out regulated procedures under the authority of this licence.

15.   The project licence holder must obtain the permission of the Secretary of State before:

   (i)   any animal undergoing regulated procedures is moved from one designated establishment to another; or

   (ii)   any animal is released for slaughter; or

   (iii)   any animal is released from the controls of the Act,

   unless this is already explicitly authorised by the project licence.

16.   At the conclusion of a series of regulated procedures for a particular purpose, protected animals which are suffering, or are likely to suffer, as a result of those procedures shall be promptly and humanely killed:

   (i)   by a competent person using an appropriate method under Schedule 1 to the Act or another method authorised in the certificate of designation; or

   (ii)   by another method authorised by the personal licence of the person by whom the animal is killed.

17.   If a veterinary surgeon, or other suitably qualified person acceptable to the Secretary of State, determines that animals are not suffering, and are not likely to suffer, as a result of the regulated procedures, those animals may be kept at the designated establishment under the supervision of that person.

18.   The licence remains the property of the Secretary of State, and shall be surrendered to him on request.

Appendix VI: Standard conditions: personal licences

The authority conferred by this licence is subject to the following conditions. Licences may be revoked or varied for a breach of conditions.

In addition, breaches of conditions 1–9 and failure to comply with a requirement under condition 10 may be criminal offences under the Act.

For the purpose of these conditions, "Inspector" means a person appointed under the terms of section 18 of the Animals (Scientific Procedures) Act 1986.

   1.   No personal licensee shall carry out a regulated procedure for which authority has not been granted in his or her personal licence.

   2.   No personal licensee shall use in any regulated procedure any type of protected animal not authorised by his or her personal licence.

   3.   No personal licensee shall carry out any regulated procedure unless authorised by a project licence.

4. No personal licensee shall carry out any regulated procedure as an exhibition to the general public or carry out any such procedure which is shown live on television for general reception.

5. No personal licensee carrying out any regulated procedure shall use any neuromuscular blocking agent in place of an anaesthetic.

6. No personal licensee shall use any neuromuscular blocking agent without express authority from the Secretary of State which must be contained in both the project and personal licences.

7. Unless otherwise authorised by the Secretary of State in both project and personal licences, personal licensees shall perform the procedures for which they have authority only at the place or places specified in their personal licences, and only in suitable areas specified in the relevant certificate of designation.

8. The personal licence holder shall arrange for any animal which, at the conclusion of a series of procedures for a particular purpose, is suffering or is likely to suffer adverse effects to be promptly and humanely killed:

    (i)   by a competent person using an appropriate method under Schedule 1 to the Act or another method authorised in the certificate of designation; or

    (ii) by another method authorised by the personal licence of the person by whom the animal is killed.

9. No animal which has completed a series of regulated procedures for a particular purpose may be re-used without express authority in the project licence.

10. If an Inspector requires that an animal must be killed because that Inspector believes that it is undergoing excessive suffering, it must be promptly and humanely killed in accordance with 8(i) or 8(ii) above.

11. It is the responsibility of a personal licensee to ensure that all cages, pens or other enclosures are clearly labelled. The labelling must be such as to enable Inspectors, Named Veterinary Surgeons and Named Animal Care and Welfare Officers to identify the project in which the animals are being used, the regulated procedures which have been performed, and the responsible personal licensee.

12. The personal licensee is entrusted with primary responsibility for the welfare of the animals on which he or she has performed regulated procedures; the personal licensee must ensure that animals are properly monitored and cared for, and must take effective precautions, including the appropriate use of sedatives, tranquillisers, analgesics or anaesthetics, to prevent or reduce to the minimum level consistent with the aims of the procedure any pain, suffering, distress or discomfort caused to the animals used.

13. It is the responsibility of the personal licensee to notify the project licence holder as soon as possible when it appears either that the severity limit of any procedure listed in the project licence (section 19a) or that the constraints upon adverse effects described in the protocol sheets (section 19b) have been or are likely to be significantly exceeded.

14. In all circumstances where an animal which is being, or has been, subjected to a regulated procedure is in severe pain or severe distress which cannot be alleviated, the personal licensee must ensure that the animal is promptly and humanely killed in accordance with 8(i) or 8(ii) above.

15. It is the responsibility of the personal licensee to ensure that suitable arrangements exist for the care and welfare of animals during any period when the personal licensee is not in attendance.

16. It is the responsibility of the personal licensee to ensure that, whenever necessary, veterinary advice and treatment are obtained for the animals in his or her care.

17. The personal licensee is subject to such supervision requirements as may be stated on the licence or which the project licence holder may deem necessary in order to ensure that regulated procedures are performed competently.

18. Before any animal, or group of animals, that has been subject to procedures is released into the wild, to a farm, or for use as a pet, the personal licensee must ensure that appropriate authority exists in the project licence for the animal or animals to be released.

19. When anaesthesia (whether general, regional or local) is used, it shall be of sufficient depth to prevent the animal from being aware of pain arising during the procedure.

19A. All authorised procedures shall, in accordance with the relevant project licence authorities, be carried out under general, regional or local anaesthesia unless:

    (i)   anaesthesia would be incompatible with the purposes of the procedures; or

    (ii) anaesthesia would be more traumatic to the animal concerned than the procedures themselves.

19B. Except where incompatible with the purposes of the procedures, when an anaesthetised animal suffers considerable pain once the anaesthesia has worn off, the personal licensee shall ensure that, wherever possible, the animal is given pain-relieving treatment in good time or that the animal is promptly and humanely killed in accordance with 8(i) or 8(ii) above.

19C. Where, in accordance with 19A above, anaesthesia is not used, analgesics or other appropriate methods must be used in order to ensure as far as possible that pain, suffering, distress and harm are limited and that in any event the animal is not subject to severe pain, distress or suffering.

20. Personal licensees must take all reasonable steps to ensure appropriate personal and project licence authorities exist before performing regulated procedures, and must be aware of the nature of the current authorities, and the conditions of issue attached to the licences.

21. The personal licensee shall maintain a record of all animals on which procedures have been carried out, including details of supervision and declarations of competence by the project licence holder as appropriate. This record shall be retained for at least five years and shall, on request, be submitted to the Secretary of State or made available to an Inspector.

22. The licence remains the property of the Secretary of State, and shall be surrendered to him on request.

Appendix 2

The following changes to the law have been made since the writing of this book.

Dogs

In spite of reports in the press (*The Sunday Times* 12/12/99) there are no Government plans to change the law on the use of dogs in research where their use is justified under ASPA. An official report was released by the Secretary of State on 8/3/00 concerning the Harlan Hillcrest affair, which had been the basis of the misleading news item in *The Sunday Times* last December (1999) (RDS News Jan. 2000 cf. p. 102–103).

The Breeding and Sale of Dogs (Welfare) Act 1999 which comes into force this year (2000) is concerned only with the pet trade. Breeding establishments for Schedule 2 animals, such as dogs, come under stricter laws (Schedule 2 of ASPA) so the 1999 Act does not apply to research institutes.

Designated Supply Establishments, approved by the Home Office, have come under continuous attack from pressure groups. These groups rejoiced in a milestone victory in the closure of a Designated Supply Establishment for Cats at Hillgrove, Oxfordshire in 1999. Already in 2000 they have triumphed in closing the Shamrock Farms Designated Establishment on 10th of March.

Charter on Licensing and Inspection

During 2000, the Code for Licensing and Inspection will be replaced by this new document. Large parts of the Charter will be similar to the Code but there will be some variations.

The list of targets is longer and more specific. The target for the time taken from receiving the Inspectorate's recommendation to issuing the licence will be increased from 10 to 15 working days. This target only applies to the Animal Procedures Section. No target has been set for the time needed by the Inspector to consider any particular application. The Inspector will be available to discuss and refine proposals regarding applications (RDS News Jan. 2000 cf. p. 132).

LD50 test

The Home Office issued a statement on 21/11/99 that no more licences for LD50 test would be granted if a suitable alternative is available. All such current licences were to be reviewed.

The Home Office has promised to press other countries to replace this test by more humane Fixed Dose Procedures. USA and Japan still demand the LD50 as a part of standard toxicity testing for new chemicals.

The LD50 Test had been designed to find the dosage level which will kill 50% of animals dosed. There are variants of the test, PD50 (Protective Dose 50%) and LC50 (Lethal Concentration 50%) for which there are no alternatives and which do not come under the definition of the LD50 Test (LASA Newsletter, Winter Issue 1999–2000 cf. p. 169).

Quarantine

What was speculated on in the text has now become reality (cf. p. 196). As from 28/2/2000 pet cats and dogs can now enter this country from other Western European Countries without being subjected to quarantine regulations as long as they have the correct documentation of vaccinations (a pet passport) and the appropriate microchip. During this year 2000, the exemption will be extended to some other pets besides cats and dogs, and the number of countries from which they may come will be increased.

Useful Addresses

Animal Health (International Trade)
Division
Animal Health and Veterinary Group
Ministry of Agriculture, Fisheries and Food
Government Buildings
Hook Rise South
Tolworth
Surbiton
Surrey KT6 7NF
Tel: 0208 330 4411

European Commission Information Office
8 Storey's Gate
London SW1P 3AT
Tel: 020 7973 1992

Office for Official Publications of the
European Union
2 Rue Mercier L-2985
Luxembourg
Tel: (352) 29 291

English Nature
Licensing Section
Northminster House
Peterborough PE1 1UA
Tel: 01733 340345

Department of the Environment
Endangered Species Branch
Tollgate House
Houlton Street
Bristol BS2 9DJ
Tel: 0117 987 8591
CITES Department of Environment,
Transport and Regions
Tel: 0117 987 8168 (Mammals)
0117 987 8691 (Other Animals)

Home Office
Constitutional and Community Policy
Directorate
Animals, Byelaws and Coroners Unit
50 Queen Anne's Gate
London SW1H 9AT
Tel: 0207 273 4000
Website for ABCU: http://
www.homeoffice.gov.uk/ccpd/abcu.htm

IATA (International Air Transport
Association)
Tabmag Publishing Ltd
Grove House
31–7 Church Road
Ashford
Middlesex TW15 2UE
Tel: 01784 255000

MAFF
3 Whitehall Place
London SW1A 2HH
Tel: 0207 270 8080
Transport Inquiries: 0208 330 8787

MAFF
Tropical, Freshwater and Ornamental Cold
Water Fish
Nobel House
17 Smith Square
London SW1P 3HX
Tel: 020 7270 8080

MAFF
State Veterinary Service
Beeches Road
Chelmsford
Essex CM1 2RU
Tel: 01245 358383

Department of Agriculture for Northern
   Ireland
Animal Health Division
Dundonald House
Upper Newtownards Road
Belfast BT4 3SB
Tel: 028 9052 0100

Information may also be available from
Northern Ireland Office
Castle Buildings
Stormont
Belfast BT4 3SG
Tel: 028 9052 0700

Scottish Office Agriculture and Fisheries
   Department
Animal Health and Welfare Branch
Pentland House
47 Robbs Loan,
Edinburgh EH14 1TW
Tel: 0131 244 6177

Welsh Office Agriculture Department
Cathays Park
Cardiff CF1 3NQ
Tel: 029 2082 5111

Research Defence Society (RDS)
58 Great Marlborough St
London W1V 1DD
Tel: No. 020 7287 2818
Website: http://www.uel.ac.uk/research/
   rds/

Libraries and sources of information

Jean Monnet House
8 Storey's Gate
London SW1P 3AT
Tel: 020 7973 1900

British Library of Political and Economic
   Science
Portugal Street
London WC2
Tel: 020 7955 7273

European Commission's Library Automated
   System (ECLAS)
Hosts Eurobases
Commission of the EU
Rue de la Loi 200 B-1049
Brussels

Communitas Europaeae Lex (CELEX)
   available on CD-ROM
Hosts Eurobases
Contex/Limited/Justis: Profile Information

Health and Safety Commission
Rose Court
2 Southwark Bridge
London SE1 9HS
Tel: 020 7717 6000

NB: Addresses are accurate at time of going to press

Bibliography

Animal Health and Veterinary Group (1993) *Implementation of the Balai Directive (92/65) in Great Britain.* MAFF handout.

Animal Procedures Committee (1989) *1988 Annual Report.* HMSO, London.

Animal Procedures Committee (1991) *1990 Annual Report.* HMSO, London.

Animal Procedures Committee (1992) *1991 Annual Report.* HMSO, London.

Animal Procedures Committee (1993) *1992 Annual Report.* HMSO, London.

Animal Procedures Committee (1997) *1996 Annual Report.* HMSO, London.

Animal Procedures Committee (1998) *1997 Annual Report.* The Stationery Office, London.

Animal Procedures Committee (1999) *1998 Annual Report.* The Stationery Office, London.

Association of Veterinary Teachers and Research Workers (1989) *Guidelines for the Recognition and Assessment of Pain in Animals.* UFAW, Potters Bar.

Barclay, R.J., Herbert, W.J. & Poole, T.B. (1988) *The Disturbance Index: A Behavioural Method of Assessing the Severity of Common Laboratory Procedures on Rodents.* UFAW, Potters Bar.

BLAVA (1998) *The Veterinary Surgeons Act 1966 and the Animals (Scientific Procedures) Act 1986 – a conflict of legislative requirements.* BLAVA Position Paper, BLAVA, London.

Brambell (1965) *Report of the Advisory Committee on the Welfare of Farm Animals.* HMSO, London.

Broom, D.M. & Johnson, F.G. (1993) *Stress and Animal Welfare.* Chapman and Hall, London.

Brooman, S. & Legge, D. (1997) *Law Relating to Animals.* Cavendish Publishing, London.

Code of Practice for the Housing and Care of Animals used in Scientific Procedures 1989. HMSO, London.

Code of Practice for Licensing and Inspection under the Animals (Scientific Procedures) Act 1986 (1994). HMSO, London.

Code of Practice for the Housing and Care of Animals in Designated Breeding and Supplying Establishments 1995. HMSO, London.

Code of Practice for the Humane Killing of Animals under Schedule 1 to the Animals (Scientific Procedures) Act 1986 (1996). HMSO, London.

Cooper, M. (1987) *An Introduction to Animal Law.* Academic Press, London.

de Smith, S.A. (1978) *Constitutional and Administrative Law.* Penguin Books, Harmondsworth.

DoH (1989) *Good Laboratory Practice: The UK Compliance Programme.* Department of Health, London.

Dolan, K. (1999) *Ethics, Animals and Science.* Blackwell Science, Oxford.

Dolan, K. & Tobin, S. (1994) *The Animals (Scientific Procedures) Act, Resource Book for Personal Licence Holders.* Spot on Training, London.

FELASA (1999) Working party report of the Federation of Laboratory Animal Science Associations working group on education of specialists. Laboratory Animals 1999 **3** pp. 1–15.

Fraser, A.F. & Broom, D.M. (1990) *Farm Animal Behaviour and Welfare.* Baillière Tindall, London.

FRAME and UFAW (1998) *Selection and Use of Replacement Methods in Animal Experimentation.* UFAW, Potters Bar.

Gordon, S., Wallace, J., Cool, A. *et al.* Reduction of exposure to laboratory animal allergens in the workplace. *Clinical Experimental Allergy* **27**, pp. 744–51.

Health and Safety Executive (1990) *What you should know about Allergy to Laboratory Animals.* HSE Books, London.

Home Office (1990) Guidance on the Operation of the Animals (Scientific Procedures) Act 1986. HMSO, London.

Home Office (1998) *Survey of Welfare Standards for Dogs within Designated Establishments.* The Stationery Office, London.

International Air Transport Association (IATA) *Live Animal Regulations 1998*, 25th Edition. IATA, Montreal and Geneva.

Kennedy Committee Report (1997) *Report of the Advisory Group on the Ethics of Xeno-transplantation.* The Stationery Office, London.

Langley, G. (1989) *Animal Experimentation: The Consensus Changes.* Macmillan Press, Basingstoke.

LASA Working Party (1990) The assessment and control of the severity of scientific procedures on laboratory animals. *Laboratory Animals*, **24** pp. 97–130.

LaFollette, H. & Shanks, N. (1996) *Dilemmas of Animal Experimentation.* Routledge, London.

Lembeck, F. (1989) *Scientific Alternatives to Animal Experiments.* Ellis Horwood, Chichester.

Linzey, W. (1984) Animal Rights. SCM Press, London.

Littlewood Committee (1965) *Report of the Departmental Committee on Experiments on Animals.* HMSO, London.

Lund, V. (1997) Postgraduate teaching in farm animal welfare and ethics. *Animal Welfare*, **6** 105–21.

Ministry of Agriculture, Fisheries and Food (MAFF) (1988) *Importing Invertebrates.* HMSO, London.

Ministry of Agriculture, Fisheries and Food (MAFF) (1995) *Pig Identification, Records and Movement: A Guide to the Legal Requirements.* MAFF Publications, London.

Ministry of Agriculture, Fisheries and Food (MAFF) (1996) *Summary of the Law Relating to Farm Animal Welfare.* MAFF Publications, London.

Ministry of Agriculture, Fisheries and Food (MAFF) (1997) *Government Response to the Farm Animal Welfare Council Report on the Welfare of Pigs Kept Outdoors.* MAFF Publications, London.

Ministry of Agriculture, Fisheries and Food (MAFF) (1998) *Code of Recommendation for the welfare of livestock.*

Ministry of Agriculture, Fisheries and Food (MAFF) (1998) *Guidance notes on The Welfare of Animals (Transport) Order 1997.* MAFF Publications, London.

Ministry of Agriculture, Fisheries and Food (MAFF) (1999) *Code of Recommendation for the welfare of livestock.* MAFF Publications, London.

Marsh, N. & Haywood, S. (1985) *Animal Experimentation.* FRAME, London.

Morton, D. & Griffiths, P. Guidelines on the recognition of pain, distress and discomfort in experimental animals and an hypothesis for assessment. *Veterinary Record*, 20 April 1985.

Orlans, B. (1993) *In the Name of Science – Issues of Responsible Animal Experimentation.* Oxford University Press, New York.

OECD (1982) *GLP in the Testing of Chemicals*, Final Report of the OECD Expert Group on GLP. Organisation for Economic Cooperation and Development, Geneva.

Paton, W. (1984) *Man and Mouse.* Oxford University Press, Oxford.

Phillips, M.T. & Sechzer, J.A. (1989) *Animal Research and Ethical Conflict. An Analysis of the Scientific Literature.* Springer-Verlag, Berlin.

Poole, T. (1997) Happy animals make good science. *Laboratory Animals* **31** pp. 116–24.

Rollins, B. (1989) *The Unheeded Cry*. Oxford University Press, Oxford.

RCVS (1999) *Legislation Affecting the Veterinary Profession in the UK*. Royal College of Veterinary Surgeons, London.

RSPCA (1994) *Ethical Concern for Animals*. Royal Society for the Prevention of Cruelty to Animals, Horsham.

Russell, W.M.S. & Burch, R.L. (1992) *The Principles of Humane Experimental Technique* (Special Edition). UFAW, Potters Bar.

Sainsbury, D. (1991) *Farm Animal Welfare: Cattle, Pigs and Poultry*. Blackwell Science, Oxford.

Short, D. & Woodnott, D. (1978) *The IAT Manual of Laboratory Animal Practice and Techniques*. Granada Publishing Ltd., London.

Singer, P. (1992) *Applied Ethics*. Oxford University Press, Oxford.

Smith, J.A. & Boyd, K.M. (1991) *Lives in the Balance*. Oxford University Press, Oxford.

Smyth, D.H. (1978) *Alternatives to Animal Experimentation*. Scolar Press, Aldershot.

Tester, K. (1992) *Animals and Society*. Routledge, London.

United Kingdom Coordinating Committee on Cancer Research (UK CCCR) (1988) *Guidelines for the Welfare of Animals in Experimental Neoplasia*. UK CCCR, London.

Table of Cases

Table of Statutes

To some readers there may appear to be gaps in the above list. Early Acts such as the Cruelty to Animals Act 1876 may be relevant to the subject and are referred to in the text. They are, however, no longer applicable having been repealed. Some Acts dealing with animals such as the Performing Animal (Regulation) Act 1925 are hardly relevant to the law on laboratory animals. Other animal Acts may look rather out of place in this list e.g. the Abandonment of Animals Act 1960. It has not been unknown for raiders to remove animals from research establishments, thus taking them into possession, and then releasing them. Such action may amount to abandonment of what could be tame rabbits. What has been said about this list is equally applicable to the following lists of Statutory Instruments and European Directives.

Table of Statutory Instruments

Table of European Legislation

European Directives

European Regulations

Index

Italic page references offer the most important information for that entry.